NO MORE A-ROVING
CONDITIONS OF AGREEMENT
SAINT'S DAY
A PENNY FOR A SONG

John Whiting

# PLAYS ONE

NO MORE A-ROVING
CONDITIONS OF AGREEMENT
SAINT'S DAY
A PENNY FOR A SONG

Edited by Ronald Hayman

OBERON BOOKS
LONDON

This collection first published in 1999 by Oberon Books
(incorporating Absolute Classics)
521 Caledonian Rd, London N7 9RH
Tel: 0171 607 3637 / Fax: 0171 607 3629
e-mail: oberon.books@btinternet.com



British Library Cataloguing-in-Publication Data.
A catalogue record for this book is available from the British Library.

ISBN 1 84002 052 0

The photograph used on the covers of the three volumes of Whiting's work published by Oberon Books is by Houston Rogers, courtesy of the Theatre Museum, London.

Cover design and typography: Richard Doust

Printed in Great Britain by MPG Ltd., Bodmin.

# Contents

ACKNOWLEDGEMENTS, 6

CHRONOLOGY, 7

INTRODUCTION, 11

Introduction to *No More A-Roving* and *Conditions of Agreement*, 19

NO MORE A-ROVING, 23

CONDITIONS OF AGREEMENT, 115

SAINT'S DAY, 205

Introduction to *Saint's Day*, 207

A PENNY FOR A SONG, 301

Introduction to *A Penny for a Song*, 303

# Acknowledgements

In the 1969 edition of John Whiting's *Collected Plays*, I acknowledged help from his widow, Jackie Whiting, who gave me access to unpublished material and newspaper cuttings, and to Dr Gabriele Scott Robinson, who showed me the thesis she had written on Whiting's work. I am still grateful to them, and to Professor Eric Salmon, who sent me a copy of his introduction to the 1975 edition of *No More A-Roving*. His 1979 book *The Dark Journey: John Whiting as Dramatist* contains more of the biographical facts than any other book on Whiting, and the chronology in this book owes a lot to Professor Salmon's extensive and meticulous research.

# Chronology

**1917** JW born in Salisbury on 15 November, the son of an army captain.

**1922** The family moves to Northampton where, discharged from the army, JW's father starts a legal career.

**1930** JW plunged into "the particularly hellish life which is the English public school" in Taunton.

**1934** He leaves school to start training as an actor at RADA.

**1937** Various acting jobs in repertory and under the direction of Robert Atkins in the Open Air Theatre at Regent's Park.

In the company at Bideford, he meets Jackie Mawson (Asthorne Mawson).

**1938** Repertory at Croydon.

**1939** Registers as a conscientious objector, but, after changing his mind, joins the anti-aircraft section of the Royal Artillery.

**1940** Marries Jackie Mawson after being promoted to the rank of corporal.

**1942** Commissioned as second lieutenant.

**1944** Begins his novel *Not a Foot of Land* while still in the army.

Discharged for health reasons.

**1944-5** Completes the novel.

Repertory in Peterborough and Harrogate, where he begins to think seriously about a career in writing – not necessarily for the theatre.

**1946** His father dies five months after Jonathan, the first of JW's four children, is born.

JW appears at the Lyric, Hammersmith, in Sean O'Casey's *Oak Leaves and Lavender.*

Writes *No More A-Roving* and *Conditions of Agreement.* He also begins some stories and plays for broadcasting, including the radio play *Paul Southman: An Appreciation for Broadcasting.*

Starts *Saint's Day.*

**1947** Repertory in York.

Writes the radio play *Eye Witness* and begins *A Penny for a Song.*

**1948** Finishes *Saint's Day* and starts *Marching Song.*

**1949** The BBC broadcasts *Eye Witness,* another radio play, *The Stairway,* and two stories, 'Valediction' and 'Child's Play'.

**1950** Repertory at Scarborough.

Finishes *A Penny for a Song.*

The BBC broadcasts the play *Love's Old Sweet Song.*

**1951** In March *A Penny for a Song* opens at the Haymarket, directed by Peter Brook.

In October *Saint's Day* is produced at the Arts Theatre and wins first prize in the play competition organised for the Festival of Britain.

He joins John Gielgud's company to play Shakespeare at the Phoenix, where JW's parts include the Gaoler in *The Winter's Tale.*

**1952** Finishes *Marching Song.*

Plays the Sexton in *Much Ado about Nothing* at the Phoenix.

In Gielgud's production of *Richard II* with Paul Scofield at the Lyric, Hammersmith, JW plays the Abbot of Westminster.

Through his agent, A.D. Peters, he gets work writing screenplays.

Reading Aldous Huxley's new book, *The Devils of Loudun*, he gets interested in its potential as a film.

The 22-year-old Peter Hall directs an undergraduate production of *Saint's Day* at Cambridge.

**1953** Starts *The Gates of Summer.*

Peter Hall directs an undergraduate production of *A Penny for a Song.*

**1954** *Marching Song* produced in the West End, directed by Frith Banbury.

**1956** In September *The Gates of Summer* starts a pre-London tour, directed by Peter Hall, but fails to reach London, partly because the leading actress, Dorothy Tutin, is taken ill.

**1957** Peter Hall, now artistic director of the Arts Theatre, commissions a one-act play. JW writes *No Why* and starts *The Nomads.*

**1960** Peter Hall, now artistic director of the Memorial Theatre, Stratford-on-Avon, commissions JW to write a large-scale play for the company's first London season. It becomes the Royal Shakespeare Company before the season starts.

**1961** In February *The Devils* opens, directed by Peter Wood at the Aldwych. It is the Royal Shakespeare Company's first production in London.

In June JW accepts the position of dramatic critic on the monthly *London Magazine.*

**1962** In August a revised version of *A Penny for a Song* is presented by the RSC at the Aldwych, directed by Colin Graham.

In November JW is taken to hospital, where cancer is diagnosed.

**1963** He works on adapting Ibsen's *The Lady from the Sea* for the screen.

He dies on 16 June at the age of forty-five.

# INTRODUCTION

Ronald Hayman

Nearly a thousand playwrights entered the competition organised in 1951 for the Festival of Britain. It was to be judged by Peter Ustinov, Christopher Fry, and Alec Clunes, artistic director of the Arts Theatre, where three prizewinning plays would each have a trial production before the judges made their final decision.

They awarded the first prize to John Whiting, a 33-year-old actor, who had been a soldier during the war. His play, *Saint's Day*, not only failed to impress the London critics – it infuriated them. In the *New Statesman,* it was condemned as the worst of the three plays; according to *The Times*, it was "of a badness that must be called indescribable".

But inside the theatrical profession, it aroused great enthusiasm. Peter Brook, John Gielgud, Peggy Ashcroft and Tyrone Guthrie were among those who wrote to *The Times* in its defence. None of these letters made a better case for the play than one published in the *Radio Times,* saying it "splits wide open the conventional forms of playwriting and allies itself with the other modern arts in a way that no other play has done. It helps the theatre to bridge the gap of time which exists between itself and other forms of artistic expression."

The letter was written by the actor-director George Devine, who within five years would be appointed artistic director of the new company at the Royal Court. In post-war France, the leading playwrights were all novelists or poets – Gide, Mauriac, Claudel, Sartre, Genet and Camus. English drama was less literary. Believing this to be the reason for "the gap of time" between it and the other arts, Devine announced that the Royal Court would be a "writers' theatre". After inviting novelists to write for it, he put on plays by Angus Wilson, Doris Lessing and Nigel Dennis. These made little impact, and the play that won prestige and financial security for the new company was a play by another young actor – John Osborne's *Look Back in Anger.* Though Devine went on running the company till 1965, he staged none of Whiting's plays.

Devine's original aims had been unpolitical, but the new voices raised in his theatre were passionately and explicitly committed to Left Wing causes – the voices of Osborne, Arnold Wesker, John Arden, David Storey and Edward Bond. Strongly influenced by his young associate artistic director, Tony Richardson, Devine, who was forty-six, employed such young directors as Lindsay Anderson, William Gaskill and John Dexter. They were all politically involved. A lot of new plays were staged; catchphrases like "angry young man" and "kitchen sink" made the writers look as if they belonged to a movement, and it became increasingly unlikely that Whiting would ever be one of them.

Asked in a 1961 interview what he hoped to achieve, he answered: "What everyone in my job hopes for, I suppose. A masterpiece." How did he hope to achieve it?

> By becoming more sceptical and less enthusiastic; by not marching anywhere; by reserving love for women and not spreading it thinly over the whole of humanity; by not going to the Royal Court Theatre; by detesting simplicity more than I do, if that is possible; by travel; by pleasure; by total rejection of the knitted woollen morality preached by Mr W, X, Y and Z; by investigation and, I suppose it will have to be so, by work.

Many of his statements about his work and his attitudes are to be found in *At Ease in a Bright Red Tie,* a volume of John Whiting's writing on theatre.

His most detailed formulation of his *credo* was made in a lecture he gave at the Old Vic in 1957. Reviewing this in *The Observer* as if it had been a theatrical performance, Kenneth Tynan, who was out of sympathy with Whiting's values, responded positively to only one brief sequence. Discussing language, Whiting dismissed "the direct unornamented speech of everyday life" as untheatrical.

> Pick up a conversation in the street and it may go something like this:
> "Now look here I said I'm not having this I said and so he says What and I says I'm not having it I'm telling you I says up and down the stairs you were four times this morning telling him I was up and down I says in your boots with little Else trying to sleep oh I told him." No, the direct unornamented speech of the theatre must be as artificial as any form.

This fragment of working-class conversation, said Tynan, was "infectiously and rivetingly alive. One longed to hear more." By making it up, Whiting had proved he was a born playwright; by rejecting it he had shown he was determined not to be a playwright at all.

It was clever of Tynan to notice in 1957 that an opportunity was being missed. When Whiting argued that dialogue could not be modelled on conversation overheard in the street, he was only echoing the opinion that was generally held. The most authoritative spokesman for it was T.S. Eliot, who had written about the syntax of theatrical dialogue. Discussing stylists such as Congreve and Shaw, he said their characters spoke in prose no less remote than verse is "from the vocabulary, syntax and rhythm of our ordinary speech – with its fumbling for words, its constant recourse to approximation, its disorder and its unfinished sentences". [T.S. Eliot *Selected Prose* p.68]

Eliot had not always practised what he was now preaching. Over twenty-five years earlier, he had abandoned the verse play that would be published in 1922 under the title *Sweeney Agonistes – Fragments of an Aristophanic Melodrama.* Depicting low-life characters, he imposed jazz rhythms on their repetitions, circumlocutions and approximations.

In the same year, he jazzed working-class speech into a comparable theatricality in a non-theatrical poem. In lines 139-172 of *The Waste Land* the only speaker is a barmaid, whose monologue reflects Eliot's impressions of working-class repetitiousness. Apart from five reiterations of "HURRY UP

PLEASE ITS TIME", the speech consists largely of fragments she quotes from quarrels she has overheard about infidelity and teeth:

> You have them all out, Lil, and get a nice set,
> He said, I swear, I can't bear to look at you.

In much of his early verse, as in this monologue and in *Sweeney*, Eliot versified the language of prostitutes, procuresses, pimps, criminals, and servants chattering about false teeth, fortune-telling and pills taken to induce abortions.

By the fifties he was focusing on more dignified characters. Trying to write plays in verse for the West End, he was also recommending verse to other playwrights. "The human soul," he wrote, "in intense emotion, strives to express itself in verse... The tendency, at any rate, of prose drama is to emphasise the ephemeral and superficial; if we want to get at the permanent and universal, we tend to express ourselves in verse."

Harold Pinter was the first British writer to make a thorough theatrical exploration of working-class repetitions, circumlocutions and approximations. Unlike Whiting, he had little respect for the literary traditions that had run through our drama from Shakespeare to Shaw, and if he learnt anything from Eliot, it was the Eliot of *Sweeney* and the monologues in *The Waste Land*, while Whiting was influenced by the 1935 play *Murder in the Cathedral* (which was written for performance in Canterbury Cathedral), and *The Family Reunion* (1939). In *Saint's Day* the pastiche of Eliot would be astonishingly direct if the play had not started as a technical exercise.

> Careful! We are approaching the point of deviation. At one moment there is laughter and conversation and a progression: people move and speak smoothly and casually, their breathing is controlled and they know what they do. Then there occurs a call from another room, the realisation that a member of the assembly is missing, the sudden shout into the dream and the waking to find the body with the failing heart lying in the

> corridor – with the twisted limbs at the foot of the stairs – the man hanging from the beam, or the child floating drowned in the garden pool. Careful! Be careful! We are approaching that point. The moment of the call from another room.

It is not only cadences and images that derive from Eliot, but the assumption that there are two levels of consciousness which can be registered theatrically. What is happening here is what happens often in the best plays of Eliot and Whiting: instead of seeming to be in full command of what he or she is saying, the speaker is suddenly possessed by a rush of abnormal awareness, but the action is not brought to a standstill, and the tension increases.

While other playwrights (including Eliot himself, Christopher Fry and Ronald Duncan) were trying to write in verse, Whiting could reach this higher level in prose. He could not have done this without Eliot's example, but while Eliot's post-war plays, from *The Cocktail Party* (1950) onwards, become progressively more prosaic, although written in verse, Whiting's plays are poetic, though written in prose. There are moments of impending violence in *Marching Song,* like this one in *Saint's Day,* when the intensity of the language brings the character's apprehensions arrestingly into close-up, while the theatrical suspense is increased by our uncertainty whether there is anything to be scared of.

With the exception of Thomas à Becket in *Murder in the Cathedral,* Eliot's characters are less interesting than what they say. Like the women who form the chorus in *Murder in the Cathedral,* the uncles and aunts in *The Family Reunion* are given some excellent lines to speak, but never come to life either collectively or individually. What goes through their consciousness is interesting; they are not. But Whiting fuses the language and consciousness of his characters with the situations he creates for them. The women of Canterbury describe their suffering, but Stella is giving us a taste of hers in the speech I have just quoted. Whiting's characters are highly conscious, touchingly vulnerable, sensitive, sometimes pathetic and (unlike Eliot's) capable of being profoundly altered by the action that involves them.

But until *The Devils* was staged by the Royal Shakespeare Company at the beginning of the sixties, Whiting's plays were dismally unsuccessful in the theatre. Did *Saint's Day* and *Marching Song* fail to achieve commercial success because he was offering something like heroic tragedy to an audience that neither believed in heroes nor wanted tragedy?

One of Kenneth Tynan's reviews in the *Observer* was titled: "No Time for Tragedy". His argument that our century is inimical to tragedy was worked out on roughly Marxist lines: "There is today hardly an aspect of human suffering (outside the realm of medicine) for which politics, psychiatry and environmental psychology cannot offer at least a *tentative* solution." His forecast was that "satire, irony, gallows-humour and other mutations of the comic spirit will be the guiding forces of our theatre in the coming years. Tragedy... has little to say to a rebellious generation obsessed by the imminent danger of mega-deaths."

For Whiting, the existence of the bomb made it all the more urgent to scrutinise destructive forces in human nature. Several of his characters are viciously aggressive, while the whole of his work is characterised by its sensitivity to the violence of unreason and the impossibility of reasoning about violence. The forces that destroy the heroes of *Saint's Day* and *The Devils* are hideously arbitrary; falling in love not so much with each other as with life and death, Whiting's characters undergo changes that can be described only as conversions. What makes them lose their faith in man or dedicate themselves to self-destruction?

None of these conversions could have been treated in simple language, and as his technique improved, Whiting became not more but less explicit about them. The obscurest of all his monologues is Robert Procathren's in the third act of *Saint's Day*. During rehearsals for the first production in 1951, both Alec Clunes and the producer, Stephen Murray, urged him to make the speech more explicit. But the problem is that it is too explanatory – Procathren is being made to explain things he does not understand. He has only just become aware of the violence in himself and in the world outside. He does not know why he is revenging himself by destroying two innocent men, but he did not understand why his own innocence had been destroyed by a pistol that went off by accident in his hand, killing an innocent woman.

From being a conscientious objector, John Whiting had become a soldier, but he cannot be accused of writing autobiographically. The main reason soldiering features so prominently in his plays is that it raises questions of discipline and destruction, order and chaos. The leader of the small group that carries out the hanging at the end of *Saint's Day* uses the argument that was used by Nazi war criminals in the Nuremberg trials and may have been used by the airmen who dropped the first atomic bombs – they were acting under orders.

Tragedy rests on a profound conviction that the universe cannot be governed by reason. The gods are not just, and no programme of political and economic change can make them alter their ways. Tragedy is a resounding vote of no confidence in the powers that be, and in any powers that might supplant them. Whiting refused to interpret human experience in social, political and economic terms. He was primarily interested in what it means to be a man. To question this in a theatrical perspective, he had to explore the empty spaces around the man-made problems and relationships. As in tragedy, he propelled man into a relationship with the totality of his existence.

He examined what it was that raised some men above the level of the rest. He also examined the lowest common multiples, but he needed a heroic yardstick to measure the ordinary inch of humanity. His heroes outgrow their fellow men before they find out how inadequate they are. If they had not isolated themselves from the human herd, they could not have felt such a strong urge to rejoin it.

Ronald Hayman
London, 1998

# Introduction to
# NO MORE A-ROVING
# CONDITIONS OF AGREEMENT

In 1947 the 29-year-old John Whiting took himself through his apprenticeship as a dramatist by writing two plays, *No More A-Roving* and *Conditions of Agreement*. If they had been produced or published, no-one could have predicted that he would develop into an extraordinarily good playwright, but it would have been clear that he would not become an ordinary one. He had a distinctive voice, a talent for arousing curiosity and drawing the audience into emotional involvement with the characters, a natural stylishness and a determination to avoid clichés of characterisation and plotting. He may have been unable to solve all the problems he set himself, but he would tackle them in his own way.

The earlier of the two plays, *No More A-Roving*, is the more congenial. Like the lilting Byron lyric that provides its title, it has charm and panache. Without being directly autobiographical, it concerns itself with an issue that must have been crucial for many young men returning to civilian life from the Second World War – is it possible to resume or renew old relationships with lovers and friends?

Angus, Benedict and the beautiful Kirsty have not seen each other for eight years. Benedict does not know that Angus and Kirsty were lovers. Angus does not know that Benedict, who was never Kirsty's lover, still believes himself to be in love with her. The audience does not find out till late in the third act that both Kirsty and Angus are now married.

Whiting's originality and sophistication are at first less apparent in his handling of these relationships than in one that carries no erotic charge. Angus has a 15-year-old servant girl called Willy Yeats. So far as he knows, this is her real name. Most plays of this period contain at least one condescendingly characterised maid or manservant, but Willy is dignified and solemn, fierce and self-sufficient, obedient and polite without being servile. She wears a fair-isle jersey and a tweed skirt. Angus has tried hard but unsuccessfully to teach her how to make tea. She is incompetent at making sandwiches, and is prone to domestic accidents, but she can recite by heart the times of the trains to London.

Another way in which Whiting distances himself from run-of-the-mill romantic comedies is by investing the characters with the sort of self-consciousness that allows them to take hold of what they are saying as if they were actors. Sometimes they even offer each other advice on how a conversation should be held. "We must behave," says Kirsty, "as if we hadn't seen each other for eight years," and some of the dialogue that follows is printed in inverted commas.

They also contrive entrances and exits for each other. Having told Kirsty that Benedict is coming to stay for the weekend, Angus sends her upstairs, telling her what time to come down again. In the second act, wanting to be alone with her, each of the men finds a pretext for sending the other to the pub.

*Conditions of Agreement* is spikier, more ambitious, more seriously flawed. Whereas *No More A-Roving* comes close to fulfilling its modest objectives, *Conditions of Agreement* tries to make a much bigger statement. At its best moments it achieves striking effects that surpass any in *No More A-Roving*, but at its worst it falls more obviously short of its intentions, and generally it fails to weld its parts into such a satisfying whole.

Readers already familiar with Whiting's later work will find them prefigured more excitingly in *Conditions of Agreement* than in *No More A-Roving*. Unlike the first play, the second contains some long monologues, and it announces several themes that will later be developed more forcefully, together with many preoccupations and many images that will recur. The dialogue is sometimes literary and deliberate, sometimes sparse and colloquial.

Unlike the charming and glamorous characters in *No More A-Roving*, the people in *Conditions of Agreement* are unsavoury – a one-eyed old man who used to be a clown in a circus, a retired grocer, a 58-year-old widow, her giant of a son, who has an artificial leg, and his 17-year-old wife, who was born illegitimate and grew up in an institution. They all have time on their hands, which is disadvantageous for the play, tending to make the action too leisurely. Nothing of any moment can be expected to happen, and the plotting of the son and the ex-clown for revenge on the ex-grocer are hardly less vague than the grudge they have against him. His main offence is to keep telling the story of how his wife was killed in an accident at the circus where the clown was performing.

Whiting succeeds in winding up some of the sequences to considerable tension and in combining comic and tragic elements. But the plot relies heavily on narrative about past action, and the most poignant combinations of comedy and tragedy occur in narrative monologues. The ex-grocer describes how the circus audience went on laughing at the clown's antics while the distressed husband tried to get help for his wife, who was hanging upside down, with her heel caught in the structure of the stand, and her skirt falling over her head.

One of the play's more interesting features is the contrast between the short speeches and the narrative monologues. In neither does Whiting approximate realistically to the speech patterns of a clown, a grocer or a girl who has grown up in an institution. At a moment of reciprocated passion, the young girl tells her husband:

> There is no cause to be afraid of the night. Why are you shy with me? You must have no shame with me. Together, we must be gay and impudent – and it must be you who comes to me to demand and be bold. I want that.

She is then given an instant of self-consciousness reminiscent of *No More A-Roving.* Jerking out of her rhetorical lyricism, she explains: "I had to say that."

All these early plays contain moments in which characters comment on themselves as if from outside, prefiguring the moment in *Marching Song* when Dido says: "I'm the girl you see on the edge of the crowd at a street accident."

# NO MORE A-ROVING

# Characters

ANGUS

KIRSTY

WILLY

BENEDICT

JAMES

ELIZABETH

The scene is a room of a house situated some thirty miles west of London on the Thames, the time being the present.

# ACT ONE

*1946: the afternoon of a Saturday in summer.*
*The scene is a room of a house on a bank of the Thames some thirty miles west of London.*
*The room itself has great charm. It was obviously designed for no other reason than to contain the delightful happenings of the next twenty-four hours. There are three entrances: a main door, leading directly into the garden stairs leading to an upper floor, and a passage-way leading to the kitchen and rest of the house.*
*ANGUS LEAROYD, aged thirty-two, is seated at a table. He is writing. KIRSTY WINTON is standing in the open doorway looking at ANGUS. She is twenty-seven, a gracious, humorous and lovely creature, dressed as befits her part in this comedy. She stands watching ANGUS for a moment, unseen by him. She speaks.*

KIRSTY: So this is where you live now!
(*ANGUS turns to her.*)
ANGUS: Hullo, Kirsty.
KIRSTY: Hullo, Angus.
ANGUS: I didn't hear you arrive. How long have you been there?
KIRSTY: A moment.
ANGUS: I didn't hear you.
KIRSTY: I'm expected to arrive, you know.
ANGUS: Oh, yes. Yes, I know.
KIRSTY: Then may I come in?
ANGUS: I'm so sorry. Of course. (*He rises and goes to her, taking from her the small case she carries.*) Do come in.
KIRSTY: (*She holds out her hand.*) Hullo, Angus. How are you? (*They shake hands.*)
ANGUS: I'm very well.
KIRSTY: Good.
ANGUS: How are you?
KIRSTY: I'm also very well. I thought this must be the house. You're rather isolated.
ANGUS: Yes, I suppose we are.
KIRSTY: We?
ANGUS: Yes. I have a girl who looks after me.

KIRSTY: I see.

ANGUS: You walked from the station. Do sit down.

KIRSTY: Thank you. Yes, I walked. It's farther than I thought.

ANGUS: I could have met you but you didn't say the time you were arriving –

KIRSTY: No.

ANGUS: – just sometime in the afternoon. There are several trains.

KIRSTY: It didn't matter. (*There is a pause.*) It's very pleasant here.

ANGUS: The house?

KIRSTY: Yes.

ANGUS: It's been lent to me for a year.

KIRSTY: Oh? Not yours?

ANGUS: No. Would you like some tea?

KIRSTY: I don't think so.

ANGUS: A drink, then.

KIRSTY: No, thank you. (*There is a pause.*) I suppose we must reconcile –

ANGUS: What?

KIRSTY: I was going to say that I suppose we must reconcile ourselves to the fact that at first conversation will be difficult. It is, isn't it?

ANGUS: I –

KIRSTY: You're trying to think of something to say.

ANGUS: Not at all. I can say this; you're very lovely.

KIRSTY: That's hardly a subject for conversation between us.

ANGUS: It was once upon a time.

KIRSTY: Once upon a time.

ANGUS: Damn!

KIRSTY: What is it?

ANGUS: Just a minute. (*He goes to the passage-way and calls to the kitchen.*) Willy Yeats!

KIRSTY: I haven't been near this part of the river for years.

ANGUS: Eight years.

KIRSTY: What?

ANGUS: Eight years. I remember perfectly.

(*WILLY YEATS has entered and stands in the passage-way leading to the kitchen. She is the maid, fifteen-years-old and, by nature, a fierce little girl: She wears no uniform but a tweed skirt and a fair-isle jersey. ANGUS turns and shouts again* Willy Yeats! *before he sees her.*)

WILLY: Yes?

ANGUS: Oh, there you are. Where have you been?

WILLY: I haven't been anywhere.

ANGUS: Haven't you? Well, will you clear that table. (*He indicates the used plates on the table.*) It looks most unpleasant.

WILLY: All right, sir.

ANGUS: The lunch was very nice. Especially the chocolate – the chocolate thing –

WILLY: Mould.

ANGUS: Mould, was it? Anyway, it was very nice. It was a good idea to put nuts in it.

WILLY: There weren't any nuts in it.

ANGUS: Weren't there? Then what were the little pieces of – well, never mind. (*To KIRSTY.*) This is Willy Yeats. She looks after me – makes me mould and things like that. Miss Kirsty Winton.

KIRSTY: How do you do.

WILLY: I'm pleased, very pleased. (*She holds up the plates.*) These'll want washing.

ANGUS: What? Yes. Yes, indeed they will.

WILLY: I'll do them.

ANGUS: Good. (*WILLY begins her return to the kitchen.*) I shall want you again in a few minutes. Come back then, will you?

WILLY: Yes, sir.

(*She goes out to the kitchen.*)

KIRSTY: Is Willy Yeats a nickname?

ANGUS: I don't think so.

KIRSTY: It doesn't strike you as being in the least strange, obviously.

ANGUS: No, because I suppose it to be her real name. You see, when I came here I wanted somebody like that –

well, not exactly like that but somebody – to come and help me here. I made enquiries in the village and I was told the local schoolmaster was the man –

KIRSTY: What!

ANGUS: To consult, I mean. So I went to see him. The next day I received a postcard from him saying, 'Am sending you Willy Yeats'. Two hours later she arrived. I said, 'Are you Willy Yeats?' and she said, 'Yes'.

KIRSTY: Then I suppose she must be.

ANGUS: I suppose so, but must we talk about her?

KIRSTY: Not necessarily. (*There is a pause.*) But we must talk about something.

ANGUS: What do you mean? Surely you must have something to say to me even though it is eight years since –

KIRSTY: Don't be angry.

ANGUS: I'm not, really. Did I sound angry?

KIRSTY: Yes. Is it really eight years?

ANGUS: You know perfectly well it is: Eight years, and that, whether we like it or not, makes me thirty-two and you twenty-seven. Now, does that fact give us a starting point?

KIRSTY: Do we need a starting point – you and I?

ANGUS: Yes.

KIRSTY: Very well. Then we must start from this moment and we must do it properly. We must behave as though we haven't seen each other for eight years.

ANGUS: Well, we haven't.

KIRSTY: Then let us behave as if we haven't.

ANGUS: You'll have to begin. I don't know how to do it.

KIRSTY: Something like this. (*She pauses.*) 'It was exciting to get a letter from you. But how on earth did you get my address?'

ANGUS: You know perfectly well the letter was forwarded to you.

KIRSTY: Oh, come along! Play up!

ANGUS: 'Well, as a matter of fact, I came across an old letter from you at the back of a drawer – and I thought how nice it would be to see you again. So I wrote to you hoping that it would find you.' How's that?

KIRSTY: Very good. Keep it up. 'An old letter from me! What did it say?'

ANGUS: 'My darling Angus, my brother, Henry, was in town last night and so I couldn't come round to you. I despise Henry but I love you – Kirsty.' (*He moves towards her.*) Kirsty.

KIRSTY: 'I was surprised when I got your letter. I've often wondered what had happened to you. Often. I kept an eye on the Personal Columns just to see if you ever married or had a baby or even died. But you wouldn't do that, would you?'

ANGUS: 'Of course not.' Must we keep this up?

KIRSTY: Yes. 'Have you seen anyone we used to know?'

ANGUS: 'No.'

KIRSTY: 'No one at all?'

ANGUS: 'No'

KIRSTY: 'Henry was killed.'

ANGUS: 'Was he really.'

KIRSTY: 'In the War.'

ANGUS: 'Fancy that!'

KIRSTY: 'Haven't you any news for me?'

ANGUS: 'No.'

(*There is a pause.*)

KIRSTY: 'Have you seen anything of Benedict? Benedict Clare.'

ANGUS: 'No, but I hope to in a few minutes.'

KIRSTY: What did you say?

ANGUS: I said, 'No, I haven't seen anything of Benedict but I hope to see something of him in a few minutes.'

KIRSTY: What do you mean?

ANGUS: What I say. Do you think it's going to rain?

KIRSTY: I don't think so. You mean Benedict's coming here, today?

ANGUS: Yes. I've asked him here, also. It's rather cloudy over there. What was it like in town?

KIRSTY: Fine. Is Benedict – ?

ANGUS: I wished you, Benedict and myself to meet again.

KIRSTY: I see. You sound pontifical.

ANGUS: After eight years. A reunion.

KIRSTY: Of course, we can't really start again.<br>ANGUS: I don't think it's going to rain. } *Spoken together.*

What did you say?

KIRSTY: I said, we can't really – never mind. When will he be here?

ANGUS: Benedict?

KIRSTY: Yes.

ANGUS: Any minute, I should think. He's coming from Devon.

KIRSTY: Where?

ANGUS: Devon.

KIRSTY: I thought you said Heaven.

ANGUS: No, Devon. The train from Reading got in about five minutes ago.

KIRSTY : It'll be nice to see him again.

ANGUS: Yes.

KIRSTY: Of course, he's very famous now.

ANGUS: Very.

KIRSTY: Those posters! Oh, dear!

ANGUS: 'Whatstheirname Films present Irresistible – '

KIRSTY : ' – indomitable – '

ANGUS: ' – impregnable – '

KIRSTY: ' – incontestable – '

ANGUS: ' – inextinguishable Benedict Clare in "Poppy".' (*They laugh.*)

KIRSTY: Oh, very famous. Still, it will be nice to see him again. Does he know I'm going to he here?

ANGUS: No. That's something I want – (*He has moved to the passage-way. He calls.*) Willy!

KIRSTY: Angus, why this – ?

ANGUS: Willy!

KIRSTY: Why this elaborate planning to get the three of us together again?

ANGUS: It isn't elaborate planning. It is merely an invitation to two people – two people I once knew – to come and spend a weekend with me. Isn't that a good idea?

KIRSTY: Very good. But why, after all these years?

ANGUS: Are you pretending you don't know?

KIRSTY: Yes.

ANGUS: Well, stop pretending. It never did any good. (*WILLY YEATS enters.*) Will you show Miss Winton to her room.

WILLY: Yes, sir.

(*KIRSTY and WILLY move to the stairs.*)

ANGUS: You've forgotten the case.

WILLY: Sorry, sir.

(*She returns to fetch it and then goes up the stairs after KIRSTY.*)

ANGUS: (*Calls.*) Kirsty!

(*She returns to the stairs.*)

KIRSTY: Yes?

ANGUS: Do you remember Benedict well? How he looks: what he says: and –

KIRSTY: Of course.

ANGUS: Have you seen him recently?

KIRSTY: No. Have you?

ANGUS: The last time I saw him was when we left him in London eight years ago.

KIRSTY: I remember. You said he doesn't know I'm going to be here.

ANGUS: No. That's why I want to – Have you a watch?

KIRSTY: Yes.

ANGUS: Come down here again, looking very beautiful, at twenty minutes to four.

KIRSTY: That's rather a long time.

ANGUS: Surely not, having waited eight years.

KIRSTY: It's a dirty trick to play on him. You'll look ridiculous if he doesn't recognize me.

ANGUS: You haven't changed, have you?

KIRSTY: No?

(*KIRSTY goes, passing WILLY who is coming down the stairs. ANGUS shouts after KIRSTY.*)

ANGUS: Don't be cryptic! Have you changed? (*But she has gone.*) Willy.

WILLY: Sir?

ANGUS: A moment. (*WILLY goes to him.*) Now, Willy, relax. Compose yourself and listen to me. Right?

WILLY: Right.

ANGUS: In the last few days, since we started our excursion into housekeeping together, you and I have got along very well. Don't you think so?

WILLY: I don't think we've done too badly.

ANGUS: Mind you, I don't think we can say there haven't been minor disasters. In fact, I think the incident of the coffee-machine might be classed as a major disaster – I still can't understand what you mean when you say the thing exploded – coffee is not an explosive –

WILLY: Well I was holding it –

(*She begins to demonstrate.*)

ANGUS: However, we'll forget that and say that generally we have managed to get along without – undue friction. But surely that is because we have both been willing to give and take. You have tolerated me when I have lost my temper and I have tolerated you when you have handed me food on a plate that was red-hot – that reminds me, when you have a minute will you try and get those stains out of the carpet – ?

WILLY: That'll need scrubbing.

ANGUS: Then scrub it. No, no! Not now. Later. Tell me – it interests me – how do you manage to hold plates as hot as that? Have you asbestos gloves permanently on your hands?

WILLY: No. It's just that I don't seem to feel anything at all.

ANGUS: Don't you? That's very interesting. But please try to remember that other people do.

WILLY: All right.

ANGUS: However, as I say, in the last few days we have not done so badly together. But Willy – and this is the point I wish to make – we have got to attempt a more concerted effort over the next two days –

WILLY: We will! We will!

ANGUS: Yes, we will, won't we? This is what I want to say. Miss Winton and Mr Clare, who are staying with me this week-end, are used to living in organized houses. Houses where the bath-water is hot but not so hot that the boiler begins to move round the kitchen under its own steam: houses where the meals are served on time but not at such a speed that the server is precipitated down the cellar steps: houses where –

WILLY: I understand what you mean.

ANGUS: You do? Good. Now, we both know from experience that there are some things you just cannot do. There are, aren't there?

WILLY: I suppose so.

ANGUS: You needn't be ashamed. There are certain things – everyday occurrences – which defeat everyone. Different people: different things. The great idea is to be able to recognize those problems when they arise and to admit oneself defeated: immediately. That is what I want you to do. We both know these things that you find difficult or impossible, don't we?

WILLY: Yes.

ANGUS: Well, over the next two days I don't want you even to attempt any of them. When you see one of these – these 'situations' approaching, go no further. Stop! Come straight to me and say, 'Mr Learoyd, I'm organized, but – ', or something like that.

WILLY: Very well, sir. I'll do that.

ANGUS: And then I'll come along and see what I can do about it. Now, I don't want you to look upon this as a lecture but rather as a little conference between us.

WILLY: I'll try! I'll try, sir! O God! I'll try!

ANGUS: I'm sure you will. Now, a few practical details. Mr Clare will be arriving very soon and then –

WILLY: Sir!

ANGUS: Willy?

WILLY: May I put a question?

ANGUS: Certainly.

WILLY: Would it be Mr Clare, the film actor?

ANGUS: Yes, it would be. I mean, it is.

WILLY: Oh.

ANGUS: Something the matter?

WILLY: It's just that I don't like him.

ANGUS: Do you know him?

WILLY: Yes, on the pictures.

ANGUS: Well, it so happens that I like him very much indeed. So we won't say any more about that. Now, we shall need some tea this afternoon and some supper this evening. And that is all you need to worry about today.

WILLY: I was cutting the sandwiches for tea when you called me.

ANGUS: Were you? What are you putting in them?

WILLY: It's a special sandwich filling, sir.

ANGUS: Oh. Well, I should think that will be very nice – yes. Don't cut them too thick, will you?

WILLY: Oh, no. they're very fine. No crusts.

ANGUS: No. No crusts. Well, I think that's everything. We've arranged a tea and a supper and there's nothing in either of those meals that you can't do, is there?

WILLY: Nothing, except make the tea.

ANGUS: No, you can't do that, I know. Just give me a shout and I'll come and do it for you. I can't understand why you can't manage that. It's just a question of boiling the water and pouring it – However, it's too late to attempt to teach you now.

WILLY: I'll learn someday! I will!

ANGUS: Yes, but not today. Give me those papers, will you? (*He points to the manuscripts on the table: WILLY hands them to him.*) Thank you. Your hands aren't very clean.

WILLY: It's the sandwich filling. (*She has been staring out of the window.*) There's a gentleman standing at the gate looking both ways.

(*ANGUS looks through the window.*)

ANGUS: Yes, that's Mr Clare. Now, remember, Willy, this is all very important to me. Mr Clare is a very old friend and – well, you do understand, don't you?

WILLY: No.

ANGUS: Never mind. (*He goes to the door and calls.*) Benedict! (*After a moment BENEDICT CLARE enters.*)

BENEDICT: Hullo, Angus. Thought this must be it. How are you?

ANGUS: Very well.

(*They shake hands.*)

BENEDICT: This is where we say to each other – 'You haven't changed a damn bit'.

ANGUS: Do we?

BENEDICT: You haven't, anyway. Have I?

ANGUS: No, I don't think so.

BENEDICT: God! I have though! For the worse. I'll tell you about it.

ANGUS: Well, stop grinning and come in.

BENEDICT: Thank you. (*He sees WILLY YEATS.*) How do you do.

ANGUS: Take Mr Clare's bag to the bedroom, Willy Yeats.

(*WILLY takes the bag from BENEDICT.*)

BENEDICT: Thank you.

(*WILLY goes up the stairs.*)

ANGUS: It's a bunk. I hope you don't mind.

BENEDICT: No I don't mind. I say –

ANGUS: Yes?

BENEDICT: What did you call the – the person who took my bag?

ANGUS: Willy Yeats.

BENEDICT: I see. Wearing a kilt. My eyes, as they say, must be deceiving me. I thought it was a girl.

ANGUS: It is.

BENEDICT: And she's called Willy Yeats.

ANGUS: Yes.

BENEDICT: That's all right. As long as I know. Well, how are you?

ANGUS: I'm very well. Won't you – ?

BENEDICT: I can't imagine why you've – What are you trying to say?

ANGUS: I'm trying to say – 'Won't you sit down?'

BENEDICT: Yes, I will. Now, before I say anything else I must ask you one thing: why haven't you got in touch with me before this?

ANGUS: Things have been rather disturbed in the last few years. There's been a war, you know.

BENEDICT: Oh, yes, I know that. When I got your letter –

ANGUS: Was it such a shock?

BENEDICT: Not at all, because I've often thought of you and presumed that one day you'd write to me again. I've wanted to get hold of you but I'd no idea where you were. It's strange that we knew each other so well and yet knew so little about each other. Relations and things, I mean.

ANGUS: I haven't any.

BENEDICT: Neither have I, since that terrible old Aunt Ellen of mine died.

ANGUS: I met her.

BENEDICT: Of course you did. (*They laugh.*) There was only one person who could have really brought us together again.

ANGUS: Who was that?

BENEDICT: Kirsty. Kirsty Winton. Do you know where she is? You haven't forgotten her?

ANGUS: No. No, I haven't forgotten her. Will you have a cigarette?

BENEDICT: Thank you. The last time I saw you was – am I right? – getting on to a train at Paddington – that was –

ANGUS: Eight years ago.

BENEDICT: Is it as long as that?

ANGUS: Don't you pretend you don't remember.

BENEDICT: Why? Has someone else been pretending?

ANGUS: Yes.

BENEDICT: Who? You know, now I see you again I realize I'm eight years older. That's curious, because – I haven't got anything to light this with.

ANGUS: Here you are.

BENEDICT: Oh, thanks. (*They light their cigarettes. WILLY YEATS comes down the stairs and goes out to the kitchen.*) No, it's curious, because, as I was going to say, I haven't been aware of my growing older in the last few years. But you – you haven't changed at all. To look at, I mean. I'm glad of that. Have you changed otherwise?

ANGUS: I'm also eight years older and actually I'm a little thinner.

BENEDICT: Yes. Yes, you are thinner. Otherwise unchanged. Good. How are you?

ANGUS: Don't keep saying, 'How are you?' I'm very well.

BENEDICT: I'm sorry. The fact is, I think I'm a little shy.

ANGUS: So am I.

BENEDICT: I'm so glad. (*They laugh.*) We show it in different ways, don't we? Have you lived here long?

ANGUS: I don't really live here. Well, I have for the last three months but, what I mean is, I don't own the place.

BENEDICT: I thought perhaps – Now I need an ashtray. (*ANGUS brings one to him.*)

ANGUS: It has been lent to me for a year. By a friend.

BENEDICT: Do I know him?

ANGUS: I don't think so. George Hellman. He's gone to the States.

BENEDICT: No, I don't think I know him.

ANGUS: There's no reason why you should.

BENEDICT: He wasn't – you didn't know him before the war?

ANGUS: No. He dates from about two years ago.

BENEDICT: I've seen no one I knew in those days with you. No one. I have an entirely new set of friends and acquaintances – and I don't like any of them very much– at least, I don't think I do. Oh, I don't know – I suppose they're all right. Have you seen anyone you used to know then?

ANGUS: You.

BENEDICT: Of course – and you remember who I am?

ANGUS: Oh, yes.

BENEDICT: Good because, you see, names – God! even faces – mean nothing to me now. I am incapable of connecting either with any period of my life. Dozens of faces keep coming up to me and saying, 'Hullo! How are you? Good to see you again'. And I say, 'Hullo! Well, Well! So it's you – ', but who, who is it? I haven't the faintest notion. It's just another face.

ANGUS: (*Laughing.*) Never mind.

BENEDICT: If you had come up to me in the street I probably shouldn't have known who you were.

ANGUS: Of course, you're very famous now.

BENEDICT: Oh, not because of that! Please, Angus!

ANGUS: I know. I was joking. Tell me what you've been doing.

BENEDICT: Well, I.......

ANGUS: Where did you go after I left you in London?

BENEDICT: I didn't go anywhere. I stayed where I was. Damn it! I couldn't move because I hadn't any money. I stayed in London – unemployed and alone – until the war started. That seemed a solution so I joined the Army.

ANGUS: What sort of thing were you in? I mean, what did you do?

BENEDICT: Well, it was a peculiar branch of the service, as they say: rather difficult to describe. I believe some of the others in it actually had guns – but, of course, I was not allowed to touch anything like that.

ANGUS: Of course not.

BENEDICT: Then, one day, I fell on my head. Three weeks later I was out.

ANGUS: – of the Army?

BENEDICT: Yes. And so I went back to the theatre and found them making do with a few strange, androgynous creatures. I passed among them and on into films – playing an unexpectedly long part in a piece of patriotic nonsense, called 'We, the Defeated'. Need I say the title is ironical?

ANGUS: I saw a picture of you in the paper attending the first night –

BENEDICT: Première, please.

ANGUS: The photographer had literally caught you on the wrong foot. I laughed.

BENEDICT: Why didn't you write to me then?

ANGUS: I don't know. I think your eminent position rather frightened me.

BENEDICT: Don't be absurd!

ANGUS: It's true.

BENEDICT: You are trying to make out that because I am what I am now I have forgotten – No, Angus! No! – we were – with Kirsty – the three of us – what am I trying to say?

ANGUS: I don't know.

BENEDICT: Damn it! You must have known how pleased I'd have been to have heard from you. (*There is a pause.*) What's the matter?

ANGUS: Nothing. Anyway, I was very pleased to see from the newspapers – I'm afraid I've never actually seen one of your films – but I was happy to hear that you'd made a success of your job. Another thing –

BENEDICT: I want to ask you something. Are you listening?

ANGUS: Yes.

BENEDICT: It was something you said to me years ago. You said, 'Benedict, you're a very nice person but your sincerity is the sincerity of a clown – exaggerated to gain favour'.

ANGUS: Did I say that?

BENEDICT: Yes, and I found only little consolation in the fact that you were rather drunk at the time.

ANGUS: You were the only person in the world I ever dare criticize – even in those days.

BENEDICT: I remind you of that because of what I'm going to tell you now – incidentally, how long may I stay here?

ANGUS: Until Wednesday.

BENEDICT: Thank you.

ANGUS: What were you going to tell me?

BENEDICT: I was going to ask you something. I was going to ask you not to laugh at me while I'm here and not to make fun of the work I'm doing now.

ANGUS: Such an idea had never entered my head.

BENEDICT: You see, I'm rather proud of myself and of what I've done in the last two or three years. (*He pauses.*) I told you I'd changed.

ANGUS: You said for the worse.

BENEDICT: Well, isn't that for the worse in your eyes?

ANGUS: No!

BENEDICT: I thought it would be. Again, I make a lot of money now and yet –

ANGUS: Well?

BENEDICT: – what can I spend it on?

ANGUS: God bless my soul!

BENEDICT: Don't laugh at me.

ANGUS: I'm not. Are you unhappy?

BENEDICT: Yes. And I thanked God when I got your letter asking me down here to see you again.

ANGUS: Why?

BENEDICT: Because I've been lonely. Yes, that's it; lonely. You remember the person I was eight years ago?

ANGUS: Yes.

BENEDICT: I was all right, wasn't I?

ANGUS: You were very much all right.

BENEDICT: I want you to make me remember, through yourself –

ANGUS: I think you're dramatizing.

BENEDICT: No, I'm not. I want you to make me remember through yourself the person I was when we knew each other before. When there were three of us: you, Kirsty Winton and myself. Let's call it an experiment.

ANGUS: But were you so very different then?

BENEDICT: I suppose it's difficult for you to judge.

ANGUS: It is, rather.

BENEDICT: I was very different then. Good enough?

ANGUS: Yes. I'll take your word for it.

BENEDICT: I can give you no explanation. Perhaps I was unconsciously hinting at it when I said that on seeing you again I realized I was eight years older. I don't want to grow old, Angus – not even middle-aged. (*There is a pause.*) Don't look so serious. Here's something to make you laugh. This morning, to travel and stay down here, I brought just as little money with me as I should have done had I been coming to see you eight years ago. Also I tried to find some clothes – clothes that I would have worn eight years ago. I failed – that is even more pathetic – because I found I had no old clothes at all. (*He pauses.*) You're not laughing.

ANGUS: I'm so sorry. (*But he does not laugh.*) Can I help?

BENEDICT: I was hoping you'd say that. Yes, you can help. By being yourself.

(*WILLY YEATS has entered: she crosses to the stairs.*)

ANGUS: Nothing simpler. I never indulge in – Where are you going, Willy Yeats?

WILLY: To the lavatory.

ANGUS: I beg your pardon – that is, I'm so sorry – I – By the way, if you want it, Benedict, it's at the top of the stairs.

(*WILLY YEATS goes up the stairs.*)

BENEDICT: Well, not at the moment.

ANGUS: As was saying, I never indulge in false reasoning about myself.

BENEDICT: Meaning that I do.

ANGUS: Yes.

BENEDICT: My dear Angus. Although I haven't seen you for eight years I have often during that time lowered the thought of you like an anchor to steady myself on the choppy sea of my introspection.

ANGUS: That's a really dreadful sentence, Benedict. Pull yourself together.

BENEDICT: Sorry. (*They laugh.*) Steady. Yes, that's the word for you. Have you remained as steady through the last eight years?

ANGUS: There was no option, because I have what is known as a 'steady' job. I help to manage a small firm of boat-builders just down the river here.

BENEDICT: Of course, you did that sort of thing before the War.

ANGUS: It was here, to this place – not this house but this part of the river – that I ran when I left London.

BENEDICT: Go on.

ANGUS: I seemed to spend years running away. First of all I ran from people and then I ran from the War. Oh, I couldn't have done anything had I stayed. 'They'd never have taken me on. Not even in your peculiar branch of the service. I'm really a weak little fellow, you know. However, when I left you in London that time I came here – stayed for a time – six weeks – and then sailed to Cornwall –

BENEDICT: Cornwall!

ANGUS: – alone. I was down there when war broke out. The reason? Because Kirsty –

BENEDICT: Kirsty? Why haven't we spoken about her?

ANGUS: I don't know.

BENEDICT: I wonder what's happened to her? Married? Maybe dead? So many people seem to be dead – quite intelligent people too. But Kirsty – darling child. Sorry. What were you talking about?

ANGUS: Myself.

BENEDICT: Of course. Go on.

ANGUS: Nothing more to tell.

(*WILLY YEATS returns: there is silence as she crosses the room and goes out into the kitchen.*)

ANGUS: (*Calling after her.*) What's the time, Willy Yeats?

WILLY: (*From the kitchen.*) Getting on for twenty to four, sir.

ANGUS: (*To BENEDICT.*) We'll have some tea in a few minutes.

BENEDICT: Good. I'd like some.

ANGUS: Then you can have a Willy Yeats's sandwich with the special filling.

BENEDICT: That'll be exciting. You know, Angus, I haven't been talking nonsense to you. About myself, I mean. I really do feel like that.

ANGUS: I think I know exactly how you feel about yourself.

BENEDICT: You should. You always did before.

ANGUS: I'll do my best to understand you again, Benedict.

BENEDICT: I shan't blame you if you don't understand. As we have said, we're both eight years older than we were at that time. We're in a different environment. I have more money than I had – you have less. Yes?

ANGUS: Yes.

BENEDICT: We have been apart and, probably very important, Kirsty Winton isn't with us now. She was important to us, wasn't she?

ANGUS: Yes.

BENEDICT: Your attitude towards her was always rather odd.

ANGUS: I don't think so.

BENEDICT: Oh, yes, it was.

ANGUS: Don't be so hectoring, Benedict. My attitude wasn't in the least odd.

BENEDICT: I was very much in love with her.

ANGUS: I know.

BENEDICT: Was it so very apparent?

ANGUS: It was up to the moment that you realized you were in love with her.

BENEDICT: I can tell you exactly when that was. You were ill with 'flu –

ANGUS: That night?

BENEDICT: I never touched her. I once kissed her. She laughed.

ANGUS: Don't go on like this. You'll make yourself ill.

BENEDICT: It was that evening you had 'flu. Kirsty and I had been to supper together leaving you alone. That evening I realized I loved her. I never told her – never had a chance. Am I being pathetic?

ANGUS: Yes.

BENEDICT: Good. On the same day that I got your letter this week I found her photograph – a coincidence – and looking at it I realized I'd never fallen out of love with her. It was strange – I couldn't remember seeing that particular photograph before – but I knew I still loved her. A slight feeling of sickness –

ANGUS: There's no need to go into the disgusting details.

BENEDICT: An odd sort of tremor when I remembered how she walked and spoke. You'd never say a thing like that, would you?

ANGUS: No.

BENEDICT: Look! I came down here with the express intention of being as miserable as hell about the past with you and as miserable as hell I'm going to be.

ANGUS: Carry on.

BENEDICT: Damn it! I thought that was why you asked me down here. So that we could be as miserable as hell together.

ANGUS: Was it so good?

BENEDICT: What?

ANGUS: The past.

BENEDICT: Well, wasn't it? Do you know, I can't remember it very clearly. Can you?

ANGUS: Yes. Very clearly.

BENEDICT: Then I –

ANGUS: Now, Benedict! Think! Was it all so uniformly good at that time? Was the sun so bright and strong that shone on us then? Were you and I so much of one mind about things? – I remember us quarrelling quite fiercely. Don't you?

BENEDICT: No, I don't! and I –

ANGUS: Wait! Was Kirsty so loving and so beautiful?

BENEDICT: Yes!

ANGUS: Was she? I remember –

BENEDICT: I don't want to hear that!

ANGUS: All right.

(*There is a pause. BENEDICT looks up at ANGUS and says.*)

BENEDICT: Damn you. Unprovoked attack. (*ANGUS laughs.*) I'd like a drink. Have you got anything?

ANGUS: There's some gin.

BENEDICT: Gin? Oh dear. Nothing else?

ANGUS: Ginger beer. And I think there's still a little Scotch.

BENEDICT: Where?

ANGUS: I'll get it. (*He fetches half a bottle of Scotch whisky from a drawer in the desk, calling.*) Willy Yeats! Bring a glass and a jug of water, will you?

WILLY: (*From the kitchen.*) Yes, sir.

BENEDICT: I think I shall go for a long swim in the river.

ANGUS: Surely it's not as bad as that!

BENEDICT: By moonlight.

ANGUS: In that case, I am happy to tell you it will be a full moon tonight.

BENEDICT: Good. That's certainly better than 'The Sun at Noonday'.

ANGUS: Obviously an allusive joke that I don't understand.

BENEDICT: I was thinking aloud. 'The Sun at Noonday' is the title of the film I've just finished.

ANGUS: Is it going to be good?

BENEDICT: I don't know. That's what I've been doing in Devonshire. We've been on location.

ANGUS: On what?

BENEDICT: Location.

ANGUS: Something else I don't understand. A technical term, I presume. Did you enjoy making it?

BENEDICT: Not very much.

ANGUS: What's it about?

BENEDICT: Are you really interested?

ANGUS: Yes.

BENEDICT: Can I have some of that whisky?

ANGUS: Of course. (*He calls.*) Hurry up, Willy.

BENEDICT: I play Marcus Cowdray. I am, myself, the 'Sun at Noonday' being an artist at the full power of his creative and erotic life. I am bursting with work and lust at my 'place' in Devon when into my life comes a strange child-wife who has run away from her husband. She is played by Jane Howe – she specializes in 'innocent' parts. Even you, Angus, must have heard of Jane.

ANGUS: Yes, I have.

BENEDICT: Poor dear! She isn't so young now and is a bit weak at both ends but all right in the middle and so she wears a bow on it. Anyway, Marcus paints her portrait and seduces her meanwhile. Time passes and she finds she is going to have a child and she doesn't seem to know if it's her husband's or Marcus's. This upsets her so she throws herself into the sea; it is conveniently handy. Marcus is left agonizing in close-up on the sea-shore in the realization that his lust has destroyed his future and only love and, less important to a certain section of our audience, his power to paint.

ANGUS: That's the end?

BENEDICT: Yes.

ANGUS: I think I've seen it.

BENEDICT: Don't be silly! It hasn't been shown yet.

ANGUS: Oh. What you might call a tragedy?

BENEDICT: Wait until you see Jane floating face upwards in the sea. I pointed out that this was impossible especially with her figure but I was ignored.

ANGUS: Well, it sounds most exciting. (*He calls.*) Willy Yeats! What about that glass? Mr Clare wants a drink.

WILLY: Coming, sir. (*She enters carrying a glass and a jug of water.*) I've been washing it, sir.

ANGUS: Well, don't make it sound as though we have only one glass in the house. You should bring these things on a tray, you know.

WILLY: Yes, sir.

(*She sets off.*)

ANGUS: No, no! It doesn't matter now. (*To BENEDICT.*) Help yourself, will you?

(*He hands BENEDICT the whisky and glass. WILLY goes out. BENEDICT begins to pour himself the whisky and speak as KIRSTY appears on the stairs looking very much more beautiful than even BENEDICT will have remembered her. She is seen by ANGUS but unseen by BENEDICT.*)

BENEDICT: You know, Angus, long, long ago, when I was a little tiny child – I am told I was very beautiful – I had a trusting nature. I retained that trust until eight years ago but I regret to tell you that it then deserted me. It raises an interesting question that I think might form a basis for discussion between us this weekend. Must we consciously reconcile ourselves as we grow older to disbelief, miscreance, doubt and suspicion – and form our lives accordingly? – or must we fight against such things knowing that we shall fail?

KIRSTY: He's obviously in a bad way. (*BENEDICT rises, turns and sees KIRSTY.*) When he feels he must tackle metaphysical problems it is a sign of the lowest ebb. It is exactly twenty minutes to four.

ANGUS: You're slow.

BENEDICT: (*Looking at her.*) I think I'm going to faint.

KIRSTY: Don't be silly! You've got a glass of whisky in your hand.

BENEDICT: Have I? So I have. Oh, well – (*He drinks.*) How do you do, Kirsty. How are you?

KIRSTY: I'm very well. (*She crosses to him and holds out her hand.*) How are you?

BENEDICT: Are you intending to shake hands with me? Absurd! (*He kisses her.*) Now kiss Angus.

KIRSTY: I already have.

BENEDICT: Have you? Would you mind very much if I sat down?

KIRSTY: Do.

BENEDICT: I think perhaps it would be better if I lay down.

KIRSTY: What's the matter?

ANGUS: He's suffering from a touch of 'The Sun at Noonday'.

BENEDICT: Angus, please! I hope I am not going to find that you, Kirsty, have grown bitter and fractious. You must understand that this trembling is the result of shock. Eight or nine years ago I might have stood up to this sort of thing but now it reduces me to – well, to this.

KIRSTY: Poor darling!

BENEDICT: What did you say?

KIRSTY: I said, 'Poor darling'.

BENEDICT: What a wonderful thing to say. (*To ANGUS.*) Isn't it? 'Poor darling'. No one has said that to me for years. Of course, that's what I need. A little pity.

ANGUS: Sit down.

BENEDICT: Thank you. I suppose you are responsible for this. I mean, it was all planned – planned to give me the maximum shock.

ANGUS: Yes.

BENEDICT: You have succeeded.

ANGUS: Kirsty nearly ruined everything by arriving before you.

KIRSTY: Sorry.

ANGUS: So I hid her.

BENEDICT: It's not a joke, is it? I say, it's not a joke?

KIRSTY: Now don't panic.

BENEDICT: What I mean is, you are Kirsty, aren't you? He hasn't gone out and found someone and dressed them up to look like you, has he? What am I talking about?

KIRSTY: I don't know.

BENEDICT: You are the Kirsty Winton I knew – however many years ago it was – when the world was gay and – what's the matter?

KIRSTY: Well, look at me. Am I so very different from the person you remembered?
BENEDICT: Yes.
KIRSTY: What?
BENEDICT: You are so very much more beautiful than I ever remembered you to be.
(*WILLY YEATS comes in.*)
ANGUS: What is it?
WILLY: Please, Mr Learoyd, I'm organized but –
ANGUS: Oh, all right.
(*ANGUS goes out to the kitchen with WILLY.*)
BENEDICT: How am I?
KIRSTY: What?
BENEDICT: How am I?
KIRSTY: Let me look at you. (*BENEDICT turns to her.*) You look very well.
BENEDICT: I think everything is going to be all right now.
KIRSTY: Why?
BENEDICT: Where have you come from?
KIRSTY: London.
BENEDICT: This afternoon?
KIRSTY: Yes. I've been away in Scotland for about a month. When I got back two days ago I found a letter from Angus waiting for me.
BENEDICT: Asking you to come down here?
KIRSTY: Yes. I wrote saying that I'd come. I don't believe he thought I would.
BENEDICT: He was always like that: never realized how fond we are of him.
KIRSTY: He's a very humble person.
BENEDICT: If I'd known where he was I'd have come unasked.
KIRSTY: How is he?
BENEDICT: Aren't we being polite to each other?
KIRSTY: Yes. How is he?
BENEDICT: Angus? Oh, I think he's all right.
KIRSTY: I only saw him for a moment when he hid me upstairs for your arrival.

BENEDICT: So it was all a plan to get us together again. Do you know, I feel almost happy.

KIRSTY: Good.

(*ANGUS has returned to the room.*)

ANGUS: (*To KIRSTY.*) What did he say?

KIRSTY: He said he feels almost happy.

ANGUS: Good.

KIRSTY: That's what I said.

(*ANGUS and KIRSTY laugh.*)

BENEDICT: I cannot see anything to laugh at.

KIRSTY: Can't you?

BENEDICT: No. (*There is a pause.*) By the way, Angus, what did that remark mean? That, 'Please, Mr Learoyd, I'm organized but – ' From – (*He points towards the kitchen.*) I can't bring myself to call her Willy Yeats.

ANGUS: It meant that she had reached a certain stage in getting tea for us and a situation had arisen with which she felt herself unable to deal. Namely, the making of the tea.

BENEDICT: I see.

ANGUS: There are certain things she can't do and making tea is one of them. Boiling an egg is another. And so I find it easier to do them myself. I've attempted to teach her but I've failed. At one time every egg she gave me was boiled to a rock. I explained to Willy that the main factor in the boiling of an egg was the length of time it was boiled. That made no impression on her. And so I bought her one of those little sand things – you know, like a –

KIRSTY: An egg-timer.

ANGUS: That's right. Well, I bought her one of those and explained how it worked. The next egg was as hard as a bullet. I again explained how the gadget worked: the following morning she boiled it with the egg. (*WILLY YEATS brings in the tea.*) Thank you, Willy. Have you got everything?

WILLY: I think so, sir.

ANGUS: The sandwiches are rather small, aren't they?

WILLY: Well, sir, I told you about the crusts.

ANGUS: Of course you did, I'm sorry. (*WILLY YEATS goes out to the kitchen.*) Would you like to do this, Kirsty? (*He indicates the tea.*)

KIRSTY: Of course.

(*She begins to pour the tea.*)

ANGUS: Will you have something to eat, Benedict?

BENEDICT: Yes. I'll have several of those little tiny sandwiches. (*ANGUS hands the sandwiches to him.*) Thank you. (*When KIRSTY has poured out the tea she hands it to ANGUS and BENEDICT: there are the usual* 'Thank you' – 'That's right, isn't it?' – 'Quite right, thank you' – 'Sorry!' – 'That's all right' – *until they are sitting. Then there is a pause.*)

BENEDICT: (*To KIRSTY.*) You came down by train?

KIRSTY: Yes.

BENEDICT: I had to change.

KIRSTY: Did you?

BENEDICT: Yes. Twice.

(*There is a pause.*)

KIRSTY: I suppose it is natural that we should be shy with each other.

BENEDICT: Why?

KIRSTY: Well, we are, aren't we?

BENEDICT: Nonsense! I'm perfectly at my ease with you. (*Pause.*) Both of you.

(*There is a pause.*)

ANGUS: What are they like?

BENEDICT: (*Holding up a sandwich.*) These?

ANGUS: Yes.

BENEDICT: Horrible. (*There is a pause: BENEDICT has been looking out of the window.*) Angus.

ANGUS: Yes?

BENEDICT: There's a horse in the garden.

ANGUS: It comes in sometimes. Doesn't do any harm. (*To KIRSTY.*) Won't you have something to eat?

KIRSTY: No, thank you.

BENEDICT: You must never be nice to horses.

KIRSTY: What are you talking about?

BENEDICT: Being nice to horses. I was nice to one yesterday and look what happened.

KIRSTY: What did happen?

BENEDICT: I was going into the hotel – I live in hotels now – and there was a horse drawing a sort of cart thing standing outside. It had that odd sort of droop that horses sometimes have – you know what I mean? – and the sun was shining and I was coming here to see Angus – and you, darling, but I didn't know that then – and so I went up to the horse and said, 'Cheer up! The sun's shining and I'm going to see Angus again – of course, his name means nothing to you but life's pretty good. So, cheer up, horse. Don't droop'. At those few kind words tears sprang into its eyes. That made me feel terrible so I patted it on the nose and then began to walk into the hotel. When I got into the revolving door it stuck – there seemed to be some kind of obstruction – I turned round and the horse was in the door with me. (*KIRSTY begins to laugh.*) You've never seen such confusion. Porters attempting to turn the door to eject the horse and only succeeding in crushing me. My terrified screams mingling with the heavy breathing of the horse who was staring at me in the most loving manner through the glass. It was awful. Finally, they got him and me out and we were both led away – drooping. So, I say, never be kind to horses. (*He watches KIRSTY and ANGUS laugh.*) That's better. Now we can talk.

KIRSTY: Yes. Yes, I think we can.

BENEDICT: Then let's start from the beginning. How are you?

KIRSTY: I'm very, very well.

BENEDICT: How are you, Angus?

ANGUS: I'm well.

KIRSTY: How are you?<br>
ANGUS: How are you? } *Spoken together.*

BENEDICT: I'm very well, thank you. I suppose you were right, Kirsty. That in a meeting after eight years there is quite a lot of ice to be broken.

KIRSTY: And that ridiculous horse broke it for us. God bless it. And God bless you.

ANGUS: God bless you.

BENEDICT: This is wonderful. You are glad to see me, both of you, aren't you?

KIRSTY: Of course we are.

BENEDICT: And I suppose you're glad to see each other? (*ANGUS and KIRSTY do not answer: in the pause they look at each other. Unseen by BENEDICT, ANGUS touches KIRSTY's hand and she takes his hand as BENEDICT continues to speak.*) I was telling Angus just before you came down, Kirsty, that I thought his attitude towards you before was damned odd. He said it wasn't. But, you know, it was – damned odd! I remember the day – Incidentally, Angus, there really is a horse in the garden.

ANGUS: What? Yes. Don't worry about it.

BENEDICT: I'm not. Your garden. Your worry. What was I saying?

ANGUS: I don't know. Was it important?

BENEDICT: I should think so. It usually is. What was I saying, Kirsty?

KIRSTY: I don't know.

(*There is a slight pause. ANGUS and KIRSTY watch BENEDICT.*)

BENEDICT: Got it! I know! I was going to say I remember the day when you and Angus were going to meet me and you didn't turn up. I waited and then came to look for you. I couldn't find you anywhere because you were – (*He stops and laughs.*) Do you remember the day? (*KIRSTY nods her head: she is smiling.*)

*CURTAIN*

# ACT TWO

*The scene is the same.*
*The time: nine-thirty the same evening.*
*KIRSTY is sitting with her face hidden in her hands. BENEDICT and ANGUS are facing each other. They are shouting.*

BENEDICT: What an argument! I've never heard such damned nonsense! Do you mean to tell me – ?

ANGUS: I mean to tell you nothing! It is impossible to reason with you when you are in this pig-headed mood. And so I am not reasoning – I am stating –

BENEDICT: I suppose I am refusing simply to be difficult?

ANGUS: Yes!

BENEDICT: Why should I go? Give me one good reason why I should go and go I will – like a lamb.

(*There is a sound of appreciation from KIRSTY.*)

ANGUS: One good reason?

BENEDICT: Yes. One good reason.

(*WILLY YEATS comes in.*)

ANGUS: Get out!

(*WILLY YEATS goes out.*)

BENEDICT: Ha! You can't think of one good reason. My dear Angus, you should...

ANGUS: Shut up! For one reason you should go because people do these things.

BENEDICT: People do these things! People do these things! If people do –

ANGUS: You damned actor!

BENEDICT: – these things I suppose I go merely to satisfy your wretched sense of decorum.

ANGUS: What I feel doesn't enter into it.

BENEDICT: It is what other people feel. Ha!

ANGUS: For God's sake stop standing there saying, 'Ha!' Whatever you may think, it is only undignified and ridiculous.

BENEDICT: Ha! Go on: strike me! (*There is a pause. To KIRSTY.*) That was the last straw. (*To ANGUS.*) That's where you went to get your coat.

ANGUS: Yes.

(*He moves across the room and picks up an imaginary coat.*)

BENEDICT: (*To KIRSTY, who looks up: she is laughing.*) Then he came back to me, shook hands, and – Well, go on, Angus, do it.

(*ANGUS returns to BENEDICT and holds out his hand: they shake hands.*)

ANGUS: Goodbye, Benedict. I shan't come back this time. Take care of yourself.

BENEDICT: I will. Goodbye, Angus. (*To KIRSTY.*) I can't tell you how noble we were.

ANGUS: It's no good going on like this, is it?

BENEDICT: I suppose not.

ANGUS: Goodbye, then.

BENEDICT: Goodbye. (*They again shake hands. To KIRSTY.*) Then he walked to the door, went out, and fell down the stairs. (*KIRSTY laughs.*) I had to go down, pick him up and put him to bed. I've never seen anybody so angry. So in the end neither of us went to the funeral.

KIRSTY: When did all this happen?

BENEDICT: Oh, about – when was it, Angus?

ANGUS: When your Aunt Ellen died. It was her funeral.

BENEDICT: Yes. That would be just after I met you, Kirsty. I've never understood why Angus was so insistent that I should go to Ellen's funeral. She was a horrible old woman. I remember when I was a child she used to take me into the garden and throw stones at me.

ANGUS: That was no reason for refusing to go to her funeral.

KIRSTY: No: then you could have thrown stones at her.

BENEDICT: Angus always had an appalling correctness about such things. With regard to funerals, marriages and births his behaviour was punctilious. He was never wrong. You must admit it is irritating.

KIRSTY: I suppose it is.

BENEDICT: Always when he made me feel I should do something I dug in my heels – it was an automatic action to disagree and refuse.

ANGUS: This afternoon you denied that we ever quarrelled.

BENEDICT: That was this afternoon. However, now – at whatever time it is – half-past nine – half-past nine! – God! that means we've been talking for – what? – five hours.

KIRSTY: I've hardly said a word.

BENEDICT: Five hours! Surely I should feel exhausted.

ANGUS: Don't you?

BENEDICT: No.

KIRSTY: Lucky fellow!

BENEDICT: And I've often wondered if I met you two again whether we should find anything to talk about.

ANGUS: Surely you didn't worry about it.

BENEDICT: Of course, I've always done all the talking. I remember, before, you both –

ANGUS: You keep saying – 'before'. Before what?

BENEDICT: I mean when we knew each other before. Before the War, if you like. I don't mind.

ANGUS: I see. Go on.

BENEDICT: I remember that you and Kirsty didn't talk together very much. It struck me as being rather strange.

KIRSTY: Why?

BENEDICT: I don't really know why.

ANGUS: Well, try and think why.

BENEDICT: It was only that –

KIRSTY: Yes?

BENEDICT: Only that –

ANGUS: Well, do go on, Benedict.

KIRSTY: Yes, do try and think why it struck you as being strange.

BENEDICT: What are you two trying to do?

ANGUS: Nothing.

(*KIRSTY and ANGUS laugh.*)

BENEDICT: And what are you laughing at?

ANGUS: Nothing.

KIRSTY: Dear Benedict.

BENEDICT: Don't be familiar. (*He laughs.*) I really feel very happy. Five hours of riotous reminiscence. Not a bad thing. Some people make a living from it. Look at our dramatic critics – well, one of them, anyway. Let's have a drink. Angus, let's have a drink.

ANGUS: You finished the whisky.

BENEDICT: And I don't like gin.

ANGUS: Ginger beer?

BENEDICT: No. Is there any chance of getting some ordinary beer? Some ale.

ANGUS: Down in the village.

BENEDICT: Oh.

ANGUS: About ten minutes there and back. (*BENEDICT is silent.*) Mention my name and they'll give it to you. (*BENEDICT remains silent and unmoving.*) Have you got any money?

BENEDICT: Yes.

ANGUS: You can't possibly lose your way –

KIRSTY: Go on the horse if he's still there.

ANGUS: Straight down and follow the river bank. It's called 'The Dolphin'.

BENEDICT: What is?

ANGUS: The pub, you fool!

BENEDICT: Can't you send Willy Yeats?

ANGUS: She's under age. They won't serve her. Anyway, I think she ought to go home now if it is really half-past nine. That's an idea. She can walk down with you and show you the way. I'll tell her.

(*He moves towards the kitchen.*)

BENEDICT: Angus!

ANGUS: Yes?

BENEDICT: You haven't offered to go, have you?

ANGUS: No.

BENEDICT: I thought I hadn't heard you.

ANGUS: (*Calling.*) Willy Yeats!

BENEDICT: Oh, well – (*He gets up.*) Can you two find something to talk about whilst I'm away?

KIRSTY: I should think so.

BENEDICT: Don't talk about anything too interesting.

ANGUS: I promise you won't miss a thing.

BENEDICT: I suppose you'll talk about me. Won't you?

ANGUS: We – (*WILLY YEATS comes in.*) Willy, I think you'd better – oh, I see you're ready to go home.

WILLY: Yes, sir.

ANGUS: Right. You'd better get along now, then. I want you to walk –

WILLY: I haven't done anything about the supper things. They'll need washing.

ANGUS: That's all right. Do them tomorrow. I want you to walk down to the village with Mr Clare and show him where 'The Dolphin' is. He wants to buy some beer.

WILLY: Very good, sir.

ANGUS: Try not to be late in the morning.

WILLY: I'll try, sir.

BENEDICT: Are you ready – er – Miss Yeats?

WILLY: Ready, sir.

BENEDICT: Shan't be long, I suppose. I don't wish to take you out of your way, Miss Yeats.

WILLY: You won't, Sir.

BENEDICT: By the way, I hear you are –

(*BENEDICT and WILLY YEATS go out. When they have gone from sight ANGUS turns from the door to KIRSTY.*)

ANGUS: Hullo.

KIRSTY: Hullo.

ANGUS: Poor Benedict. (*They begin to laugh together.*) That was always said in a situation like this. Remember? (*KIRSTY nods her head.*) By the way, you didn't kiss me.

KIRSTY: When?

ANGUS: When you arrived. You told Benedict that you had. You didn't, you know. You shook me almost heartily by the hand.

KIRSTY: And said, 'Hullo, Angus, how are you'.

ANGUS: Yes. Just like that.

KIRSTY: Sorry. Come here. (*He moves to her and she kisses him.*) I think you're making an awful fuss.

ANGUS: I am, in a very quiet way. Will you have some gin?

KIRSTY: No. I'll have a cigarette.

ANGUS: Don't get up. Here you are.

(*He hands her the cigarettes and takes one for himself.*)

KIRSTY: Thank you.

ANGUS: I thought he ought to be here at this time.

KIRSTY: Benedict?

ANGUS: Yes.

KIRSTY: I think I know why now.

ANGUS: Having thought it over?

KIRSTY: Having thought it over.

ANGUS: Well, why?

KIRSTY: Because he is Benedict. Benedict, who was, after all, our background. Wearing, sometimes irritating but, nevertheless, a background. It might have been strange as well as dangerous to have been with you again without the accompaniment of that continuous flow of words.

ANGUS: Dangerous?

KIRSTY: We were without it once and you remember what happened? We lost each other.

ANGUS: Good God! Do you mean to say our happiness together was dependent on Benedict?

KIRSTY: It seems so. We were together – however many years ago it is –

ANGUS: Eight.

KIRSTY: We were together – Benedict prattling to us – we were laughing and we were in love – how strange it feels to say that again! – we were in love – you and I in love then – and so to solve our problems we came away together to – to the house – (*She points.*) – over there, is it?

ANGUS: No. Over that way.

KIRSTY: You with your little boats and me –

ANGUS: You sound almost –

KIRSTY: What?

ANGUS: Never mind.

KIRSTY: Unhappy?

ANGUS: I was going to say bitter – but, go on.

KIRSTY: You remember what happened. I don't have to tell you. (*She holds up her unlighted cigarette.*) May I have something to light this?

ANGUS: I'm so sorry.

(*He lights her cigarette.*)

KIRSTY: Thank you. I can make a suggestion.

ANGUS: Then please do.

KIRSTY: About Benedict.

ANGUS: Yes?

KIRSTY: He's a baby – a child. Certainly in manner and, in many ways, in mind. He has an amazing aptitude for making all the people who know him behave like children – like himself. Perhaps that is what he did to us eight years ago. Took us with him to his own remote world of fantasy by his laughter, his wonderful schemes and his unlimited exaggeration. And it was in that world we fell in love: not this world at all. Once removed from the Benedictine Heaven to the world of reality with its practical details – do you remember the food question, the furniture question, the money question in our house over there? – well, once among that we quarrelled, were miserable and, very wisely, we parted.

ANGUS: Do you believe that?

KIRSTY: What? That we – ?

ANGUS: That it was very wise of us to part?

KIRSTY: Well, wasn't it? You must admit that that six weeks together was hell. Go on, admit it.

ANGUS: Yes, it was.

KIRSTY: Therefore surely it was very wise to part.

ANGUS: You are suggesting that to have been happy we should have kept Benedict under the bed.

KIRSTY: Probably. You see he – well, look at him now – it's eight years since we've seen him – and has he changed?

ANGUS: He swears he has.

KIRSTY: In what way?

ANGUS: He says for the worse.

KIRSTY: You know – you must know, that he hasn't changed at all. He is one of those God-gifted creatures who will never change. The only risk he runs by that is that he may be rather pathetic in his old age – he'll probably start playing practical jokes –

ANGUS: Dear God!

KIRSTY: But now – well, how old is he?

ANGUS: Two months younger than I am. Nearly thirty-two.

KIRSTY: Now he runs no risks, he has commercialized his world and it can be seen at the cinema. But we're not concerned in that –

ANGUS: I've never seen him on the films.

KIRSTY: I have (*She laughs.*) – but I shan't let it influence me. I think, Angus, you underestimate his power.

ANGUS: Power over us?

KIRSTY: Yes. For us he is the only remaining link with a past that was predominantly happy. You admitted that when you gave your reason for asking him here today.

ANGUS: That wasn't my reason. It was your conjecture.

KIRSTY: But you confirmed it. It hurts you to admit his necessity to us because I think you despise him a little.

ANGUS: No, no! I'm –

KIRSTY: Just a little?

(*There is a pause.*)

ANGUS: He said we'd talk about him.

KIRSTY: Yes.

ANGUS: If you feel like this why have you come here?

KIRSTY: Because you asked me to come.

ANGUS: I'd like to ask this –

KIRSTY: And because I wanted to see you again.

ANGUS: Would you have come if I hadn't asked Benedict as well?

KIRSTY: You're forgetting something. I didn't know he was going to be here. (*There is a pause.*) Why did you ask me? (*He does not answer.*) Angus.

ANGUS: What?

KIRSTY: Why did you ask me down here? Did you think I might still be in love with you?

ANGUS: Are you?

KIRSTY: I don't know. (*ANGUS moves from* her.) Angus.

ANGUS: Yes?

KIRSTY: Are you in love with me?

ANGUS: I don't know, either.

KIRSTY: Eight years.

ANGUS: Long time.

KIRSTY: To remain faithful. But then we haven't, have we? (*There is a pause.*) What is that music?

(*Dance music has been playing distantly.*)

ANGUS: What? Oh, it's a dance – village 'hop' – they have it over that way on Saturday nights. Remember? Horrible affair. It's been playing for some time.

KIRSTY: I've only just heard it.
ANGUS: That tune wasn't written eight years ago.
KIRSTY: No.
ANGUS: Another cigarette?
KIRSTY: No, thank you. You haven't asked about me, you know. About what I've been doing.
ANGUS: I don't want to know.
KIRSTY: I'm quite prepared to tell you.
ANGUS: I just don't want to know.
KIRSTY: All right.
(*There is a long pause.*)
ANGUS: Kirsty.
KIRSTY: Yes?
ANGUS: Darling.
KIRSTY: You're going to make me cry! It's absurd! But you're going to make me cry!
ANGUS: No. You're not going to cry. (*He holds her to him.*) Anyway, we made a magnificent effort to rationalize this situation.
KIRSTY: Damn it! I'm not nineteen now. It is to be expected that I should make some attempt to be rational at my age.
ANGUS: You were wonderful. All that about Benedict and us. I almost believed it.
KIRSTY: I've believed it for eight years.
ANGUS: Why?
KIRSTY: Because I couldn't bring myself to believe that it was our fault that we quarrelled.
ANGUS: So you blamed Benedict?
KIRSTY: Yes. I blamed him for not being there.
ANGUS: What tortuous reasoning.
KIRSTY: I'm given to it.
ANGUS: Poor Benedict! Blamed for not being there like some awful old Madame.
KIRSTY: Did he ever know about us?
ANGUS: No. From what he's said I'm sure he didn't. I've always wanted him to know. About our running away from him. About our being in love with each other.
KIRSTY: So have I. Why did we never tell him?
ANGUS: I've never told anyone in the world.

KIRSTY: Neither have I. But I wish Benedict knew. I do like him so much.
ANGUS: You do?
KIRSTY: And you. I like you too.
ANGUS: Thank you. Would you like me to kiss you?
KIRSTY: Yes, please.
ANGUS: Very well. I will.
KIRSTY: Thank you.
(*ANGUS kisses her.*)
ANGUS: You do that very well now.
KIRSTY: Was I so bad before?
ANGUS: Yes, very bad. I can see you now. Stand up.
KIRSTY: Well?
ANGUS: Let me see. No, no! Stand away! That's better. You dress better. And you're wearing jewellery. You used not to do that.
KIRSTY: No.
ANGUS: What's the matter?
KIRSTY: Nothing. Go on.
ANGUS: Turn round. And again. Yes.
KIRSTY: What?
ANGUS: You're fatter.
KIRSTY: Quite right. I am.
ANGUS: You've more bottom.
KIRSTY: I've reduced round the bust.
ANGUS: Is it dropping?
KIRSTY: No!
ANGUS: Good.
KIRSTY: Well, is it?
ANGUS: I can't really tell yet.
KIRSTY: Anything else?
ANGUS: I like your hair. You were inclined to screw it back.
KIRSTY: This is better?
ANGUS: Much better. You were a little dowdy in the old days, darling.
KIRSTY: I was not!
ANGUS: Oh, yes, you were. I remember one day Benedict came up before lunch and said he had invited Kirsty

Winton to have tea with us. I imagined anyone with such an imposing name must be very wonderful. I thought you were one of Benedict's strange theatrical friends. When you arrived Benedict was out, you remember. You stood in the door looking at me, and said, 'I suppose I've come to the wrong house again'. And then you began to talk at the top of your voice while you removed and replaced your right glove at least a dozen times.

KIRSTY: You looked so angry.

ANGUS: I was. Until I looked at you properly and saw your rather shapeless tweed suit and, what I think are called, sensible shoes: your hair screwed back into that absurd little bun and your 'afternoon tea' make-up.

KIRSTY: Did I look so dreadful?

ANGUS: So dreadful that I fell straight in love with you. I half hoped at that moment that Benedict would fall under a bus with the cream cakes. But he didn't. He might fall in the river tonight.

KIRSTY: Would it be worth our throwing him in?

ANGUS: But surely I've told you all this before?

KIRSTY: No, never.

ANGUS: Haven't I? God bless my soul!

KIRSTY: So I've changed?

ANGUS: Oh, yes. You're not Benedict, you know. There's only one thing.

KIRSTY: What's that?

ANGUS: Your name.

KIRSTY: What?

ANGUS: What is your name?

KIRSTY: What do you mean?

ANGUS: Well, you have a second Christian name. Kirsty or Christiana, Something Winton. I'm sorry but I've forgotten it.

KIRSTY: Caroline.

ANGUS: Of course. C.C. It was on your luggage. I remember everything else about you. It's just that I couldn't remember that. One of the absurd things that can worry you. Does it shock you so much that I should forget?

KIRSTY: No. Why?

ANGUS: You look rather shocked. In fact, you look very serious.

KIRSTY: I need Benedict here.

ANGUS: No, you don't. But I need you. Come back! Where have you gone?

KIRSTY: What? Oh, I'm sorry.

ANGUS: Mustn't go into trances. Where were you?

KIRSTY: In time: eight years back. In place – Oh Angus!

ANGUS: Darling!

KIRSTY: But it was good then, wasn't it?

ANGUS: Very good, surely.

KIRSTY: Until that Friday afternoon.

ANGUS: Until then.

KIRSTY: Where did you go that afternoon? (*There is a pause.*) Don't tell me if you don't want to.

ANGUS: I don't mind. I took the boat and went to Cornwall. Falmouth. I was there when war started. I left the boat and came back by train.

KIRSTY: Came back – ?

ANGUS: To our house, yes. You had gone, of course, and you had left the place in an awful state. There was a detective novel you had been reading still lying in a chair – Wait! I can remember the title – 'Murder must Advertise' – you had left your dog's lead behind –

KIRSTY: I couldn't find it.

ANGUS: It was hanging over one of the pipes in the kitchen. The radio was still tuned to Milan: we'd been listening to Mozart's Requiem the evening before I left and you hadn't touched it after that.

KIRSTY: I never wanted to hear music again.

ANGUS: There was half a glass of water and a bottle of aspirin on the table by the bed and behind the bed some underclothes of yours. The clock had stopped at three minutes to five. There was one of your shoes standing upright on the third stair. And my revolver had been taken out of the desk and left on the little round table. Very frightening.

KIRSTY: But there was no body.

ANGUS: No. That was something.

KIRSTY: Were you very angry?

ANGUS: Not then, no. I looked everywhere for a letter – a note. There was nothing.

KIRSTY: I didn't think you'd come back.

ANGUS: When did you leave?

KIRSTY: The day after you – and I remember nothing more than the clouds being very high and very white above the house. Nothing more.

ANGUS: How long did it take you to forget me?

KIRSTY: About a year.

ANGUS: And you did forget me?

KIRSTY: I wanted someone.

ANGUS: Someone other than me?

KIRSTY: Yes.

ANGUS: I don't want to hear about it.

KIRSTY: All right.

ANGUS: Damn! Don't let us talk too much of the past or those are the things we shall say. Let's stay in the present.

KIRSTY: Well, in the present –

ANGUS: Yes?

KIRSTY: – I think I want you. (*She kisses him. They are sitting now and fall into each other's arms. After the kiss this is what they say.*) It's ridiculous but we can say none of the usual things.

ANGUS: Such as?

KIRSTY: Such as – 'Have you missed me?' or 'Does this eliminate eight years?'

ANGUS: That's not the usual thing to say, anyway. No one in their senses –

KIRSTY: Nevertheless, we can't say it. Neither can we say, 'We're going to be so happy now', nor, that most important –

ANGUS: What? (*She does not answer but holds ANGUS to her, he kisses her and then says.*) Still. Be still. You're trembling. Dear Liz.

KIRSTY: My name happens to be Kirsty.

ANGUS: Of course – dear Kirsty.

KIRSTY: An echo from the more recent past, I imagine.

ANGUS: Yes. Sorry. (*They laugh.*) It's getting dark. And you can hear the river now. Listen.

KIRSTY: I can't.

ANGUS: Listen.

KIRSTY: My heart is beating in my ears.

(*His hands are on her breasts.*)

KIRSTY: Darling, Benedict will be back.

ANGUS: Yes, I'm afraid he will be. (*He releases her.*) We don't want to upset him.

KIRSTY: Would it upset him?

ANGUS: I should think so, because he's in love with you.

KIRSTY: I –

ANGUS: Thinks he's in love with you.

KIRSTY: I didn't know that. No! We mustn't laugh. We mustn't be malicious. Not about Benedict. About ourselves but not –

ANGUS: No, we must not. You didn't know?

KIRSTY: No. Poor Benedict.

ANGUS: Why? He's quite happy about it. Apparently it was the evening –

KIRSTY: Will he tell me himself?

ANGUS: (*Laughing.*) My dear – !

KIRSTY: (*Suddenly angry.*) Don't joke! (*Pause.*) I'm sorry. He told you?

ANGUS: Yes. Apparently it was an evening he took you out to supper. I had the 'flu.

KIRSTY: What!

ANGUS: Quite. An evening you've not yet forgotten – not because of Benedict but because of me. You remember? Benedict asked to borrow my car – I lent it to him and you went off together – look at me! – you went in the early afternoon – it was raining – became much worse in the evening – when you came back you left Benedict and drove the car round to me – visiting a sick friend –

KIRSTY: Was it raining?

ANGUS: Yes. Let me see – you had your dog with you and he was very hungry but we could find nothing to give him to eat except baked beans. He had such terrible wind after them that we had to shut him in the cellar.

KIRSTY: I'd forgotten that.

ANGUS: You were dressed almost entirely in black that evening – I remember thinking how very unsuitable that was for visiting an invalid. After all, I'd only got 'flu. You were very quiet – almost resigned – but, God knows! we seemed to have waited so long.

KIRSTY: Five weeks from the day we met.

ANGUS: I worried as to whether you'd catch the 'flu.

KIRSTY: Someone had to stay the night with you. You were almost delirious.

ANGUS: Well, that was the evening Benedict fell in love with you.

KIRSTY: What? Oh, yes. I'd forgotten Benedict.

ANGUS: Good.

(*He is about to kiss her.*)

KIRSTY: There's one thing we should admit.

ANGUS: What's that?

KIRSTY: That both of us – and, for that matter, Benedict as well, at this moment, today – are practising some form of subterfuge. And we are closing our eyes to our own trick as well as to the tricks being played on us. True?

ANGUS: We were never honest with each other before, were we?

KIRSTY: Would it have helped?

ANGUS: Helped us to stay together?

KIRSTY: Yes.

ANGUS: I don't think so.

KIRSTY: Would it help now?

ANGUS: To be honest?

KIRSTY: Yes. To tell the truth.

ANGUS: No. It would merely blow everything sky-high.

KIRSTY: You don't want that?

ANGUS: No! Let's each pull the wool over our own eyes.

KIRSTY: If we don't consider our motives our conduct can be nothing but moral.

ANGUS: It can only be said that we didn't know any better. (*They laugh.*) Satisfied?

KIRSTY: Completely.

ANGUS: It is always pleasant to be able to rationalize a situation to one's own advantage.

(*He kisses her.*)

KIRSTY: Angus, why didn't we get married?

ANGUS: We both said – oh, yes, you said it – we decided that we were too young.

KIRSTY: As good an excuse as any, I suppose.

ANGUS: I think Benedict must be lost. I wish he'd either come back or stay away altogether.

KIRSTY: He's here.

(*BENEDICT enters.*)

ANGUS: Hullo.

BENEDICT: These riverside pubs. Really!

ANGUS: Where's the beer?

BENEDICT: I haven't got any.

ANGUS: What!

BENEDICT: They wouldn't give me any. Not unless I had some bottles. Have you got any?

ANGUS: What damned nonsense! Did you mention me?

BENEDICT: Yes. They'd never heard of you. I gave your name three times quite distinctly – they laughed and said, 'No beer'.

ANGUS: There are two or three bottles in the kitchen.

BENEDICT: Are there? Hullo, Kirsty. I've just seen a dog like the one you had. It reminded me. What was it called?

KIRSTY: Umbrage.

BENEDICT: That's night. I remember. 'Are you going out?'

KIRSTY: 'Yes.'

BENEDICT: 'Well, take Umbrage.'

(*Their laughter is quite disproportionate to the joke.*)

ANGUS: I said, there are two or three bottles in the kitchen.

BENEDICT: Yes. I heard that.

ANGUS: Would you like to get them?

BENEDICT: No.

ANGUS: What?

BENEDICT: Would you like to go this time?

ANGUS: Not a bit.

BENEDICT: Go on. Please!

ANGUS: Do you really want the beer?

BENEDICT: Yes.

ANGUS: Well, why the hell didn't you have some whilst you were in the pub?

BENEDICT: I had a pint but I want some for tonight.

KIRSTY: Go on, Angus.

BENEDICT: I suppose, looking at the matter objectively, Angus is the modern type of host.

ANGUS: Now, look here – !

BENEDICT: You'd better hurry or they'll be shut.

(*ANGUS goes out to the kitchen.*)

KIRSTY: I think I'll walk down with Angus.

BENEDICT: No!

KIRSTY: No?

BENEDICT: No. Please!

KIRSTY: All right.

(*ANGUS returns from the kitchen, he goes straight across the room and out of the house. BENEDICT follows him to the door and calls after him.*)

BENEDICT: The walk will do you good. (*He turns back to KIRSTY.*) Hullo.

KIRSTY: Hullo.

BENEDICT: I have an admission to make.

KIRSTY: I should think so.

BENEDICT: What do you mean?

KIRSTY: I mean that you went down to the village: that the pub sold you some beer: that you brought it back with you and that this little scene we've just had was a trick to get Angus out of the house.

BENEDICT: You're quite right, of course.

KIRSTY: I'll accept all that if you'll tell me why.

BENEDICT: Because I want to talk to you alone.

KIRSTY: I gathered that. I mean, why do you want to talk to me alone?

BENEDICT: Well, really, Kirsty! – just a minute. (*He goes out of the house and after a moment returns with two hottles of beer.*) Do I have to give a reason for talking to you?

KIRSTY: (*Laughs.*) I suppose not.

BENEDICT: I should think not. Have some?

(*He holds up a bottle.*)

KIRSTY: No, thank you.

BENEDICT: I'm going to.

KIRSTY: Good.

(*BENEDICT goes out into the kitchen.*)

BENEDICT: It was very much further than Angus said. Willy Yeats took me across the fields. We hardly spoke a word the whole way. (*Something falls in the kitchen.*) Damn! She wasn't going home, anyway. She was going to some local dance.

KIRSTY: I can't hear the music now.

BENEDICT: What music?

(*He comes back into the room carrying two glasses. He is rubbing a stain on his coat.*)

KIRSTY: What have you done?

BENEDICT: I've upset a dish containing some really dreadful looking vegetables.

KIRSTY: What was it you – ?

BENEDICT: Are you sure you won't have some of this? I've brought another –

KIRSTY: Quite sure. What was it you wanted to talk to me about?

BENEDICT: Just a minute. Let me get myself 'settled', as they say. (*He pours out the beer and sits down.*) Oh, dear! It's warm. Still, I'd better get rid of it before Angus comes back.

KIRSTY: You needn't bother. The trick was quite transparent.

BENEDICT: Was it? I'm not very good at that sort of thing. Especially with Angus.

KIRSTY: No, you're not.

BENEDICT: It's Angus I want to talk to you about. That is, first of all. How have you felt about him since you've been here? (*KIRSTY does not reply.*) Would you say he's happy?

KIRSTY: Would you?

BENEDICT: No

KIRSTY: Of course, he's told me very little about himself. About himself in the last eight years, I mean.

BENEDICT: He's told me very little. He's been doing this business with the boats, you know. He always used to be happy doing something that was connected with such things. I shouldn't think he makes much money but he's got some, hasn't he?

KIRSTY: I believe so.

BENEDICT: Do you think there's much else for him to tell?

KIRSTY: Eight years is a long time to people like us.

BENEDICT: You mean you think there is something else?

KIRSTY: I don't know.

BENEDICT: Do you think he might be unhappy over some woman?

KIRSTY: Maybe he is.

BENEDICT: It might very well be that. His attitude towards women was always rather odd.

KIRSTY: Yes, it was.

BENEDICT: You agree?

KIRSTY: Most certainly.

BENEDICT: I've always thought that Angus is rather the sort to be put upon by women: unlike myself, he is over honest and quite scrupulous in his dealings. For that reason I've always tried to protect him. Yes, it might very well be a woman. I wonder what she'd be like?

KIRSTY: What? Yes, I wonder.

BENEDICT: Are you listening to me?

KIRSTY: Of course.

BENEDICT: Please do, as this is very important. You may have realized by now that I am very fond of Angus. I know that you're fond of him too – but when we knew each other before it was more you and me and me and Angus than Angus and you. That's very complicated but you know what I mean.

KIRSTY: Yes, I know what you mean.

BENEDICT: But you must remember that it was Angus who provided us with the – well, the background to the period when we knew each other. We owe him a lot. Don't forget that. However, I'll speak about you in a minute: at present I'm dealing with Angus.

KIRSTY: Rather roughly. Go on. I'm listening.

BENEDICT: I believe he's lonely. Now that you and I have met again I expect we shall be seeing quite a lot of each other. I hope so, anyway. I hope we can pick up where we left off.

KIRSTY: Where did we leave off?

BENEDICT: Well, for me it was an evening – but I'll come to that in a minute. I was about to say something: what was it? I do lose track awfully easily. Oh, yes, I know –

KIRSTY: Now that we've met again –

BENEDICT: Yes! Yes, I know! I hope that we shall be seeing a lot of each other – (*He pauses, hoping: KIRSTY does not speak.*) – and I want to include Angus because, as I said before, I think he's lonely. You don't seem very enthusiastic.

KIRSTY: I –

BENEDICT: But you must be. You see, we should do something for him if he's miserable. (*He pauses.*) You don't think I'm a fool, do you? (*KIRSTY shakes her head and moves to him.*) Do you?

(*KIRSTY kisses him.*)

KIRSTY: Something may not have occurred to you.

BENEDICT: What's that?

KIRSTY: You say that Angus seems unhappy. Do you think he was unhappy before we came here today?

BENEDICT: Am I being very stupid?

KIRSTY: Don't let it worry you.

BENEDICT: I'd like to know.

KIRSTY: Sometime: perhaps sometime.

BENEDICT: I am, on occasion, very stupid. (*He has risen and is moving about the room.*) May I give you an instance? (*He has stopped before the book-case.*) What a lot of books Angus has here. I don't remember him reading so much. (*He takes down a book.*) 'The Voyages of Dr Doolittle'. Have you ever read that? I have. What I'm going to tell you concerns you and myself – an evening together over eight years ago – a summer evening – you'll have forgotten – Angus was ill – I think he had the 'flu – something like that –

KIRSTY: This is where I came in.

BENEDICT: Why do you say that?

KIRSTY: I'm sorry. A silly, unfunny joke. Go on.

BENEDICT: Don't joke just for a few minutes.

KIRSTY: Go on.

BENEDICT: Angus was ill – 'flu – you went to see him and then came on to meet me – we went together – it was somewhere like this – somewhere on the river – a river – I think Angus had lent us his car – yes, he had – (*He remains looking at the books.*) 'A Voyage Round the World'. (*He takes down the book.*) I always like the maps in these sort of books. I remember that evening you were very gaily dressed and you laughed a good deal – you had flowers in your hair –

KIRSTY: What?

BENEDICT: I said, you had flowers in your hair.

KIRSTY: Nonsense! I've never worn flowers in my hair.

BENEDICT: Haven't you? I thought you did that evening. I thought I remembered it all so clearly. It was a fine evening – the weather, I mean –

KIRSTY: It was summer.

BENEDICT: Warm – and you were most lovely – there was a delightful air of anticipation, of expectancy about you – as if something of tremendous importance was about to happen –

KIRSTY: I was only nineteen.

BENEDICT: What did you say? (*KIRSTY does not reply.*) I fell in love with you that evening. (*He pauses: KIRSTY does not speak.*) I said –

KIRSTY: Yes, I heard what you said.

BENEDICT: You drove the car back – dropped me at my place – and then went on to take the car round to Angus and to find out how he felt. Before you left me you kissed me and said, 'You'll be all right, Benedict'. That made me think you knew and so I didn't say anything. Before I knew what had happened you had gone – left me in London alone. (*He pauses.*) Kirsty, are you crying?

KIRSTY: No.

BENEDICT: Oh, I thought you were crying. (*He pauses.*) I shall always pretend that had I told you that evening you wouldn't have laughed at me. That's all I have to say.

KIRSTY: And you said it beautifully.

BENEDICT: Darling, you are crying. (*KIRSTY makes no attempt to hide her tears.*) Don't do that. I'm so helpless about tears. (*He holds out his handkerchief.*) The only gesture I know in such a situation.

KIRSTY: I've got one.

BENEDICT: Darling, I didn't want this to happen.

KIRSTY: Poor Benedict. It's all right.

BENEDICT: Better?

KIRSTY: Yes. I don't really do that sort of thing, you know.

BENEDICT: What was it?

KIRSTY: Just that ridiculous story of yours.

BENEDICT: I thought it would make you laugh.

KIRSTY: You said I mustn't laugh. Anyway, I didn't want to.

BENEDICT: Oh, I don't know. I suppose it is rather comic. But then whatever I'd done you would have laughed at me.

KIRSTY: In the kindest way. The laughter has mostly been with you, not against you. You know that.

BENEDICT: Perhaps. But – seriously, if only for a moment – there's something I have never understood. Why did you go away like that? I thought it was because you knew I was in love with you and so you – well, ran away. But it wasn't that, was it?

KIRSTY: No.

BENEDICT: I was very lonely: quite naturally. For some time I'd had you and Angus as an audience and then suddenly there was no one. At one moment there was all that we had together and the next moment you had gone with never another word from you until today. After you, Angus disappeared. I saw him off on the train but there was no explanation, nothing until some weeks later when there was a letter from him: a letter I didn't understand at all – apparently begging forgiveness for something. I was left alone. I didn't understand it. You went and then Angus went and I – (*He stops.*)

KIRSTY: What's the matter?

BENEDICT: Shut up a minute! I'm putting two and two together.

KIRSTY: (*Not harshly or unkindly.*) I trust they'll eventually make four.

(*There is a long pause as BENEDICT stares at KIRSTY.*)

BENEDICT: Was that it?

KIRSTY: Yes.

BENEDICT: Do you know when you are reading sometimes and you go over a sentence again and again and each time completely misread one word? That's what I've been doing, isn't it?

KIRSTY: Are you very angry?

BENEDICT: No, I'm not angry. Suddenly I said, 'You went away and then Angus went away and I was left in London'. I've said that before but this time, for the first time, I saw that it meant – you and Angus went together.

KIRSTY: Yes.

BENEDICT: You went together.

KIRSTY: You are angry.

BENEDICT: No, I'm not. Just a minute. (*There is silence whilst BENEDICT stands with his hands covering his face. KIRSTY makes* a *half-movement towards him but remains silent. At last, BENEDICT takes his hands from his face and says.*) Why didn't you tell me?

KIRSTY: We didn't tell anyone. We've never told anyone. It was a very secret and – and frightened thing altogether.

BENEDICT: Yes. Yes, I understand. But there's one thing. You must answer 'Yes'. Tell me that you were very much in love with each other.

KIRSTY: Yes, we were.

BENEDICT: Then what happened?

KIRSTY: We quarrelled and parted after six weeks.

BENEDICT: I see.

KIRSTY: We didn't meet again until today.

BENEDICT: What am I doing here?

KIRSTY: You're here because we love you.

BENEDICT: (*He laughs.*) This makes all that I've said to you this evening seem rather ridiculous, doesn't it?

KIRSTY: We've bungled it horribly. We should have told you. But don't be angry.

BENEDICT: Stop saying that. I'm not angry.

KIRSTY: You have every right to be.

BENEDICT: Nonsense! I've no right at all. Come here. (*KIRSTY moves to him.*) Is it good to see him again?

KIRSTY: Of course.

BENEDICT: Has he changed?

KIRSTY: A little.

BENEDICT: But you remembered him much as he is.

KIRSTY: Yes.

BENEDICT: Let me look at you. The point is that you haven't gone back to the time that you knew me but to the time just after you left me.

KIRSTY: Don't, please!

BENEDICT: It's true. It doesn't matter but it's true.

KIRSTY: (*Crying out.*) For God's sake! You're so tolerant, it's nauseating! (*There is a pause: then BENEDICT laughs aloud.*) I can't understand why you're not angry. You should be.

BENEDICT: I've never been angry. Even in the old quarrels with Angus I was never angry. It is something that is sadly lacking in me. (*He has turned away to the window.*) He should be back in a moment.

KIRSTY: He seems to have been gone hours.

BENEDICT: No. Only a few minutes. By the way, we mustn't let him know.

KIRSTY: Know what?

BENEDICT: That I know about you – and him – and everything.

KIRSTY: Why not?

BENEDICT: You know perfectly well why not. Promise me.

KIRSTY: I promise.

BENEDICT: We'll have a little conspiracy against Angus for a change. He'll probably see through it but never mind.

KIRSTY: You never see through plots against you, do you?

BENEDICT: Very rarely.

KIRSTY: But then, Benedict, you are not possessed by those insects of doubt and suspicion which worry people like myself and Angus. Little buzzings permanently disquieting the mind.

BENEDICT: I think I'd be most unhappy if I were.

KIRSTY: Yes, one is.

BENEDICT: You really wanted me to know about yourself and Angus being in love, didn't you?

KIRSTY: Yes. If I'd not wanted you to realize it I could have easily turned the conversation.

BENEDICT: Yes.

KIRSTY: You know how bad you are at sticking to the subject in hand. Of course we both wanted you to know, not only today but eight years ago – only we hadn't the courage to tell you. That's a thing we lack – courage.

BENEDICT: Funny! Had I been in Angus's place – had it been you and me – I should have been so happy to tell everyone – especially Angus.

KIRSTY: Don't be hurt about it.

BENEDICT: I'm not, because I think I understand. You said yourself that it was a very secret and frightened thing. That is what I understand. Not about myself. Love with me would never be secret or frightened but between you and Angus – yes, I understand, my dears.

KIRSTY: It is really you who are of the practical world –

BENEDICT: Why do you say that?

KIRSTY: And we who are of the heaven we credit to you.

BENEDICT: Once you spoke of the three of us together. Now it is you and Angus and, a little way off, rather cold and quite alone, myself.

KIRSTY: Can we avoid speaking of it like that?

BENEDICT: I suppose not. And now, until he comes back, a little light conversation between us.

KIRSTY: Oh, no!

BENEDICT: Oh, yes! Come along, you can manage it. You mustn't look like that when Angus comes in.

KIRSTY: How do I look?

BENEDICT: Lost. Have a drink.

KIRSTY: Yes, please.

BENEDICT: Beer?

KIRSTY: Please.

(*BENEDICT pours out two glasses of beer. He gives one to KIRSTY.*)

BENEDICT: Here you are. God bless you.
KIRSTY: God bless you. (*They drink.*) Here's Angus.
BENEDICT: There's just one more thing I should say –
KIRSTY: What is it? Quickly! What is it?
BENEDICT: Only that – (*ANGUS comes in.*) Welcome!
KIRSTY: Welcome!
ANGUS: Thank you very much.
BENEDICT: You've been quick.
ANGUS: As a matter of fact, I thought I'd been rather a long time. I mean, I didn't want to come back too soon after your elaborate plans to get me out of the house.
BENEDICT: Well, after all, it's a very nice walk to the village.
ANGUS: Yes.
BENEDICT: Along by the river.
ANGUS: Yes.
BENEDICT: At this time of the evening.
ANGUS: Quite.
BENEDICT: Does you good.
ANGUS: Shut up! (*He laughs.*) Here's your beer.
BENEDICT: We have some at the moment but that'll do for me to take to bed.
KIRSTY: Have you started drinking in bed?
BENEDICT: I don't sleep very well.
ANGUS: What shall I do with it?
BENEDICT: Put it down there. Have some.
ANGUS: No, thank you. Why are you two standing up like this?
BENEDICT: I don't really know.
ANGUS: Have you been having a row?
BENEDICT: No. (*To KIRSTY.*) Why are we standing up like this?
KIRSTY: We stood up to get the beer.
ANGUS: Well, please sit down again. (*They do so.*) I hope I didn't come back too soon. I can go out again if you like.
BENEDICT: (*To KIRSTY.*) I'd forgotten that he indulged in this form of heavy irony.
KIRSTY: I remembered it.

BENEDICT: Did you? I suppose I remembered only the pleasanter things about him.

KIRSTY: You're inclined to do that.

BENEDICT: Remember the – yes, I am. Oh, Angus – where are you? – oh, there you are – we've been talking whilst you were out.

ANGUS: Oh yes?

BENEDICT: I've been telling Kirsty that I was in love with her.

ANGUS: Really?

BENEDICT: I've been telling her of the evening I fell in love with her. You had 'flu –

ANGUS: Yes. You've told me.

BENEDICT: Of course I have. She took it very well.

KIRSTY: I cried.

BENEDICT: But those were only tears for what might have been: not real tears at all.

KIRSTY: That's certainly one way of looking at it.

ANGUS: As a viewpoint it is nonsense. There are no other tears.

BENEDICT: Wait a minute. You're sidetracking me. I have something else to say. I was about to tell Kirsty this when you came in and interrupted me.

ANGUS: Well, tell her now.

BENEDICT: I intend to. I was going to tell her that for a long time past I've believed myself to be in love with her. I don't know why I've believed that. (*He pauses and then continues to speak to ANGUS.*) Of course I know why, really. Because I've often thought, 'Must tell Kirsty that' – thought it in the fraction of time before remembering that she was no longer with me: because I've mistaken strangers for her – a common failing in such cases, I believe. Again, because I need to be praised all the time for each thing I do: I need to be laughed out of the pretensions I've assumed in the last few years and I believed Kirsty could do that. Because I have been lonely. (*He turns quickly from ANGUS to KIRSTY.*) Don't say, 'Poor Benedict!'

KIRSTY: I wasn't going to.

BENEDICT: (*To ANGUS.*) I've known all these symptoms and then today I see Kirsty again. I see her today and she is just as I remember her but I find I am not in love with her. Just not in love with her. (*To KIRSTY.*) Should I apologize?

KIRSTY: Not necessary.

BENEDICT: She is quite unchanged. The change obviously is in me. I'm no longer in love with her. (*There is a respectful silence.*) I'm in love with Daphne.

ANGUS: Who?

BENEDICT: Daphne Foggater.

ANGUS: You're making it up!

BENEDICT: I'm not. She's a very nice girl. Simple.

KIRSTY: Do you mean she's half-witted?

BENEDICT: I do not! I mean she's simple in her tastes and way of life.

KIRSTY: Very nice.

BENEDICT: Not like you two.

ANGUS: Have another drink, Benedict?

BENEDICT: I'm going to bed. (*He picks up the beer ANGUS has brought back with him.*) May I take this glass with me?

ANGUS: Certainly.

BENEDICT: One more thing. Have you a good book I can read?

ANGUS: Do you mean a 'good' book or a good book?

BENEDICT: Either. I think something concerned with self-sacrifice.

ANGUS: There's a bible.

BENEDICT: Excellent. I'll take that.

ANGUS: Lower left shelf.

BENEDICT: Got it. Goodnight.

ANGUS: }<br>KIRSTY: } Goodnight.

(*BENEDICT goes upstairs.*)

ANGUS: He has too.

KIRSTY: What?

ANGUS: Taken the bible. (*He laughs.*) Benedict in bed with beer and a bible! What will he be like in the morning? (*He pauses.*) I wonder, am I quite as fond of him as I used to be?

KIRSTY: The same thought passed over me – but only like a shadow. Because of course I'm just as fond of him as I ever was.

ANGUS: Does he make us laugh just as much as ever he did?

KIRSTY: No, perhaps not. But then, we are older – not so likely to be amused.

ANGUS: That sounds dreadful. 'We are older, not so likely to be amused.' I remember he used to make me laugh very much. By the way, what was all that about? Did you really cry?

KIRSTY: Yes, a little.

ANGUS: Why?

KIRSTY: For the reason he gave: tears for what might have been.

ANGUS: For what might have been with Benedict?

KIRSTY: Of course, you fool!

ANGUS: You never once wept with me: not even tears of rage.

KIRSTY: And God knows! there were plenty of opportunities for those.

ANGUS: We're in the past again.

KIRSTY: I know.

ANGUS: Let's come into the present. Listen! You are here with me and Benedict and it is a fine warm evening. To particularize: Benedict is upstairs pouring out a glass of beer and probably preparing to read Ecclesiastes; you are sitting there older and, perhaps, wiser; I am standing here older but no wiser. That is the present.

KIRSTY: 'Even of present things we have no other hold but by our fantasy.'

ANGUS: Don't quote things at me! Detestable habit!

KIRSTY: Sorry.

ANGUS: You should have been an English mistress.

KIRSTY: I was.

(*She has risen and they stand looking at each other in silence. Suddenly ANGUS speaks.*)

ANGUS: Come here, for the love of God!

KIRSTY: You flatter yourself.

(*But she laughs and moves quickly to him.*)

ANGUS: You're very lovely.

KIRSTY: I *am* very lovely?

ANGUS: You *are* very lovely.

KIRSTY: We have achieved the present.

ANGUS: I may say it now?

KIRSTY: Yes. Whenever you like. But another thing you said –

ANGUS: What?

KIRSTY: That I'm older and, perhaps, wiser.

ANGUS: Well?

KIRSTY: I'm not. Not a bit wiser.

ANGUS: I'm so glad.

KIRSTY: So am I. I should be a fool to be wiser. (*She suddenly laughs.*) You have got a ridiculous face. As solemn as a pudding.

ANGUS: I was trying to disentangle the paradox of its being foolish to *be* wiser.

KIRSTY: Because then I couldn't be so happy.

ANGUS: And you are happy? At this very moment?

KIRSTY: Yes.

ANGUS: Then why those tears?

KIRSTY: They're not real tears.

ANGUS: You've never cried with me before.

KIRSTY: I know.

(*There is a pause.*)

ANGUS: I can't say anything else.

KIRSTY: I don't think there is anything else to say. Except, having achieved the present – let us make some use of it.

ANGUS: We could go out.

KIRSTY: Yes.

(*ANGUS has moved to the door.*)

ANGUS: It hasn't rained. I said it wouldn't.

KIRSTY: The dancing has ended.

ANGUS: Listen! (*Very distantly and played at extreme speed can be heard 'God Save the King'. KIRSTY and ANGUS embrace: There is a long kiss between them. The kiss and the National Anthem end simultaneously.*) Now the dancers are saying goodnight –

KIRSTY: Foolish people!

ANGUS: And whether happy or unhappy, they are preparing to go home.

KIRSTY: Let us go home.

ANGUS: Where is that?

KIRSTY: (*She points through the door.*) Somewhere out there. I don't quite know where – but somewhere. After all, we don't ask for much.

ANGUS: It's no good. However hard we try we can't make a tragedy out of this.

(*They laugh at themselves.*)

KIRSTY: We should be ashamed!

(*Their laughter stops suddenly: they kiss again.*)

ANGUS: Come along. We can go by the long lane.

KIRSTY: Yes, I remember. I remember the way.

ANGUS: Don't say that! (*There is a pause.*) Don't say that. Please!

(*They go out: there is a pause.*)

*CURTAIN*

# ACT THREE

*The scene is the same.*
*The time: ten-thirty the following morning – that is, Sunday.*
*The table is laid for breakfast.*
*BENEDICT, dressed in pyjamas and dressing-gown, is sitting at the table. A Sunday newspaper is before him. WILLY YEATS is just leaving the room for the kitchen. BENEDICT calls after her.*

BENEDICT: Don't disturb yourself about it. Mr Learoyd explained to me about your difficulty in making tea and I quite like coffee. (*But WILLY YEATS has gone. BENEDICT opens the newspaper and, after a moment, WILLY YEATS returns with a pot of coffee which she puts on the table.*) Thank you. You're not upset, are you? I'm very sorry. It was just that I wasn't thinking when I asked for tea. Of course, a solution would have been for me to come into the kitchen and make the tea myself, wouldn't it? But we didn't think of that, did we? Never mind. I'm sure it will be very good coffee. (*He begins to pour it out.*) Have some.

WILLY: No, thank you.

BENEDICT: When are Mr Learoyd and Miss Winton going to get up?

WILLY: Mr Learoyd is up: he's gone out.

BENEDICT: What?

WILLY: I met him going out as I was coming in. At about half-past eight.

BENEDICT: Two hours ago! Where's he gone?

WILLY: He said he was going down to the village.

BENEDICT: What for?

WILLY: I don't know.

BENEDICT: What about Miss Winton?

WILLY: She's still in bed. I shook her about half an hour ago.

BENEDICT: What did she say?

WILLY: 'Go away!' Do you want anything to eat, sir? (*She waits in anguish until BENEDICT answers.*)

BENEDICT: No. I don't think so. I'd like a cigarette. Are there any?

WILLY: I expect so: in that box.

BENEDICT: Get me one, will you? (*WILLY fetches him the cigarettes.*) Does Mr Learoyd treat you well?

WILLY: Oh, yes.

BENEDICT: Surprising. You can tell me the truth, you know.

WILLY: He shouts at me sometimes.

BENEDICT: Why don't you shout back? You'd frighten him to death.

WILLY: I did once.

BENEDICT: What did he do?

WILLY: He said, 'Willy Yeats! Leave this house at once!'

BENEDICT: Did you?

WILLY: No. There's nothing else, is there, sir?

BENEDICT: I don't think so. Why does he call you Willy Yeats?

WILLY: Because it's my name.

(*She goes out to the kitchen.*)

BENEDICT: Sound reason. (*He again opens the newspaper and, after a moment, calls.*) Miss Yeats!

WILLY: (*From the kitchen.*) Sir?

BENEDICT: Are you interested in pictures? That is, films, movies, flicks.

WILLY: Not much.

BENEDICT: Oh.

(*There is a pause as he reads: suddenly WILLY puts her head round the corner of the passageway.*)

WILLY: I'm very sorry.

BENEDICT: What? Oh, I don't mind, really. I just wondered. (*WILLY goes: BENEDICT continues to read. Unseen by him KIRSTY comes down the stairs: she is wearing a dressing-gown. Suddenly BENEDICT shouts at the top of his voice.*) Kirsty! Get up! (*There is an appalling crash from the kitchen.*) Careful!

KIRSTY: Good morning. I am up. What's the matter?

BENEDICT: I just wanted someone to talk to, that's all.

KIRSTY: What was all that noise?

BENEDICT: Willy Yeats. Have some coffee?

KIRSTY: Please.
BENEDICT: There's nothing to eat.
KIRSTY: I don't want anything to eat. But I want a cigarette.
BENEDICT: Here you are.
KIRSTY: Thank you.
BENEDICT: Angus has gone out. (*KIRSTY does not answer this.*) Kirsty!
KIRSTY: What?
BENEDICT: You're asleep.
KIRSTY: I know.
BENEDICT: I said, Angus has gone out.
KIRSTY: Has he?
BENEDICT: He went out two hours ago.
KIRSTY: Oh?
BENEDICT: Have you upset him?
KIRSTY: In what way?
BENEDICT: Well – he may have thrown himself in the river.
KIRSTY: Yes, he may have done that.
BENEDICT: Kirsty!
KIRSTY: What?
BENEDICT: Wake up!
KIRSTY: I'm sorry.
BENEDICT: I want to talk to you.
KIRSTY: Go ahead.
BENEDICT: I heard you and Angus go out last night.
KIRSTY: Did you?
BENEDICT: I don't wish to pry into what is, after all, a very private affair but – What are you giggling about?
KIRSTY: Nothing. Go on.
BENEDICT: As I say I don't wish to pry but I do want to ask you this: What are you going to do?
KIRSTY: I haven't the faintest idea.
BENEDICT: Well, haven't you discussed it with Angus?
KIRSTY: Don't be silly, old man.
BENEDICT: Now, look here, Kirsty, I rather resent –
KIRSTY: Give me some more coffee.
BENEDICT: What?
KIRSTY: Give me some more coffee.

(*He does so.*)

BENEDICT: I rather resent –

KIRSTY: And my cigarette seems to have gone out. (*BENEDICT lights it for her.*)

BENEDICT: Don't blow down it! Draw on it! I rather resent this attitude of yours. I am prepared to be noble, not to say self-sacrificing, about you. I am only concerned with your future happiness. You and Angus made a mess of things before and I can see you doing it again. Well, I don't want that to happen and I feel that I might be able to –

KIRSTY: Benedict.

BENEDICT: Yes?

KIRSTY: Is your pomposity inherited?

BENEDICT: Yes, from my father. You won't believe this but – his last words were, 'Tell the world my final thoughts were of Shakespeare'. Then he died. Mother was furious. (*There is a pause.*) You've changed the subject.

KIRSTY: I know. Don't go back to it, please.

BENEDICT: Very well. (*Pause.*) Would you like to see the paper?

KIRSTY: No.

BENEDICT: Oh.

KIRSTY: You read it if you want to.

BENEDICT: I've read it. By the way, I haven't told Angus yet, but I must get back to town this morning.

KIRSTY: Is that a decision taken at this moment?

BENEDICT: No, no! I –

KIRSTY: Last night?

BENEDICT: No. I had intended to get back soon. There are a lot of things I've got to do and, one way and another, I –

KIRSTY: Don't!

BENEDICT: I really must go.

KIRSTY: I don't mean don't go. I mean don't pretend with me. It hurts.

BENEDICT: All right. I thought perhaps it would hurt less if I pretended. I don't want to hurt you.

KIRSTY: Thank you.

BENEDICT: Of course I decided last night. What else could I do?

KIRSTY: Nothing else, I suppose.

BENEDICT: I'll get out of the way. Perhaps you'll let me come and see you both sometimes.

KIRSTY: You said you didn't want to hurt me.

BENEDICT: I don't; so I won't say any more. But I'd like to ask you one question: you are going to be happy together this time, aren't you? (*KIRSTY does not answer.*) But I don't understand. You must have made some plans together. People don't fall in love and not think of the future.

KIRSTY: Don't they?

BENEDICT: Surely that's the big part of falling in love. (*ANGUS comes into the room.*) The business of what we are going to do together.

KIRSTY: Not what we have done together?

BENEDICT: Come now, can you look forward to the love and kisses you gave and received yesterday?

KIRSTY: Of course not.

ANGUS: I'm sorry. I was kept longer than I thought I should be. Good morning Benedict.

BENEDICT: Good morning.

ANGUS: Good morning, Kirsty.

BENEDICT: She's not awake yet.

ANGUS: Isn't she?

BENEDICT: Certainly not from the nonsense she's been talking.

ANGUS: Has Willy Yeats managed breakfast all right?

BENEDICT: Yes. There was the usual difficulty about tea so I had coffee. Do you want some?

ANGUS: Yes, please. (*BENEDICT pours the coffee for ANGUS.*) It's going to be a lovely day, I think.

BENEDICT: Is it? Good. (*There is a pause.*) There doesn't seem to be anything to eat.

ANGUS: I'm so sorry. Do you want something?

BENEDICT: No.

ANGUS: Well, I don't. (*There is a pause.*) Kirsty?

KIRSTY: What?

ANGUS: Do you want anything to eat?

KIRSTY: No.

(*There is a pause.*)

BENEDICT: Well, I must –

KIRSTY: We're back where we started and this time there's no horse in the garden.

BENEDICT: This time it would make no difference if there were. I must go and get dressed. (*He rises from the table and crosses to the stairs.*) Oh, Angus –

ANGUS: Yes?

BENEDICT: I'm afraid I must get back to London this morning.

ANGUS: Must you?

BENEDICT: I meant to tell you yesterday that I'd have to go but there just didn't seem any opportunity.

ANGUS: You said you could stay until Wednesday. However – are you quite sure you must go?

BENEDICT: Yes, I'm afraid so.

ANGUS: All right. I believe there's a train about midday. You'd better check it with Willy Yeats. Strangely enough, she knows all about such things.

BENEDICT: Good. I'll do that. I'm going to dress.

ANGUS: All right. (*BENEDICT goes up the stairs.*) Good morning, Kirsty.

KIRSTY: Good morning, Angus.

ANGUS: Are you awake?

KIRSTY: Yes. Where have you been?

ANGUS: To speak to a man.

KIRSTY: What sort of man do you speak to at half-past eight on a Sunday morning?

ANGUS: A man with a very long beard, very short legs and a very great deal of money.

KIRSTY: Just the sort of man to speak to at half-past eight in the morning. Nice conversation?

ANGUS: Short but to the point.

KIRSTY: I heard you go, darling.

ANGUS: I thought you were asleep.

KIRSTY: No.

ANGUS: Why didn't you say something?

KIRSTY: I hadn't anything to say.

ANGUS: I might have known you weren't asleep. You were looking so very lovely.

KIRSTY: Meaning that I'm not when I'm really asleep?
ANGUS: Exactly. Yours is a very conscious beauty.
KIRSTY: How do I look at the moment?
ANGUS: Dreadful. Give me a cigarette.
KIRSTY: You don't want a cigarette.
ANGUS: Don't I?
KIRSTY: No. Come here. (*ANGUS rises and moves round the table to her.*) Kiss me.
ANGUS: Mind the coffee pot!
KIRSTY: Damn the coffee pot! (*ANGUS kisses her.*) Now look at me. Well?
ANGUS: You haven't got any make-up on.
KIRSTY: No. I've washed my face.
ANGUS: It's a very good face. (*He pushes back her hair.*) I can feel the pulse in your temple. One – two – three – four – five – six – seven – eight –
KIRSTY: That's very quick, isn't it? Apart from the lack of make-up can you see nothing else?
ANGUS: Stand up. (*She does so.*) Not really, darling. Darling. My very sweet and unaware darling.
KIRSTY: And you. And you, my darling. (*She puts her arms around him and they kiss. After the kiss they stand staring at each other in silence until KIRSTY says.*) Damn!
ANGUS: What's the matter?
KIRSTY: It's no good, is it?
ANGUS: No.
KIRSTY: There's no hope of its ever being good, is there?
ANGUS: No.
KIRSTY: I wonder why not?
ANGUS: We said we would never examine our reasons.
KIRSTY: The bloody old moralists would say it was just physical attraction between us.
ANGUS: You sound like an angry child. Yes, that's what they'd say.
KIRSTY: And they'd be quite right. You're very good in that sense. But there was something more – surely something more.
ANGUS: Friendliness, perhaps.
KIRSTY: A desire to please. (*They laugh.*) It's quite useless trying to explain it.

ANGUS: Quite useless.

KIRSTY: Other people would say we've just fallen out of love – they would say that we fell out of love eight years ago when you left me. (*ANGUS turns away.*) Darling, don't! Don't turn away from me. (*ANGUS turns back to her.*) That's what other people would say but it's not true, is it?

ANGUS: No. To hell with other people.

KIRSTY: It's not just this morning, you know.

ANGUS: I know that.

KIRSTY: It was last night –

ANGUS: And every night and day in the last eight years.

KIRSTY: You see! It is obvious to us both. And there's something that proves it –

ANGUS: Do we need anything else to prove it?

KIRSTY: Perhaps not but, do you know, since I have been here, since we have met again, neither of us has said to the other, 'I love you'. Not even in moments of – well, moments –

ANGUS: You're shy.

KIRSTY: Yes, I am. Moments when there is nothing else can be said.

ANGUS: I know.

KIRSTY: Neither have we mentioned the future.

ANGUS: No.

KIRSTY: We've both known the whole time.

ANGUS: Yes. Something you said.

KIRSTY: What?

ANGUS: Last night. You said, 'And in the present I think I want you'. I *think* I want you. You were unsure.

KIRSTY: No! No, you're wrong. Last night I was certain I wanted you but I could see no further. You must know I wanted you. Darling, I've always found great delight in you. And it was that delight combined with a desire to please and friendliness that made us.

ANGUS: Made us what we are or what we were? (*He does not wait for her to answer.*) You are standing there as I remember you one morning but you are saying things you have never said before.

KIRSTY: After all, we are told that love can never give us all we wish; therefore we must be grateful for the little it does give.

ANGUS: Which of your bloody old moralists is that?

KIRSTY: And it has given us each other – for a time. We should be grateful.

ANGUS: We have each other but we're just no good together.

KIRSTY: No good at all. Funny! We haven't quarrelled this time and yet we know more surely.

ANGUS: More surely than when we did quarrel.

KIRSTY: (*After a pause.*) Angus –

ANGUS: Yes?

KIRSTY: Nothing. I must go and get dressed.

(*She begins to move to the stairs.*)

ANGUS: Kirsty! Just a minute! (*She turns.*) Just a moment to look at you now that you're going away.

KIRSTY: Am I going away?

ANGUS: I think so. Soon.

KIRSTY: How soon?

ANGUS: Within an hour.

KIRSTY: In that case, I'd better go and dress now. (*But she remains standing there, facing ANGUS.*) You're all right, aren't you?

ANGUS: What? Yes, I'm all right.

KIRSTY: Then I'm going to dress now.

ANGUS: Yes, run along.

(*But neither of them move.*)

KIRSTY: I remember that blue jersey you're wearing.

ANGUS: It's not the same one. It's another one like it.

KIRSTY: Not the same one?

ANGUS: No.

KIRSTY: Sorry. I thought it was.

ANGUS: Don't apologize.

KIRSTY: I didn't mean to. (*KIRSTY half-turns to the stairs.*) I'm going upstairs now.

ANGUS: You're so lovely.

KIRSTY: What?

ANGUS: You're so very lovely.

KIRSTY: (*Whispers.*) I can't really hear what you're saying.

ANGUS: You're very lovely.

(*He holds out his hands to her: she looks at him for a moment and then cries out.*)

KIRSTY: Please! Angus! Please!

ANGUS: Isn't she, Benedict?

(*He speaks to BENEDICT who has come down the stairs behind KIRSTY.*)

BENEDICT: What?

ANGUS: Kirsty. Isn't she a lovely person?

BENEDICT: Yes, she is. She – (*He turns to her but she has gone up the stairs.*) Angus, does Willy Yeats really know about the train times?

ANGUS: Yes.

BENEDICT: Haven't you got a time-table?

ANGUS: No. I keep Willy Yeats instead.

BENEDICT: Can I ring up the station?

ANGUS: There's no telephone here.

BENEDICT: Damn! Then it will have to be Willy Yeats.

ANGUS: And why not? I'll send her in to you.

BENEDICT: Thank you.

ANGUS: There's no need for you to go. You do understand that, don't you?

BENEDICT: I really think I ought to go. I've got a lot of things to do.

ANGUS: All right.

(*He begins to move to the kitchen.*)

BENEDICT: Oh, Angus.

ANGUS: Yes?

BENEDICT: May I see you again sometime?

ANGUS: Most certainly. Whenever you like. I shall be here.

BENEDICT: Here?

ANGUS: Yes. For the rest of this year, anyway.

BENEDICT: You're not thinking of moving?

ANGUS: No, I don't think so.

BENEDICT: That's all right, then.

ANGUS: I'm going through to the garden. I'll send Willy in to you.

(*He goes out to the kitchen. Almost immediately WILLY YEATS appears and stands in the passageway.*)

WILLY: Sir?

BENEDICT: What? Oh.

WILLY: Sorry, sir. Did I make you jump?

BENEDICT: Yes.

WILLY: Mr Learoyd said you wanted to speak to me.

BENEDICT: That's right. I do. I believe you know about the trains to London.

WILLY: Yes, sir. Eleven twenty-eight. One twenty-eight. Three five. Seven –

BENEDICT: This morning. I want to go this morning.

WILLY: Eleven twenty-eight. One twenty-eight. Change at Twyford.

BENEDICT: Are they good trains?

WILLY: Oh, very good, sir. The very best they have, sir.

BENEDICT: (*After a pause.*) Are you laughing at me, Willy Yeats?

WILLY: No, sir.

BENEDICT: I shall be able to catch the eleven twenty-eight, shan't I?

WILLY: I should think so. If you hurry.

BENEDICT: Good. I'll do that.

WILLY: Are you packed, sir?

BENEDICT: Yes, there's very little. (*There is a pause.*) Well, that's it, then. Eleven twenty-eight.

WILLY: That's it, sir. Eleven twenty-eight.

(*She turns to go.*)

BENEDICT: Oh – er –

WILLY: Sir? (*BENEDICT is holding out a pound note to WILLY: with terrifying suspicion she asks.*) What's that?

BENEDICT: (*Speaking at great speed and obviously under stress.*) It's usual, Willy. I can assure you it is quite usual. I should like to say how very comfortable I've been here: everything you have done for me has been excellent – quite excellent – and this is merely a small indication of my appreciation. Please take it now and let me go.

(*WILLY comes forward and takes the note.*)

WILLY: It has been very pleasant having you here.

BENEDICT: Not at all.

WILLY: I only wish you could stay longer.
BENEDICT: I wish I could. I would, I assure you, if –
WILLY: It's very nice down here.
BENEDICT: Charming! Charming!
WILLY: However, you must come again.
BENEDICT: I shall be delighted. It's extremely kind of you.
WILLY: Not at all. Goodbye.

(*She holds out her hand.*)

BENEDICT: Goodbye. (*They shake hands and WILLY goes out to the kitchen. BENEDICT stands for a moment staring after her and then calls, rather weakly.*) Angus! Angus! (*A pause.*) No one about?

(*JAMES answers from the front door.*)

JAMES: Yes, I – er
BENEDICT: Oh! Good morning.
JAMES: Good morning.
BENEDICT: What? –
JAMES: Mrs Sotheran?
BENEDICT: Who?
JAMES: Mrs Sotheran.
BENEDICT: I think you must have the wrong house.
JAMES: I don't think so. This is Mr Learoyd's house, isn't it? Mr Angus Learoyd.
BENEDICT: Yes.
JAMES: How do you do.
BENEDICT: How do you do. I'm not Mr Learoyd.
JAMES: No?
BENEDICT: No. My name's Clare. Mr Learoyd's out at the moment. In the garden, I think.
JAMES: Anyway, if this is Mr Learoyd's house I'm right. My wife, Mrs Sotheran, is staying here.
BENEDICT: Is she? But I'm afraid there's only myself, Mr Learoyd and –

(*He stops.*)

JAMES: Yes?
BENEDICT: What is your wife's name?
JAMES: Christiana. Some people call her Kirsty.
BENEDICT: Yes. Yes. In that case, you'd better come in.

JAMES: Thank you.

(*He comes into the room.*)

BENEDICT: I think – I think your wife is dressing. I'll tell her you're here.

JAMES: Thank you.

BENEDICT: Is she expecting you?

JAMES: What's that?

BENEDICT: I said, is she expecting you?

JAMES: Oh, yes.

BENEDICT: She is?

JAMES: Yes.

BENEDICT: Then I'll tell her you're here. (*He goes to the stairs.*) Kirsty! (*To JAMES.*) She had a very late night last – (*He calls.*) Kirsty!

KIRSTY: (*From her bedroom.*) What is it?

BENEDICT: Your – there's someone to see you.

KIRSTY: What?

BENEDICT: There's someone to see you.

KIRSTY: Who?

BENEDICT: Come down, will you?

KIRSTY: All right. I shan't be a minute.

BENEDICT: (*To JAMES.*) She'll be here in a minute.

JAMES: Good. Thank you.

BENEDICT: Do sit down.

JAMES: Thank you. Is Mr Learoyd about?

BENEDICT: I think he'll probably be in soon.

JAMES: Good.

BENEDICT: Have you had some breakfast?

JAMES: Yes, thank you. I had it before I started.

(*There is a pause.*)

BENEDICT: You've come down from London?

JAMES: Yes. (*There is a pause.*) Haven't we met before?

BENEDICT: No, I don't think so.

JAMES: Your face seems very familiar. What is your name again?

BENEDICT: Clare. Benedict Clare.

JAMES: I don't seem to know your name but your face – it seems very familiar to me.

BENEDICT: How very strange.
JAMES: I don't forget people.
BENEDICT: Don't you?
JAMES: No. I thought we might have met at work.
BENEDICT: What is your work?
JAMES: I'm a schoolmaster. But I've been doing educational work for the Government recently. You don't do anything like that?
BENEDICT: No, I don't do anything like that at all. Will you have a cigarette?
JAMES: I don't smoke.

(*A pause.*)

BENEDICT: Interesting, I should think.
JAMES: What?
BENEDICT: Your work.
JAMES: Yes, very.
BENEDICT: Have you – ?

(*ANGUS comes in from the kitchen.*)

JAMES: Have I what?
BENEDICT: This is Angus Learoyd. Mr Sotheran.
JAMES: How do you do.
ANGUS: How do you do. (*ANGUS shakes hands with JAMES.*) You got here quite easily?
JAMES: Yes. I came down by car.
ANGUS: Good. It's not really a long run. Do sit down.
JAMES: Thank you.
ANGUS: Your wife knows you're here, does she?
JAMES: Yes. Mr – I'm sorry.
BENEDICT: Clare.
JAMES: Mr Clare told her. I believe she's dressing.
ANGUS: I expect she'll be down in a moment. Have you had breakfast?
JAMES: Yes, thank you.
ANGUS: Cigarette?
JAMES: I don't smoke, thank you very much.
ANGUS: Benedict?
BENEDICT: What? No, thank you.
JAMES: Mr Learoyd –

ANGUS: Yes?

JAMES: There's nothing wrong, is there? I mean –

ANGUS: I can assure you everything is perfectly all right.

JAMES: I just wondered. It was when you said – no, it's foolish of me – but, you see, this is the first time Christiana has ever been away on even a short visit or holiday without me. Under those circumstances perhaps you can regard my anxiety as –

ANGUS: I can quite understand.

JAMES: I am not the sociable type, I'm afraid. When Christiana told me she knew you some years ago and you had invited her down for the week-end I felt –

ANGUS: Hullo, Christiana.

(*She has come down the stairs – she is dressed. After the shortest pause she says.*)

KIRSTY: Hullo, Angus. Hullo, James.

JAMES: Good morning, my dear. (*He goes to her and kisses her.*) We have been waiting for you.

KIRSTY: Have you?

ANGUS: Not really.

KIRSTY: I'm sorry. You've met Angus and –

JAMES: Oh, yes. We've been talking. I was telling Mr Clare that I'm sure he and I have met before. Do you think that's possible?

KIRSTY: I don't know. (*To BENEDICT.*) What do you feel about it?

BENEDICT: What do I feel?

KIRSTY: Yes.

BENEDICT: Nothing at all.

(*There is a pause.*)

JAMES: Well, my dear, if you're ready –

KIRSTY: Yes, I am.

JAMES: Good. Then I think we ought to be moving.

KIRSTY: Are we going back to London?

JAMES: Well, that's what you want, isn't it?

KIRSTY: Yes.

JAMES: Surely that is the message you gave to Mr Learoyd to give to me on the phone this morning. (*He turns to ANGUS.*) I haven't got this all wrong, have I? The message you gave to me was that Christiana wished me to come down here and fetch her as she had decided she ought to be back in London by this evening. That is right, isn't it? I mean –

KIRSTY: Quite right, James.

JAMES: Good. For a moment I thought I'd made some dreadful mistake. I'm not very good on the telephone at any time. I'm a trifle deaf.

KIRSTY: Well, James, you needn't worry this time because you have got it quite right.

JAMES: Excellent. Shall we get along? Have you a bag, my dear?

KIRSTY: Yes, it's upstairs.

JAMES: Is it packed?

KIRSTY: Yes. I'll get it.

ANGUS: Don't bother! (*There is a pause.*) We'll have Willy Yeats get it. (*He calls.*) Willy!

BENEDICT: Come along, Mr Sotheran. While your wife gets her bag and says her goodbyes I'll come down with you and help you turn the car round. It's rather tricky.

JAMES: Thank you. It's very nice of you. Goodbye, Mr Learoyd. I hope we can meet again sometime.

ANGUS: I hope so. Goodbye.

JAMES: (*To BENEDICT.*) I don't wish to labour the point of our having met before but may I ask what your job is?

BENEDICT: I'm in Cold Storage at the moment.

JAMES: Really!

(*They go out together. ANGUS and KIRSTY stand looking at each other.*)

KIRSTY: (*She begins to laugh.*) That was a damnable trick to play.

ANGUS: Surely it was the only way.

KIRSTY: But how did you know?

(*WILLY YEATS comes in from the kitchen.*)

WILLY: I thought I heard you call me.

(*She is about to retire.*)

ANGUS: Come here! I did. Some minutes ago.

WILLY: Well, I didn't come before because I wasn't sure whether I heard you or not.

ANGUS: Willy.

WILLY: Sir?

ANGUS: Stop talking nonsense.

WILLY: Yes, sir.

(*Throughout this conversation with WILLY, ANGUS remains looking at KIRSTY.*)

ANGUS: Upstairs, in Miss Winton's room, probably standing by the bed, is a small suitcase.

WILLY: Yes, sir.

ANGUS: Get it. (*WILLY moves to the stairs.*) Willy!

WILLY: Yes Sir.

ANGUS: Do you smoke? (*There is a shamed silence from WILLY.*) I said, do you smoke?

WILLY: Yes, sir.

ANGUS: Then take this – (*He takes a cigarette from his case and holds it out to WILLY.*) – go upstairs, sit on the bed, smoke the cigarette and when you have finished it bring down the bag.

WILLY: Yes, sir. (*She again moves to the stairs but stops.*) Sir.

ANGUS: Willy?

WILLY: No matches.

ANGUS: Dear God!

(*He throws a box of matches at WILLY which she catches.*)

KIRSTY: (*As WILLY passes her.*) Do you play cricket?

WILLY: Yes, Miss.

(*She goes up the stairs.*)

KIRSTY: I can't wait as long as that.

ANGUS: Why not? We're not to blame for Willy's dilatory service.

KIRSTY: Still shifting the responsibility on to someone else?

ANGUS: As ever.

KIRSTY: How did you know?

ANGUS: About – ?

(*He points through the door.*)

KIRSTY: Yes.

ANGUS: Well, I – Sit down.

KIRSTY: Darling, I can't stay now. James will be sitting out there in the car getting angrier and angrier.

ANGUS: Does he? Get angrier and angrier, I mean.

KIRSTY: Sometimes. Tell me how you knew.

ANGUS: I guessed.

KIRSTY: When?

ANGUS: I don't really know. As to the practical details – after you were asleep last night I went to your bag – ostensibly to get a cigarette – and I found an unsealed and unstamped letter addressed to some charity organization. It was in your handwriting and signed – Christiana Sotheran. At the letterhead was a telephone number. I took a chance and rang it this morning. James answered me.

KIRSTY: But he hasn't got a very long beard or very short legs.

ANGUS: No, but I thought he might have.

KIRSTY: I see.

ANGUS: Has he got a very great deal of money?

KIRSTY: Yes.

ANGUS: I'm glad. You had to go, you know. And, besides, I wanted to see him.

(*He turns away.*)

KIRSTY: You're laughing!

ANGUS: No, I'm not.

KIRSTY: Don't, please!

ANGUS: But I'm not laughing. (*There is a pause.*) We have settled all our reasons, you know.

KIRSTY: I know.

ANGUS: We can talk of other things now. He calls you Christiana.

KIRSTY: Yes.

ANGUS: Never Kirsty?

KIRSTY: No, he doesn't like it.

ANGUS: I'm glad.

KIRSTY: Angus, I must go.

ANGUS: Don't worry. (*He is at the window.*) They've turned the car round. Benedict is talking to him. He is laughing. James – James is laughing. Is that usual?

KIRSTY: Not very. Oh, he laughs quite a lot, really. But not at the same things as we do – I do. He has a more academic humour – but that's probably his job.

ANGUS: What is his job?

KIRSTY: He's an educationalist.

ANGUS: Is that the same as a schoolmaster?

KIRSTY: Yes, really, I suppose. But he doesn't have to make a living from it.

ANGUS: Small boys?

KIRSTY: Yes. Very small, recalcitrant boys.

(*WILLY YEATS comes down the stairs carrying KIRSTY's bag.*)

ANGUS: Take it out to the car, Willy.

KIRSTY: No. I'll take it

(*She takes the bag from WILLY.*)

ANGUS: All right, Willy. That's all. (*As she is going.*) How do you feel?

WILLY: Fine.

ANGUS: Good.

(*WILLY goes out to the kitchen.*)

KIRSTY: Now I must go.

(*She moves to the door.*)

ANGUS: Kirsty!

KIRSTY: Yes?

ANGUS: What's he like?

KIRSTY: Oh – all right. (*They laugh very gently at JAMES.*) What do we say?

ANGUS: I don't really know. 'Farewell' is so affected.

KIRSTY: Surely not at a moment like this.

(*And so, after a pause, ANGUS says.*)

ANGUS: Farewell, Kirsty.

KIRSTY: Farewell, Angus.

(*She goes out: ANGUS does not watch her go to the car but stands unmoving. After a moment WILLY YEATS returns to the room. She waits silently until ANGUS turns and sees her.*)

ANGUS: Unless it's very important don't bother me, there's a good girl.

WILLY: I'm sorry, sir.

ANGUS: What are you sorry about?

WILLY: Something terrible has gone wrong, hasn't it, sir?

ANGUS: Something terrible – ?

WILLY: I did try, sir! Really, I did try very hard!

ANGUS: I don't quite understand you, Willy.

WILLY: Well, sir, they're both leaving.

ANGUS: Yes.

WLLLY: Then something terrible must have gone wrong. I've tried to think what it is, sir, but I can't. I've tried to keep my mind on the things that matter and I thought I had done but I can't have done because they're both going and they wouldn't do that unless –

ANGUS: Willy! (*He moves to her and puts an arm round her shoulders.*) Willy, dear child! It's not your fault. They're going – that's true – and they're going because things have gone wrong – but nothing for which you were responsible. Really and truly, they're not. Come along, now. Look up. You believe me, don't you?

WILLY: Truth, sir?

ANGUS: Of course. There was something I'd intended to tell you later but I'll tell you now instead – and don't think I'm saying it just because you're miserable at the moment. It is this: I'm very pleased with the way you've done your job about the house in the last day. You have carried on quite excellently. I'm afraid I've not helped you as much as I said I would but you've done magnificently on your own. I'm very proud of you. (*BENEDICT comes in from the garden.*) Very proud of you, indeed. If you don't believe me ask Mr Clare.

BENEDICT: What?

ANGUS: Am I not very proud of Willy?

BENEDICT: Well, you should be.

ANGUS: There you are. Now, run along – and Willy! –

WILLY: Sir?

ANGUS: Don't worry so much about things. I don't.

WILLY: No, sir.

(*She goes out to the kitchen. There is silence between ANGUS and BENEDICT for some moments: until BENEDICT speaks.*)

BENEDICT: They've gone.

ANGUS: Have they?

(*There is a pause.*)

BENEDICT: I haven't been so near to tears for a long time. Eight years to be precise.

ANGUS: It's always good to be precise about such things.

BENEDICT: You mustn't let this make you angry and bitter.

ANGUS: It doesn't.

BENEDICT: I thought, perhaps, –

ANGUS: After all, I sent for her husband.

BENEDICT: That's right. You did. I was forgetting that.

ANGUS: I thought you were.

BENEDICT: Why did you?

ANGUS: Send for him? What else could I do?

BENEDICT: Nothing, I suppose. Did you know about him before she came? Surely not.

ANGUS: No. I knew last night.

BENEDICT: She couldn't expect to keep it from you.

ANGUS: She didn't wish to keep it from me. Both of us pretended but really we kept nothing from each other. It was a conscious deception that we both understood must fail to deceive. We wanted it to be like that. No, we kept nothing from each other – only from you, Benedict.

BENEDICT: You loved her?

ANGUS: Yes.

BENEDICT: You still – ?

ANGUS: Don't ask that!

BENEDICT: Very well. I must go –

ANGUS: Yes.

BENEDICT: Or I shall miss that train. Eleven twenty-eight. (*He remains unmoving.*) Angus, do you remember we once – jokingly – spoke of Kirsty being married?

ANGUS: Yes.

BENEDICT: Do you remember what we said we'd do if we met her – what was then hypothetical – husband?

ANGUS: Yes. We said we'd laugh at him.

BENEDICT: I didn't feel I wanted to laugh at Sotheran.

ANGUS: Didn't you?

BENEDICT: Do you think he ill-treats her?

ANGUS: In what way?

BENEDICT: Beats her or anything like that.

ANGUS: I didn't notice any marks. Do you think he might?

BENEDICT: Quite capable, I should say. He's got a mouth like a pocket. (*ANGUS laughs.*) And his finger-nails weren't very clean. And – what else was there about him? This, anyway: an absurdly proprietary air towards Kirsty.

ANGUS: Well, damn it, she is his wife.

BENEDICT: Nevertheless, we should resent it.

ANGUS: Nonsense!

BENEDICT: But –

ANGUS: You mustn't allow this to make you angry and bitter, Benedict.

BENEDICT: I've got nothing against the man. I was only saying these things because I thought it might make you feel better.

ANGUS: Don't bother. I've nothing against the man, either.

BENEDICT: Except that he married Kirsty.

ANGUS: Not even that. (*There is a pause.*) Hell! These roses are falling.

(*There is a rose-bowl on the table.*)

BENEDICT: I should be able to read some miserable symbolism into that fact. But I can't see – I can't see – (*He stops.*) Oh, Angus! Angus, I do hope she's happy with him.

(*ANGUS moves to him and is about to speak when WILLY YEATS comes into the room.*)

WILLY: Sir!

ANGUS: Yes?

WILLY: No. Mr Clare, sir.

BENEDICT: Yes?

WILLY: Eleven o'clock, sir. Twenty minutes walk to the station.

BENEDICT: God, I must –

WILLY: Eleven twenty-eight train, sir.

BENEDICT: Yes. I must run. I'm almost packed.

WILLY: I'll get your bag, sir.

BENEDICT: No, I'll get it.

(*He runs up the stairs.*)

ANGUS: Well, Willy, my dear, it looks as if we are going to be left on our own for the rest of the weekend. What are we going to do with ourselves?

WILLY: I don't know, sir.

ANGUS: Let's go fishing.

WILLY: All right, sir. I've got my rod in the kitchen.

ANGUS: Good. We'll catch our supper, then come back here and I'll show you how too cook it.

WILLY: Right, sir. I suppose I should clear these breakfast things away.

ANGUS: Yes, I suppose you should. (*WILLY begins to collect the plates and cups. After a pause ANGUS says.*) Willy.

WILLY: Sir?

ANGUS: Have you ever been in love?

WILLY: Not yet, sir.

ANGUS: But you think you will be one day?

WILLY: I expect so, sir.

ANGUS: May I moralize to you for a few minutes? About being in love.

WILLY: I don't understand what that means, sir.

ANGUS: What? Moralize? You understand what morals are, don't you?

WILLY: No, sir.

ANGUS: You don't? (*He laughs.*)

WILLY: Why do you laugh, sir? Should I know?

ANGUS: Of course not.

WILLY: I'd like to know, sir. I'd like to know everything.

ANGUS: No, you wouldn't, Willy. Remain ignorant and remain happy. Discover morality and you'll discover a conscience.

WILLY: Oh, I have a conscience, sir.

ANGUS: Have you? Tell me about it.

(*ELIZABETH is standing in the doorway. She is twenty-one years of age: she wears spectacles. She remains unseen by ANGUS and WILLY.*)

WILLY: Well, sir, we were told at school that it was an 'inner voice'.

ANGUS: And what does it say?

WILLY: Usually – 'Don't!'

ANGUS: When I was at school there was a boy named McIntosh who was given to (*He senses ELIZABETH standing at the door and turns to her.*) Hullo.

ELIZABETH: What are you two talking about?

ANGUS: We were discussing Willy's conscience – her 'inner voice' which is always saying 'don't!'

ELIZABETH: Does it say, 'Don't clear away breakfast until eleven o'clock in the morning'?

WILLY: Of course not. I'm sorry.

(*She collects some plates and cups and hurries away into the kitchen.*)

ELIZABETH: Surprised to see me?

ANGUS: A little – but you know I'm never really surprised at anything.

(*ELIZABETH comes into the room.*)

ELIZABETH: How are you?

ANGUS: I'm all right.

(*They kiss.*)

ELIZABETH: Has Willy Yeats been behaving herself?

ANGUS: Oh, yes.

(*BENEDICT comes down the stairs: He is carrying his bag.*)

BENEDICT: I shall have to run to catch that damned train. I – (*He sees ELIZABETH.*) I'm so sorry.

ANGUS: Oh, Benedict – this is Elizabeth.

BENEDICT: How do you do.

ELIZABETH: How do you do.

BENEDICT: I'm terribly sorry but I must go. A train, you know.

ELIZABETH: Yes.

BENEDICT: Goodbye, Angus. God bless you. (*They shake hands.*) Shall I see you again?

ANGUS: I don't know. Will you?

BENEDICT: Let's see, should we? Let's wait and see.

ANGUS: Yes.

BENEDICT: It may all come right.

ANGUS: Perhaps it will.

BENEDICT: Goodbye. (*To ELIZABETH.*) Goodbye.

ELIZABETH: Goodbye. (*BENEDICT goes out.*) I know that man's face, don't I?

ANGUS: It's Benedict Clare.

ELIZABETH: The film actor?

ANGUS: Yes.

ELIZABETH: I didn't know you knew him.

ANGUS: Oh, yes. I've known him since he was so high.

(*He indicates just how high: it is about two and a half feet.*)

ELIZABETH: You've never told me.

ANGUS: Haven't I?

(*BENEDICT puts his head round the door.*)

BENEDICT: Angus.

ANGUS: Yes?

BENEDICT: There's a baby in the garden.

ELIZABETH: Yes. It's mine.

BENEDICT: Oh, that's all right, then. Well, goodbye, again.

ANGUS:<br>ELIZABETH: } Goodbye.

ELIZABETH: He's been staying here?

ANGUS: Yes. For the weekend. But he's had to get back to town. How's Judith?

ELIZABETH: She's got the measles.

ANGUS: What?

ELIZABETH: Yes. Absurd, isn't it? That's why I'm back today instead of Thursday. I didn't want to keep Christopher there in case he caught them. Of course, he may have done so already but we must hope for the best.

(*ANGUS has moved to the door and, looking into the garden, calls.*)

ANGUS: Christopher! (*He waves to the child.*) Good God! He can wave his hand now.

ELIZABETH: Yes. He started that the day before yesterday. (*WILLY YEATS comes into the room to fetch the remaining breakfast dishes.*) He's also started to say something that sounds remotely like your name. How are you, Willy Yeats?

WILLY: I'm very well, thank you.

ELIZABETH: Has my husband been good to you?

WILLY: Oh, yes. We've got along very well. Haven't we, sir?

ANGUS: I think so, Willy.

WILLY: Of course, we've had a pretty busy time but I think we managed all right. At least, Mr Learoyd said we did. We've had –

ELIZABETH: What have you done with Christopher's photograph, Angus?

ANGUS: I took it upstairs.

ELIZABETH: Any special reason?

ANGUS: No. (*WILLY goes out to the kitchen with the remaining breakfast dishes.*) Has Judith got anyone to nurse her?

ELIZABETH: She's not as ill as all that. She can move about. I attempted to show sisterly devotion but you know how she hates that sort of thing. I must get Willy to make me some coffee.

(*She begins to move to the kitchen.*)

ANGUS: Can I bring Christopher in here?

ELIZABETH: No, darling. I think he may go to sleep.

ANGUS: All right.

ELIZABETH: I hope by coming back like this I haven't upset any of your plans.

ANGUS: What? No. I wasn't intending to do anything. Willy and I were going fishing, that's all.

ELIZABETH: Were you? Can I come?

ANGUS: Of course.

ELIZABETH: Good. I'll tell Willy. (*She goes to the passageway and calls.*) Willy Yeats! I'm coming fishing with you so hurry and get the place tidied up – and will you make me some coffee?

WILLY: (*From the kitchen.*) I am making some.

ELIZABETH: Good girl. Bring it in, will you? (*She turns to ANGUS.*) Ah! It's good to be back. Do you know this is the first time I've been away without you since we've been married?

ANGUS: God bless my soul! The first time in four years? I hadn't realized that.

ELIZABETH: Have you missed me?

ANGUS: Not a bit. I've had a most beautiful woman staying here with me.

ELIZABETH: Oh? Who was that?

ANGUS: I'm quite serious. Someone called Christiana Winton.

ELIZABETH: She sounds very –

ANGUS: Sit down.
ELIZABETH: Why?
ANGUS: Because I've got something to tell you.
(*ELIZABETH sits.*)
ELIZABETH: Well?
ANGUS: Well, once upon a time –
ELIZABETH: Angus! Angus, I –
ANGUS: Yes?
ELIZABETH: (*She laughs.*) How absurd! When you said that I suddenly remembered the day –
ANGUS: What did you say?
ELIZABETH: I said, I suddenly remembered the day –
ANGUS: Liz!
ELIZABETH: What's the matter?
ANGUS: Say it again.
ELIZABETH: Don't be absurd!
ANGUS: Please!
ELIZABETH: All right. I suddenly remembered the day when –
(*She stops.*)
ANGUS: Go on.
ELIZABETH: When I was ill – and you came to see me and sat by my bed and said, 'I've got something to tell you'. For a moment I was so frightened because I thought you had come to tell me that you didn't love me any more – but you began, 'Once upon a time – ', and it was only some ridiculous story. Do you remember how I laughed? You thought I was delirious but it was only relief.
ANGUS: Liz!
(*He goes to her.*)
ELIZABETH: What is it?
ANGUS: I love you, that's what it is.
ELIZABETH: Well, I love you. (*ANGUS laughs.*) Why are you laughing?
ANGUS: It's just relief.
ELIZABETH: Relief at what?
ANGUS: Relief at finding that you are as – that you are – that you are Elizabeth.

ELIZABETH: I think we're both rather inclined to hysteria. What were you going to tell me?

ANGUS: Well, once upon a time –

(*WILLY comes in with the coffee.*)

WILLY: Will you be fishing from the boat?

ANGUS: I should think so.

WILLY: Then I shall want my trousers.

(*She goes back into the kitchen.*)

ANGUS: Dear Liz, I had meant to make a tragedy out of this but I can't because Willy wants her trousers and your glasses are slipping towards the end of your nose.

ELIZABETH: What are you talking about?

ANGUS: I'll tell you sometime.

ELIZABETH: Now.

ANGUS: No. We're going fishing. Coffee?

ELIZABETH: Yes, please.

ANGUS: (*Shouts.*) Willy! Sugar!
ELIZABETH: You love to create a mystery, don't you? } *Speaking together.*

ANGUS: Did you get that stuff in London for me?

ELIZABETH: Yes, but I could only get them in brown.

ANGUS: Brown! Oh God!

ELIZABETH: It was all they had.
ANGUS: Willy! Sugar! } *Together.*

WILLY: Coming, sir.
ELIZABETH: I'm sorry. (*The curtain begins to come down.*) You should buy the damned things yourself. } *Together.*

ANGUS: Are you taking Christopher fishing?
WILLY: Here, sir. } *Together.*

ANGUS: Thank you.

WILLY: No lump.

ANGUS: No what?

WILLY: Lump.

ANGUS: Lump what?

WILLY: Lump sugar!

ANGUS: Never mind. (*WILLY goes out.*) Are you taking Christopher?

ELIZABETH: I should think so.

ANGUS: I hope he won't be sick again.
*(ANGUS is pouring out the coffee.)*
ELIZABETH: Willy can look after him.
ANGUS: She'll want to fish. (*He looks at the bowl of sugar.*) Oh, God! Willy!
WILLY: Sir! (*In she comes.*)
ANGUS: It's salt.
WILLY: Sorry, sir. (*Out she goes.*)
ANGUS: Really! Really! Really! I don't know.
*(ANGUS and ELIZABETH are laughing.)*

*CURTAIN*

So, we'll go no more a-roving
    So late into the night,
Though the heart be still as loving,
    And the moon be still as bright.

For the sword outwears its sheath,
    And the soul wears out the breast,
And the heart must pause to breathe,
    And love itself have rest.

Though the night was made for loving,
    And the day returns too soon,
Yet we'll go no more a-roving
    By the light of the moon.

*George Noel Gordon, Lord Byron.*

# CONDITIONS OF AGREEMENT

## Characters

EMILY DOON

PETER BEMBO

A.G.

NICHOLAS DOON

PATIENCE DOON

*Conditions of Agreement* was first performed at the Bristol Old Vic in October 1965, with the following cast:

EMILY DOON, Eithne Dunne

PETER BEMBO, Terence Hardiman

A.G., Frank Middlemass

NICHOLAS DOON, David Burke

PATIENCE DOON, Jane Lapotaire

Director, Christopher Denys

The scene is laid in the living-room of Emily Doon's house, in the present.

# ACT ONE

*Time is the present. The scene is the large living-room on the ground floor of Mrs Doon's house in a small town near Oxford. The house was built in 1740. The room is of great beauty. Details of decoration are a massive fireplace with plasterwork overmantle and an exceptional rococo doorcase for the only door into the room. The wooden panelling of the walls is painted white. Four windows are set to look over the street: the room, although on the ground floor, is set above the street. The furniture is of a period: there is a piano. Set beside the fireplace is an oil-painting of a woman. It is the afternoon of a Thursday in September. The sun is shining strongly through the drawn curtains.*

*EMILY DOON is asleep in a chair, her feet resting on a low stool. A thin woollen shawl covers her. As she sleeps, her mouth slightly open, there is only the faintest whisper of a snore from her. A small, cheap alarm clock stands on the arm of her chair. On a low table before her a tray of tea is set with a silver kettle over an unlit spirit lamp. EMILY is fifty-eight years of age. Beneath her shawl covering she is gaily dressed. The alarm clock rings, waking EMILY. She starts up: 'What!' she cries and then, realizing her position and that no one has spoken, taps herself reprovingly on the forehead. She switches off the alarm of the clock. Rising, she takes up the shawl, folds it and places it beneath the cushion of the chair. She stands before the tea-table taking a rapid inventory of the contents: she is satisfied. She goes to the mantelpiece, looks at herself again and grimaces. She then replaces both spectacles and mirror on the mantelpiece. EMILY goes to the window and, slightly drawing back the curtain, looks into the street. She is blowing her nose when she sees someone known passing in the street. She hurriedly steps back and regards this person furtively until they are out of sight. She pulls back the curtains and then comes down to her former chair and takes up the alarm clock: this she puts to her ear as she carries it to, and places it away in, the desk. From the desk she takes a powder-box and powders her face, running her fingers over her lips. After putting the powder back in the desk she goes to the table and takes up the teapot and the kettle. She goes out of the room. The telephone rings immediately. EMILY returns to the room and carries the kettle and teapot to their places before answering the telephone.*

EMILY: Hullo – yes, this is Emily. That's A.G., isn't it? You might have known it would be me. You know there's no one else in the house. What? I don't know anything about that. You'd better ask Nicholas – he made it. Yes, I expect him this afternoon. Well, I suppose so. It's usual to bring one's wife back from the honeymoon, isn't it? Look, A.G. It seems absurd for you to ring me up as much as you do when you live next door. Five times in the last two days. I mean, if I go to the window now I can see you talking on the phone. Why don't you call and talk to me? Yes, I know that, but – What's that? Coming to my door now? On the steps? Is it anyone you know? What's he look like? Yes, I am expecting someone. (*The front doorbell rings.*) He's just rung the bell. I must go and answer it. Yes, well, come and see Nicholas about that, A.G. Any time. I must go now. (*The doorbell rings again.*) Yes. Yes. Goodbye.

(*She puts down the receiver and goes quickly out of the room, leaving the door open. There is a pause. PETER BEMBO enters. He slowly crosses the room. A moment later EMILY returns, coming into the room and shutting the door behind her.*)

PETER: (*He turns, smiling, to face her.*) How are you, Emily?

EMILY: I'm well, thank you, Peter.

PETER: You expected me this afternoon, didn't you?

EMILY: Yes. That is, I didn't know it would be you. I knew someone was coming but I didn't know who.

PETER: You got my letter.

EMILY: Yes. This morning. But you know I always found your signature completely illegible and you can't expect me to remember your handwriting after twenty-three years.

PETER: I'm sorry. I wrote the letter in a train – perhaps it was worse than usual. It is my precaution always to type the envelopes.

EMILY: Surely there's no point in that as when the letter arrives it can't be read. Sit down. (*PETER sits.*) We'll have some tea. (*She puts her hands to her eyes.*) I'm so sorry but I've been asleep and I'm not really awake. Yet I am awake, aren't I, Peter?

PETER: Oh, yes. Twenty-three years since we've seen each other but in this moment we are both here, both awake and I'd like some tea very much indeed. (*He takes up a small hand-bell from the tray and rings it.*)

EMILY: I'm alone here. I must go myself. (*She takes up the teapot and kettle. She indicates the spirit lamp.*) That thing never works. (*She goes out of the room. PETER rises to look at the portrait of the woman. He reverses the picture to examine the frame. An opened letter is on the mantelpiece. He picks this up, peeping into the envelope. He takes two snap shots from the envelope, and looks at them. He does all this unhurriedly, with no secrecy and it is only by coincidence he has returned the photographs and letter to the mantelpiece when EMILY re-enters.*)

EMILY: I found your letter in the kitchen.

(*She unfolds it. PETER returns to his chair.*)

PETER: Should I pour this out?

EMILY: No. Leave it for a moment. I've only just made it. Now! How anyone could be expected to read that signature as Peter Bembo is beyond me. It looks like a prescription for something.

PETER: If it's so very peculiar I should have thought you'd have remembered it – or remembered me –

EMILY: In the three years I knew you your signature changed about fifteen times.

PETER: Unintentionally. Probably my signature lacked uniformity because my life lacked stability.

EMILY: You must have been the despair of your bank.

PETER: I didn't have a bank.

EMILY: Have you one now?

PETER: No.

EMILY: Anything in the old sock or under the mattress?

PETER: If that is a joke I don't understand it.

EMILY: Have you any money?

PETER: No. (*EMILY rises and goes to the window. She stands looking down into the street. There is a pause.*) Can I have some tea now?

EMILY: Of course. I'm sorry. (*She returns slowly to the tea-table.*) What has happened to your eye? (*She refers to the black patch worn by PETER over his left eye.*)

PETER: It's a permanent loss. From about ten years ago.

EMILY: How? (*She is pouring the tea.*)

PETER: A long and, I think, very funny story –

EMILY: Bembo would have sawn off his legs to make the children laugh so it is only right he should think losing an eye very funny. You're still the clown.

PETER: One cannot follow the profession of circus clown and for forty years rely on physical deformity and grotesque mischance for success without retaining some –

EMILY: There's been no mention of you for years. In the press.

PETER: I am old: done with. (*Pause.*) Still laughable, perhaps. Yes?

EMILY: (*She smiles.*) Yes. When did you retire?

PETER: About fifteen years ago.

EMILY: And what have you been doing since?

PETER: Nothing. I've been living in Armenia.

EMILY: (*She looks at the envelope of PETER's letter.*) I hadn't noticed this. It's not addressed to Emily Doon but to Emily Heitland.

PETER: What?

EMILY: My name is Doon now.

PETER: Oh, yes. Lambert mentioned your marriage –

EMILY: Lambert? Good gracious!

PETER: Yes. I went to see him to get your address.

EMILY: I haven't seen him since I – Of course, he was our only mutual acquaintance. What's he doing now?

PETER: He's editing a hairdressers' trade journal.

EMILY: Poor Lambert! Probably still combining the brain and manners of a sparrow with an abundance of misdirected energy. I remember my mother telling me one day, 'If you're lucky you'll marry a man like Mr Lambert.' That's what she said. Lambert was nineteen at the time. Worthy! Oh, dear me, worthy! (*She pauses.*) I married John.

PETER: John, was it?

EMILY: John Doon. He was a soldier.

PETER: You –

EMILY: He was killed. He was a hero.

PETER: What?

EMILY: (*Loudly.*) He was a hero. (*She takes up PETER's letter again.*) This letter of yours came and I thought at first it was a bill or circular. I nearly didn't read it immediately. No one except tradesmen address their letters to me on a typewriter.

PETER: Don't you look at bills?

EMILY: Of course I do. And I pay them.

PETER: He left you money?

EMILY: Don't be a fool, Peter. What soldier has ever died and left any money?

PETER: Soldiers and circus clowns, eh? The understanding of their affinity might be difficult by any but their widows.

EMILY: Listen. Is there anything in this to indicate who you might be? (*She reads.*) 'Dear Emmy – '

PETER: That should have been a clue. Does anyone else call you Emmy?

EMILY: Sometimes my son.

PETER: Ah! You have a son?

EMILY: Yes. Nicholas.

PETER: The dark boy with the girl in the photographs? (*He indicates the mantelpiece.*)

EMILY: What? Oh, yes. Yes, that's his wife. They're on their honeymoon. They come back today. (*She pauses.*) When did – ?

PETER: I had a look at them when you were out of the room. (*He points to the portrait.*) Who's that?

EMILY: Me.

PETER: I'm so sorry. I – (*Breaks off.*) Nicholas is a good-looking boy.

EMILY: I suppose you must say that. Yes, he's – I don't like him very much. (*She reads.*) 'Something hotel. Something Street, London. (*She makes a resigned gesture.*) Dear Emmy – I am in London after – '

PETER: Yes. I remember exactly what I said. More important, I remember exactly what you said the last time we met. You said, 'Goodbye, you damned old clown.' Those were your last words to me before I went to – Where on earth was I going that time?

EMILY: You were fooling about to the last moment.

PETER: Never thought I'd see you again. I have not come back to disturb you but I can tell you your first words to me. 'Please stand up.'

EMILY: (*She begins to laugh.*) At the Charity Dance for Crippled Children. 'Mr Peter Bembo, the famous clown,' the Lady Mayoress said, introducing us.

PETER: 'This is Miss Emily Heitland, one of our committee,' she said.

EMILY: And you said, 'How d'you do,' and stood on your head. Your trousers slipped down to your knees and showed your yellow socks. I stood before you, your face at my feet, with my hand stretched out like a fool. All around us the children laughed and clattered their little wooden legs.

PETER: Such antics were expected of me.

EMILY: Yes, I remember. (*She pauses.*) Dear Bembo. I was a little afraid of you and I couldn't understand then why the children were not afraid.

PETER: The children were never afraid.

EMILY: I only realized that from performances. There was your trick of leading a child from the audience whilst the band – what was that tune?

PETER: 'The Hill where Melchen Lives.' A child's song – forgotten now.

EMILY: You led the child out to hold your paper hoop. Never once in all the times I saw you do that was the child afraid.

PETER: Never once at any time was the child afraid. There was never a tear shed, except of laughter, at my performances.

EMILY: You're boasting.

PETER: God knows, Emmy, I have little enough to boast of now. Leave me that.

EMILY: I meant it most gently. (*She looks towards the window.*)

PETER: You are expecting someone. Who is it?

EMILY: Nicholas and Patience.

PETER: No one else? (*EMILY does not answer.*) Someone else is expected here. (*He rises, speaking.*) So, quickly! My intention was to talk about the present, not the past. And so, Emmy, my love – (*There are three short, nervous rings at the doorbell. Simultaneously with the first ring of the doorbell the telephone begins to ring.*)

EMILY: Nonsense, Peter! (*She points to the portrait.*) You had forgotten me.

PETER: No! (*There is a pause.*) Which shall I – (*EMILY goes quickly from the room. PETER answers the telephone.*) Hullo. Yes, this is Mrs Doon's house. No. No, I am not A.G. My name is Bembo. Would you like to – Who is that? Nicholas? Oh, yes; your mother will only be a moment – I say she'll be back in a moment. What? Very well. I'll tell her. (*EMILY and A.G. enter.*) Here she is. Will you speak to her? Oh. Oh, very well. A quarter of an hour. Yes. Yes, I'll tell her. Goodbye. (*PETER puts down the receiver and turns to EMILY. He is startled to see A.G. standing beside EMILY who he thought to be alone.*) I – Your son, Emily – Nicholas. He'll be here in a quarter of an hour. I asked him if he would speak to you but he said, no.

EMILY: Thank you, Peter. This is A.G. Our neighbour. He lives on that side – No! on that side. A.G., this is Peter Bembo, a very old friend of mine.

A.G.: How do you do.

PETER: How do you do. (*They shake hands.*)

A.G.: (*There is a pause.*) Emily, I really came to return this. (*He is carrying a strange piece of machinery.*) It doesn't work.

EMILY: So you said on the phone. Did you try it clamped to the edge of a table?

A.G.: Yes. I followed the instructions you wrote out for me most carefully but I can't get it to work at all.

EMILY: The electric current is the same in both our houses, isn't it?

A.G.: I think so. I don't really know.

EMILY: It worked all right in this house. We'll ask Nicholas when he comes in. Have you had tea?

A.G.: Yes, thank you.

EMILY: Well, sit down. You're not in any hurry, are you?

A.G.: No. (*He sits, holding the machinery on his knees.*)

EMILY: More tea, Peter?

PETER: No, thank you. (*He turns away to the window.*)

A.G.: (*After a pause.*) It's a special reading lamp Nicholas has invented for me.

PETER: (*Suddenly realizing he is being spoken to and not having heard.*) What's that?

A.G.: (*Louder.*) It's a special reading lamp Nicholas has invented for me. My eyes are not at all good now and I am engaged on work needing much reading and writing.

PETER: I see.

A.G.: Yes, I am writing my memoirs and I had hoped this lamp would help me when I work at nights but I can't get it to light. I clamped it firmly to the edge of the table and followed the instructions. (*He takes a slip of paper from his pocket.*) These are the instructions Emily wrote out for me. One: clamp to edge of table by means of screws. Two: connect –

EMILY: You still have your hat on, A.G. Take it off. (*He does so, placing it on the lamp on his knees.*)

A.G.: I did all this and yet it wouldn't work.

EMILY: We'll ask Nicholas when he comes in.

A.G.: I'll leave the instructions too. Nicholas may find them wrong.

EMILY: He dictated them to me. I wrote exactly what he said.

A.G.: I'll leave them, though. (*He puts the lamp, his hat and the instructions on the floor beside his chair.*) Mrs Barton tried it but it didn't work.

EMILY: How is Mrs Barton?

A.G.: She's very well, thank you. She had a cold but she's better now.

EMILY: I haven't seen her for some time. (*To PETER.*) Mrs Barton looks after A.G. She's quite an oddity. How many children has she now, A.G.?

A.G.: Nine. Do you know, I have to give each of them a birthday and a Christmas present. Eighteen presents a year and each one different. I am just beginning to note down ideas for Christmas presents now, three months before: but I've got two birthdays before Christmas. It makes it almost a life work. (*He begins to feel for his notebook but EMILY interrupts him.*)

EMILY: Is the husband out of prison yet?

A.G.: Barton? Oh, yes. He does odd jobs for me.

EMILY: Are you sure you won't have some tea?

A.G.: Quite sure, thank you. (*Speaking very much louder than he had intended to PETER.*) Who are you? What are you doing here?

PETER: I beg your pardon.

EMILY: A.G.! You mustn't shout at Peter like that.

A.G.: I'm so sorry. I thought Mr Bembo was deaf.

(*PETER and EMILY look at each other.*)

PETER: What gave you that idea?

A.G.: I don't really know. You gave the impression when I first spoke to you that you didn't hear me.

PETER: You spoke very quietly.

A.G.: Yes, I suppose so. I'm sorry. Tell me, are you – ? But it was years ago. There was a circus clown, Bembo. He was called, 'Bembo, The Clown' – almost as if to – well, to imply there was no other clown in the world. I saw him once as 'Bembo, El Bufoncillo'. That's Spanish. Many years ago now. Must be dead now.

PETER: I am 'Bembo, The Clown'.

A.G.: Are you? Not dead, then?

PETER: Not yet, no.

A.G.: But you haven't performed –

PETER: For fifteen, sixteen years. No, I am, as they say, retired.

A.G.: It is most startling. (*To EMILY.*) My wife, you know – (*To PETER.*) She died many years ago before I came to live here. She –

EMILY: Of course! But not at one of his – (*As she indicates PETER she is interrupted by A.G.*)

A.G.: She died, sir, at the circus during one of your performances.

(*There is a pause.*)

PETER: What did you say?

A.G.: She died, sir –

PETER: A death! It was never mentioned to me.

A.G.: Please! You mustn't distress yourself.

PETER: Distress myself! But this is most important. 'Never a tear except of laughter.' (*To EMILY.*) You remember I said that was the only remaining boast I could make.

EMILY: Ask him.

PETER: I will. Now, sir. I want you to tell me when and where this death of your wife occurred. The remembering of such things may make you unhappy but it is important to me. I am a stranger to you and I realize such things are difficult to retell to a stranger. But if I can impress upon you the importance of this knowledge to me I am sure –

A.G.: Certainly I will tell you.

(*EMILY suddenly laughs aloud.*)

PETER: Thank you.

A.G.: Twenty years ago. I was forty. I had been married three years. (*PETER is listening intently. EMILY lights a cigarette. As she is doing so A.G. stops speaking until the cigarette is lit. PETER regards her during the interruption with a sudden hostile irritation.*) Helen – the name has never become strange to me – (*He stops.*)

PETER: Go on.

A.G.: Helen was ten years younger than me. We had wished during the three years of our marriage for children. In that third year Helen underwent an examination which proved that she was unable to bear children.

PETER: I can dispense, sir, with these more personal details. I only wish to know –

A.G.: The knowledge of this distressed her considerably.

PETER: But of course. I understand. It is natural in a woman –

A.G.: This distress, probably not apparent to a casual observer at the time, manifested itself in a highly nervous state. So much so that I determined to take her for a holiday in an attempt to divert her brooding. I was also determined to prove to her that she and I, alone, were self-sufficient and could live full and definite lives although childless. We travelled to Spain. For the first few weeks it appeared that my resolves generally were to be realized. She was almost happy. My mind was at rest as to my business in England – my brother was left in charge – and I was able to attend to her and give her my interest and understanding. After the third week we went to Burgos. When we entered the city by car we saw the advertisements for the circus. 'Bembo, El Bufoncillo' greeted us. There was one show to be given in the evening of the following day.

PETER: (*With almost a shout.*) Yes! I remember! Yes!

A.G.: She had a strange liking for the circus –

PETER: Ha!

A.G.: – and an almost childlike understanding of the clown's antics which have always remained completely incomprehensible to me. We spent that night at an hotel and I remember that, although we were both tired after the journey, I made love to her. The last thing she said to me before falling asleep was, 'Will you take me to the circus tomorrow?'

(*There is a long pause until A.G. continues.*)

The following evening we went to the circus. You say you remember, Mr Bembo. Perhaps you remember the stands around the open-air ring you used that day.

PETER: The local authorities would not –

A.G.: There was a fault in the erection of those stands. It went unnoticed. Helen and I were forced by being late to sit far from the ring and high in the back row of the stand. Thirty feet up – would you say thirty feet, Mr Bembo?

PETER: Don't be absurd! You can hardly expect me to remember. (*He speaks to EMILY in defiance.*) This is only a most trivial incident to me.

A.G.: I should say quite as high as that. We sat and watched the beginning of the performance. Mr Bembo, the stands were most ill-constructed for Helen's feet as she sat were clear of the planking – a fact which touched me considerably at the time. Admittedly, she was a small woman but you must confess, Mr Bembo, it is not comfortable to sit without your feet firmly planted. (*He pauses.*) You, sir, had begun your antics. You had crawled beneath the horse, examined its mouth and had been snapped at, examined its feet and had been stamped upon. You had mounted and fallen; remounted with aid and again fallen. The child had come forward from the audience to hold that great paper hoop before you. The horse had charged forward, halted, and you had sailed from his back, through the air, through the hoop and had landed in the sand. There was such laughter at that!

It was then, during the laughter, that Helen turned to me and complained of sickness. She said she could not hear the laughter she recognized in the faces around us. Immediately I took her hand to lead her away but the passage on the high stand was narrow and she was forced to loose my hand and go before me, alone. Then she fell. From the narrow passage-way above the seats she fell outward. The shoe on her right foot caught in a brace of the stand structure and she hung, head downward, above the drop of – oh, I should say quite thirty feet. I went towards her: I was mortally afraid of the height. Looking down I could not see her face as her skirts had fallen about her head. I could make no attempt to raise her. I was not a strong man: I have grown stronger since then to meet a similar eventuality which may never arise. I could make no attempt to hold her to her position for the terror of the notion that she might drag me down. She made no sound. I appealed for help to some men and women sitting below us. They were half-turned to watch our antics but had made no movement towards us. My Spanish was poor – I can now speak it well – but there must have been some implication of my terrible position in my face and manner. The response of these men and women – I can never be quite sure of this – but I believe their response to my call was laughter: the sound was laughter and the grimaces seemed to be caused by mirth. It was not until some years after that I came to the charitable conclusion that their not coming to my aid – indeed, sir, they turned back to watch you at your antics – was because they could see me gesticulating but could not see Helen hanging by her heels. Then the strap of Helen's shoe – an old shoe, worn for comfort – broke and she fell. They tell me she was killed instantly – her hat was driven into her head. When I climbed down to her she lay terribly disordered in the sand. The soldiers picked her up –

PETER: Did you cry?

A.G.: – and arranged her. I could not –

PETER: Did you cry? There at the circus – did you cry? (*A.G. does not answer. PETER speaks with great urgency.*) Tell me, did you cry?

A.G.: You must remember my position.

PETER: It is a well-known fact, is it not, that shock caused by an incident such as you have just told us does not occasion precipitate tears? Was this so in your case? Did the emotional impact causing tears or grief strike you immediately or – Do you understand me? Did you stay and weep or wait until you had left the crowd?

A.G.: Yes.

PETER: Well, which?

A.G.: I wept bitterly on being told she was dead. I was told by an official of the circus. Perhaps you remember him? A garish uniform with buttons of –

(*PETER is obviously not listening. A.G. makes an appeal to his understanding.*)

You must remember. It was the death of my wife. She was beloved of me.

PETER: I quite understand.

(*PETER moves to the window. There is a pause. A.G. picks up his hat and looks at EMILY. She is staring at her hands stretched on her lap. A.G. puts down his hat again on the reading lamp.*)

(*To EMILY.*) A car has just driven up.

(*A.G. rises.*)

A.G.: I must be going, Emily.

EMILY: What? Oh, very well, A.G. Goodbye.

A.G.: Goodbye. (*They shake hands.*) Goodbye, Mr Bembo.

(*PETER murmurs an inaudible goodbye. A.G. goes to the door. As he reaches it the door is opened and NICHOLAS stands there.*)

NICHOLAS: Hullo, A.G. Going?

A.G.: Yes, I –

NICHOLAS: Back in a minute. Patience has gone to her room. (*He goes. A.G. hesitates a moment.*)

A.G.: I shall not wait. No. (*He goes, unanswered. EMILY looks up at PETER and smiles.*)

EMILY: Peter.

PETER: Yes?

EMILY: Turn round.

(*He turns from the window.*)

You must not allow it to affect you so deeply.

PETER: Emily. Emily, it was always understood that any incident among the audience of my performance should be reported to me. If they kept this from me what other things may have happened without my knowledge? Always I was told, 'Success! Success and nothing but laughter!' You remember, Emmy, my only boast.

EMILY: Don't worry, Peter. You can still vaunt the greatest talent.

PETER: Can I? The mechanics, Emmy. If I were to jump from that chair now I'd probably break both my legs. I'm an old man now. I pity myself. Who is he?

EMILY: A.G.?

PETER: Yes.

EMILY: A neighbour.

PETER: What is he?

EMILY: A retired grocer.

PETER: He's a friend of yours?

EMILY: I suppose so. Nicholas –

PETER: I presume that was Nicholas who came in just now?

EMILY: Yes. Nicholas says A.G. calls so often and stays so long because he's in love with me. It may be true. Nicholas plays jokes on him – he won't leave A.G. and me alone together. One night A.G. made no attempt to go until two-thirty and then it was Nicholas who showed him to the door. But again Nicholas has been away for ten days and I've been alone in the house but A.G. hasn't called here. He waited until you arrived. He saw you come in from his window.

PETER: All this about his wife –

EMILY: Pay no attention to that. He loves telling the story. He must have told me twenty times – without the references to you, of course.

PETER: Is it true?

EMILY: I should think so. The details never vary. He showed me some photographs of her once. She looked a dowdy little thing. I believe she served behind the counter in his shop or something. Did he tell me that or did I imagine it from looking at her? I don't know.

PETER: Have you known him long?

EMILY: About three years now. He introduced himself to me one morning. It was not until some time afterwards I knew that that in itself was an extraordinary thing. I really know very little about him.

(*NICHOLAS's voice is heard off, calling.*)

NICHOLAS: (*Off.*) I can manage. I'm very good on these stairs.

PETER: Emily, may I stay here for a while?

EMILY: Why, yes, I suppose so. Yes, of course.

PETER: If you, with your ever passionate demand for motives –

EMILY: No, no!

PETER: – want my reasons they are these: (*He is hesitant, unsure.*) I have travelled a long way – I am tired – it is natural at my age – I have no money but I expect a small sum to be made available to me in a matter of a week or so – there is you and – I want to interest myself in others – perhaps your son – I want –

EMILY: Have you been very lonely?

PETER: Not so much lonely as alone. I am not, by nature, taciturn. My work as a clown demanded that I should amuse by my very silence. And recently, in my retirement, there have been incidents too horrible to – (*NICHOLAS and PATIENCE enter. NICHOLAS is a giant of a man who walks with the aid of a heavy stick. He limps badly. PATIENCE, his wife, aged seventeen, is attempting to support him when they enter the room. When they are within the room he, without speaking, pulls himself from her.*)

PATIENCE: I was only trying to help, dear.

NICHOLAS: Hullo, Mother. (*He makes no movement towards her.*)

EMILY: Hullo, Nicholas.

NICHOLAS: Have you any cigarettes? We ran out on the journey and haven't yet had time to get any.

(*As EMILY indicates the cigarettes on the tea-tray NICHOLAS becomes aware of PETER BEMBO standing by the window. For a moment the two men stare at each other.*)

Emily.

EMILY: My son, Nicholas. Mr Peter Bembo. And –

NICHOLAS: (*Pointing at her with his stick.*) My wife, Patience. How do you do.

(*PATIENCE and PETER greet each other. NICHOLAS turns to the tray, takes and lights a cigarette.*)

EMILY: (*To PATIENCE.*) Come and sit down.

(*PATIENCE and NICHOLAS sit.*)

NICHOLAS: Whose cup of tea is this?

PETER: I think it must be mine.

NICHOLAS: (*He holds the cup out.*) Here you are.

EMILY: It must be quite cold by now.

PETER: Yes, it is.

NICHOLAS: Patience will go and make some more – and we shall need another cup.

EMILY: I'll –

NICHOLAS: Patience will go. Run along.

PETER: I'll go and get it. (*He picks up the teapot.*)

NICHOLAS: Oh, all right.

EMILY: The kitchen is – (*But PETER has gone.*) Did you have a nice time?

(*There is a pause.*)

PATIENCE: Very nice, thank you. (*They speak together.*)

NICHOLAS: Who is he?

EMILY: Good. What did you say, Nicholas?

NICHOLAS: Who is he?

EMILY: Who?

NICHOLAS: Mr Rainbow.

EMILY: Bembo: Peter Bembo.

NICHOLAS: Well, Bembo then. Who is he? He's gone out to give you an opportunity to say something about him.

EMILY: He's a very old friend of mine. I knew him many years ago – before you were born.

NICHOLAS: Another one, eh?

EMILY: Don't be silly, Nicholas. (*To PATIENCE.*) Did you like Bath? You hadn't been there before, had you?

NICHOLAS: You will find, Patience, that we are often attended by elderly gentlemen with a kind of fading love-light in their eyes.

EMILY: Shut up!

NICHOLAS: They will be introduced and explained to you by Mother as, 'A very rare old friend of mine. I knew him many years ago – before you were born.' That formula introduces each one. There was Harry or Henry or whatever his name was – ten years ago when I was a child – Harry died but he didn't leave us any of his money. Then there was Andrew – one of the hearty kind – he used to frighten me – he died but he didn't leave us any money: it wasn't until after he was dead that we found he hadn't any money to leave, was it, Emmy? There were others in varying stages of wealth and penury. All acquaintances of my mother until she met my father and became respectable. I must say she still appears to possess great charm. There's A.G. next door who in the last three years has become passionately attached to her. Poor old A.G. He thinks Mother is 'such a lady'. He told me so.

EMILY: Have you taken the car back to A.G.?

NICHOLAS: Mother has given up saying to me, as she used to say to me when I was a child, 'Be nice to So-and-so. Behave yourself in front of him and show him what a sweet, clever little boy you are.' Implying that So-and-so had money and that we were very poor and that if by some artifice I could touch a streak of sentimentality in So-and-so by my charming antics So-and-so might be very kind and give me fifty pounds down and remember me in his will when he died.

EMILY: (*To PATIENCE.*) Are you hungry?

NICHOLAS: I used to sing for them, the Harrys and the Andrews. A little song called, 'The Hill where Melchen lives'. Emily used to accompany me on the piano while I piped away in a whining falsetto and Harry or Andrew used to sit in a state of profound embarrassment. I tell you now, Emmy, that singing – I used to round it off with a little dance, remember? – It was a mistake.

EMILY: I realize that now. You've always been very nice as long as you kept your mouth shut.

NICHOLAS: (*Laughs.*) Good for you. Cheer up, Emmy. I forgive you everything.

PATIENCE: Can I have a piece of cake?

EMILY: Do, my dear. (*She passes the cake.*)

PATIENCE: I'm really very hungry.

NICHOLAS: What are we going to do with Bembo?

EMILY: What do you mean? What are we going to do with him.

NICHOLAS: I mean is he staying at an hotel in the town or what.

EMILY: He's staying here. (*She suddenly laughs quietly.*)

NICHOLAS: What are you laughing at?

EMILY: I think you two should get on well together.

NICHOLAS: Do you mean Patience and I should get on?

EMILY: No, no! You and Bembo.

NICHOLAS: What on earth makes you say that?

(*He is staring at EMILY when PETER comes in with the teapot which he puts on the table. EMILY begins to pour out the tea for PATIENCE and NICHOLAS.*)

Thank you, sir.

EMILY: Will you have some tea now, Peter?

PETER: No, I think not, thank you. (*To PATIENCE.*) I hear you two have just got married.

PATIENCE: Yes.

PETER: My congratulations to you both.

PATIENCE: Thank you.

NICHOLAS: Have you come far today, sir?

PETER: From London.

NICHOLAS: By road?

PETER: No, train. I arrived this afternoon.

EMILY: I'll go up and get your room ready in a minute, Peter.

PETER: (*After a pause.*) Thank you. Thank you, Emily.

(*The realization that this is a definite invitation to stay at the Doons' house has a perceptible physical effect on PETER. He leans back in his chair and rests his head, his arms stretched and relaxed before him.*)

It is very pleasant to be –

(*The telephone rings. NICHOLAS answers it.*)

NICHOLAS: Hullo. Yes, Nicholas here. Hullo, A.G. You've left what? The reading lamp? Oh, yes. Why didn't you wait?

(*As he is speaking he holds out his burnt-through cigarette. PATIENCE rises and takes an ashtray to him. EMILY is speaking to PETER.*)

Well, come round some time. You're what? Going to bed? Oh, I'm very sorry. What's the trouble? I see. Is Mrs Whatshername there – Mrs Barton? Would you like one of us to come round? No. Very well. Goodbye. (*He puts down the receiver.*) A.G. is not feeling well so he's going off to bed.

EMILY: I'm sorry to hear that.

NICHOLAS: Have you upset him?

EMILY: I don't think so. I'll go up and get your room ready, Peter.

PETER: Thank you.

EMILY: Will you come and help me, Pat?

NICHOLAS: Who are you speaking to?

EMILY: Your wife.

NICHOLAS: Pat! Pat! This damned use of diminutives making nonsense of names. Her name is Patience and she will be called so.

PETER: You are inconsistent. (*He speaks quietly.*) I believe you sometimes call your mother Emmy.

(*NICHOLAS does not reply.*)

EMILY: Will you come and help me make the bed, Patience?

PATIENCE: Of course, Mrs Doon.

(*EMILY and PATIENCE go out.*)

NICHOLAS: Has Mother been talking to you about me?

PETER: No.

NICHOLAS: She does to most people – at length.

PETER: Does she?

(*NICHOLAS waits for PETER to continue.*)

Why? Are you an interesting person?

NICHOLAS: She doesn't like me, you know.

PETER: She mentioned that she didn't.

NICHOLAS: Did she? You must be a very 'old friend' to be told that. With most people she has a fine attitude of affection for me. Did she say anything else about me?

PETER: No.
NICHOLAS: She said something rather odd to me.
PETER: What?
NICHOLAS: She said she thought you and I would get on well together.
PETER: Really?
NICHOLAS: Yes.
PETER: I wonder why she should think that?
NICHOLAS: (*After a pause.*) Should we try and find out? You're staying here for a while, aren't you?
PETER: You're thinking that – Yes, your mother has been kind enough –
NICHOLAS: You invited yourself.
(*PETER takes out a cigarette case.*)
PETER: Yes.
(*They both take and light cigarettes.*)
NICHOLAS: Why?
PETER: Have you your mother's passion for reasons?
NICHOLAS: I like behaviour that is understandable.
PETER: And mine is not?
NICHOLAS: Frankly, no.
PETER: I shall not explain. I can see no foundation for your mother's assumption that we should have anything in common. Indeed, I am beginning to find your attitude detestable.
NICHOLAS: What are your interests?
PETER: Very few. Eating and sleeping.
NICHOLAS: At least your digestion has survived. How old are you?
PETER: Sixty-eight.
NICHOLAS: I'm twenty-two. Do you drink?
PETER: Not excessively.
NICHOLAS: What is your job?
PETER: I've retired.
NICHOLAS: What was your job?
PETER: I was a clown.
NICHOLAS: A what?
PETER: A clown in a circus. 'Bembo, The Clown'. Have you never heard of me?

NICHOLAS: No.

PETER: Has your mother never spoken of me?

NICHOLAS: Never. (*He pauses.*) There's nothing there. I have never been to a circus in my life and if I had I'm sure I'd have disliked it intensely – especially the clowns.

PETER: (*He leans forward.*) And what are your interests?

NICHOLAS: Well, I – You must realize that at my age they are constantly changing.

PETER: Do you work at anything?

NICHOLAS: No. I am slightly incapacitated. (*He hits the lower part of his right leg with his stick.*) It is artificial below the knee.

PETER: Not a very great incapacity.

NICHOLAS: No, but it is an excuse. I see your eye –

PETER: Yes. An accident some years ago. (*He smiles: pointing to NICHOLAS's leg.*) How did it happen?

NICHOLAS: (*He smiles.*) They all think I lost it in a war.

(*PETER laughs. NICHOLAS laughs.*)

But it must be something more than that. The loss of an eye and the loss of a leg are not enough foundation for an understanding between us.

PETER: I think you place too much importance on it.

NICHOLAS: Not at all. Emily has an acute mind. She is not given to making loose remarks. Have you a lot of money?

PETER: I have none at all.

NICHOLAS: Then why? Why? Why? (*He moves away from PETER.*)

PETER: I don't think we want to prolong this any longer. I shall go up to my room.

NICHOLAS: Wait a minute! (*He stops.*)

PETER: Well?

NICHOLAS: What did you and Emily talk about?

PETER: When?

NICHOLAS: When you were alone together. You must have arrived before A.G.

PETER: Mostly about ourselves.

NICHOLAS: And the past. It's always in the past, isn't it, with you people?

PETER: Why not? It is a healthy memory.

NICHOLAS: Nonsense!

PETER: Really! I cannot see what –

NICHOLAS: The past for me as you old people consider it is corrupt but terrifyingly productive of one thing. That one thing is hope. Hope that some incident of the past will produce us some money for the present. Hope that some acquaintance of the past will offer me some sedentary job in the future. For years now Emily and I have lived together in this house supported by her pension and the small sums I have managed to earn by the very odd jobs I have done. I have been brought up to believe that the past is our god and that that god will provide. But my faith is failing. None of the supposed benefactors have come forward with money or jobs or even common acts of kindness. And it was on these people my childhood trust and affection were squandered. (*He pauses.*) In affection I have recently made a gesture to the present by my marriage. Do you know what my wife, Patience, is? She was brought up in an institution because she was born a bastard: she was completely friendless. I met her at a local dance hall where she was working as a cashier. We were married and she has nothing to remember before the day she met me. This makes her an ideal companion for Emily, whom I love. But you! You people of the past sometimes come this way: all you wish to do is to talk of the past. You revivify Emily's memory and her faith in the better dead and forgotten. And that is a most criminal thing to do! (*He turns sharply away from PETER and in doing so his leg buckles and he falls to the floor. PETER makes no movement to assist him. After a slight cry of pain NICHOLAS looks up at PETER.*) Will you help me? I am unable – (*PETER moves to help him.*) Very kind of you – now I can manage – sometimes happens this – distressing – I can manage now. (*He is on his feet.*) Thank you. May I sit down for a minute? (*He sits. PETER picks up the cigarette NICHOLAS has dropped in his fall and puts it in an ashtray.*) Well, Mr Bembo, I hope you enjoy your stay with us. As you have undoubtedly noticed I shall do my best to make it entertaining for you. Emily was quite wrong. If you and I talk we shall only do so at cross purposes. But A.G. will suit you. You must meet A.G. He has a fund of anecdote both comic –

PETER: I have already met him.

NICHOLAS: Of course, he was here when –

PETER: I hate him.

NICHOLAS: (*After a pause.*) Poor little man. Why? (*Pause.*) What did you say?

PETER: I hate him.

NICHOLAS: I'm so sorry. I thought you said you hit him.

PETER: I very nearly did.

(*NICHOLAS is about to speak.*)

I shall give you only one reason. To tell you it is based (*He covers his face with his hand.*) in some half-forgotten professional pride that he has destroyed. Unforgivable clumsiness.

NICHOLAS: In return for this confidence I shall give you my definite reason for hatred of A.G. I hate him because in his ignorance he cannot see our want. He avails himself of our company because he is a lonely man: we prove ourselves friends by giving him an audience for the continually reiterated story of the death of his wife: we allow him the impression that he is associated with gentlefolk –

(*PETER laughs.*)

– an intentional irony, Mr Bembo – we give A.G. all this and in return get nothing. He continually tells us he is fond of us but his stupidity does not allow him to see how he can practically express that affection – by hard cash. Even for a wedding present – an excellent opportunity for him – he gave Patience the most Godawful sort of water-jug. We cannot parade our poverty before him in any more obvious way than we do at present. He is aware of my dislike but again his stupidity is such that he cannot understand the cause. Undoubtedly, if ever the light did dawn on him he would present us, quite happily, with a cheque for several hundred pounds. But, Mr Bembo, the apparent lack of pride allowing me to tell you this is counterbalanced by a fierce and active pride preventing me from telling, in plain terms, a retired grocer the direction in which his duty lies.

(*PETER stands shaking his head.*)

Well?

PETER: A more prolix and fantastic reason than mine. You realize, I hope, that neither of these are sane causes. For hating a man, I mean.

NICHOLAS: I realize nothing of the kind.

PETER: Good.

NICHOLAS: My hatred is the only active thing within me. (*In sudden despair.*) I must attempt a future as well as a present.

(*A pause.*)

PETER: Can I help you?

NICHOLAS: (*In complete acceptance.*) Shall we begin our acquaintance from here? How do you do, Mr Bembo.

(*PATIENCE enters.*)

PATIENCE: Mr Bembo, sir. Mrs Doon says will you go up now and she will show you your room.

PETER: Thank you. My luggage is at the station. How can I – ?

NICHOLAS: I'll go and fetch it for you before I return the car to A.G.

PETER: Thank you.

NICHOLAS: Is there much?

PETER: Three suitcases.

(*NICHOLAS, who has his back to PETER, smiles. PETER gives NICHOLAS the cloakroom tickets.*)

NICHOLAS: All right.

(*PETER goes out. PATIENCE moves to the window and looks into the street.*)

PATIENCE: When are you going to fetch the luggage and take the car back?

NICHOLAS: In a few minutes. (*He takes a small notebook from his pocket and begins to write.*)

PATIENCE: Can I come with you?

NICHOLAS: Of course.

(*PETER can be heard calling* 'Emily! Emily!')

PATIENCE: It was nice of the gentleman next door to lend us his car for the honeymoon.

(*NICHOLAS continues to write.*)

NICHOLAS: Patience.

PATIENCE: Yes?

NICHOLAS: Come here.

(*PATIENCE comes down from the window and stands directly before NICHOLAS who continues to write. He speaks with great gentleness.*)

Try not to behave as if you were a servant. You are a married woman now and this is your home. The people who happen to stay here are as much your guests as they are Emily's. There is no need to call them 'sir' – and when you come into a room come right in, don't stand just inside the door. (*He puts the notebook back in his jacket pocket and looks up at her.*) Why don't you talk more?

PATIENCE: I don't seem to have anything to say to people like that. Mr Bembo, I mean.

NICHOLAS: You talk nineteen to the dozen to me when we're alone. What is it about other people?

PATIENCE: I don't know.

NICHOLAS: When we were having tea, for instance. Hadn't you anything definite to say then except whatever it was you said – about the cake? What were you thinking?

PATIENCE: Oh, I don't know. Why Mr Bembo wears that black patch over his eye. Whether I should call your mother Mrs Doon or Mother or what. Whether I couldn't have some more sugar in my tea – I like a lot of sugar in my tea. (*She takes hold of the walking-stick and pulls* NICHOLAS *from the chair.*) And I was thinking about you.

NICHOLAS: What about me?

PATIENCE: Nothing.

NICHOLAS: Why didn't you say any of these things?

PATIENCE: You were talking too much.

NICHOLAS: (*Laughs.*) Yes! Yes, I do, you know. (*He goes to the desk and taking out a small knife begins to sharpen the pencil with which he has been writing. PATIENCE goes to him and receives the parings in her cupped hands.*)

PATIENCE: Who is Mr Bembo?

NICHOLAS: A friend of Emily's, a friend of yours and a friend of mine.

PATIENCE: He's old, isn't he?

NICHOLAS: Nearly seventy.

PATIENCE: I say! As old as that!

NICHOLAS: (*He mimics her.*) I say! Yes! Over two and a half times older than you.

PATIENCE: I say! That's some age, my man, some age!

NICHOLAS: How right you are.

(*They laugh. NICHOLAS replaces the pencil in his pocket and the knife in the desk. PATIENCE carries the wood parings and throws them into the fireplace.*)

PATIENCE: Does he make you want to laugh?

NICHOLAS: Who? Bembo?

PATIENCE: Yes.

NICHOLAS: Not particularly.

PATIENCE: He does me.

NICHOLAS: You should have told him.

PATIENCE: That I wanted to laugh at him? No!

NICHOLAS: He likes being laughed at.

PATIENCE: Even when he's being serious?

NICHOLAS: At all times.

PATIENCE: Nicholas! Nobody likes being laughed at.

NICHOLAS: Shall I tell you a secret? About Emily and Peter?

PATIENCE: Yes, please.

NICHOLAS: Come here.

(*She moves to him and he whispers to her.*)

PATIENCE: (*She screams with laughter.*) But they're old!

NICHOLAS: They weren't always old. Ssh! Don't make such a row.

(*PATIENCE is on sure, known ground with this mention of the physical. She moves to NICHOLAS and puts her hands into his jacket pockets, pressing her body to him, sure of her behaviour.*)

PATIENCE: But, there, you see, Nicholas, I can never imagine old, cold bodies doing what we've done, can you? It's like a true story I once read of two people in love, loving. It wasn't until the end of the book I found out they were both dead and that made it horrible.

NICHOLAS: 'Peace, good reader, do not weep;
Peace, the lovers are asleep.
They, sweet turtles, folded lie
In the last knot that love can tie.'

PATIENCE: What's that?

NICHOLAS: It was written by a bloke who lived round here. Don't worry. He's dead, too.

(*PATIENCE has pulled the notebook from NICHOLAS's pocket. She holds it in her hand. The conversation between the living of the dead is beyond her limited understanding. She takes her only refuge.*)

PATIENCE: Kiss me.

NICHOLAS: (*He kisses her.*) Oh, my own lass. God save us both.

PATIENCE: God save us indeed.

(*They embrace. She speaks to him, returning his gentleness.*)

There is no cause to be afraid of the night. Why are you shy with me? You must have no shame with me. Together, we must be gay and impudent – and it must be you who comes to me to demand and be bold. I want that.

(*She steps back from him. He stands motionless, leaning forward on his stick. Suddenly he looks up at her.*)

I had to say that.

NICHOLAS: I'm all right, really, you know.

PATIENCE: Of course you are. Come along.

NICHOLAS: Are you going to put on a coat?

PATIENCE: No. (*She holds up the notebook.*) What were you writing in this?

NICHOLAS: How much I've spent today. Patience.

PATIENCE: Yes?

NICHOLAS: Pay attention.

(*She is reading the notebook.*)

PATIENCE: I'm listening.

NICHOLAS: You remember I explained to you the other morning about your behaviour now we're married with regards to money and things like that?

PATIENCE: Yes.

NICHOLAS: We must be careful.

PATIENCE: I don't spend much.

NICHOLAS: No, I don't mean that at all. You remember what I said – you mustn't let anyone know we're poor.

PATIENCE: Are we? Mrs Doon gave me ten pounds for the honeymoon. I've never had so much money.

NICHOLAS: Yes, I know, but – (*He stops, realizing the impossibility of an explanation.*)

PATIENCE: What are you trying to tell me? I'm listening.

NICHOLAS: It doesn't matter. Don't use that dreadful perfume you have on, there's a good girl.

PATIENCE: It's 'Sweet Jasmine'.

NICHOLAS: I don't care what it is.

PATIENCE: It was a present from the girls at the hall. I've got ever such a lot left. Seems a pity to waste it.

NICHOLAS: I'll buy you some more.

PATIENCE: Will you? I'll put it down in your book. 'La-di-da perfume for Patience – twenty pounds.'

NICHOLAS: Behave yourself.

(*PETER comes in.*)

I'm just going to fetch your luggage.

(*The telephone rings.*)

PETER: Thank you. Shall I – ? (*He goes to the telephone.*) Hullo – oh, hullo, A.G. (*PETER has an easy familiarity.*) How are you feeling? Good. You haven't gone to bed yet? This is Peter Bembo.

(*EMILY enters.*)

EMILY: How long will you be, Nicholas?

NICHOLAS: Not long.

PETER: (*At phone.*) He can bring it round. (*To NICHOLAS.*) You can take the reading lamp round to A.G., can't you? He wants you to try it there.

NICHOLAS: Certainly, certainly. (*He picks up the lamp from the floor.*)

PETER: He'll bring it round now.<br>
NICHOLAS: Can we have a fire, Emily? } *Together.*

EMILY: I'll light one.

(*PATIENCE has been staring at PETER. She suddenly bursts into laughter.*)

PETER: You must take care of yourself, you know, A.G. (*To PATIENCE.*) What are you laughing at?

PATIENCE: You.

(*PETER makes a clown's grimace at her which increases her laughter. NICHOLAS and EMILY also laugh. PETER increases his facial antics also elaborating strange, stilted gestures. He pulls a false nose from his pocket and puts it on. He continues to speak on the telephone to A.G. NICHOLAS and PATIENCE begin to move to the door.*)

PETER: What's that you say? What's that? No. No, we're all laughing here, A.G. So hurry up, get better and come round: come round.

*CURTAIN*

# ACT TWO

## Scene 1

*The same, three days later: that is, the Sunday. The time is ten-thirty in the morning. The sun is shining into the room with an unnatural brightness. Church bells are ringing. A.G. is sitting alone in the room. He is wearing an overcoat and holds a hat and stick. Beside him, on the arm of the chair, is a large, ivory-bound prayer-book. After a moment A.G. turns his head to stare at the portrait of EMILY. As he stares at the picture his lips begin to move but the words are inaudible. He rises to move towards the picture and in doing so knocks the prayer-book to the floor. He picks up the book and putting it beneath his arm moves to stand before the portrait. He stretches out his hand and touches the face of the picture. In sudden, unreasoning panic he turns to the door.*

A.G.: (*His voice thin with fear.*) Emily! Emily! (*He remains staring at the door. In a whisper.*) Emily!

(*There is a sudden strident burst of laughter from beyond the door. A.G. moves slowly towards the door: he opens it. Standing in the hallway with their backs to the room are PETER BEMBO and NICHOLAS DOON. They are talking together. When the door is fully open they turn to face into the room but they do not enter.*)

NICHOLAS: Good morning, A.G.

A.G.: Good morning, Nicholas. Good morning, Mr Bembo.

PETER: Good morning.

(*There is a pause whilst the two men silently regard A.G.*)

NICHOLAS: Are you better?

A.G.: Oh, yes.

NICHOLAS: You were never really very ill, were you?

A.G.: You mean – When?

NICHOLAS: On Thursday. When you rang up to say you were going to bed and rang again asking me to come round and then wouldn't see me when I arrived.

A.G.: Why do you say that?

PETER: You were afraid.

A.G.: (*Pauses.*) Do you know if Emily is ready? We haven't much time.

NICHOLAS: Why were you afraid, A.G.? Why have you stayed away?

A.G.: You should grow up, Nicholas. That's what you should do – grow up.
PETER: That's not applicable to me. What should I do?
A.G.: You, Mr Bembo, should practise tolerance and –
PETER: Yes?
A.G.: – and respect.
PETER: Tolerance and respect.
A.G.: Yes.
PETER: (*To NICHOLAS.*) And you must grow up.
NICHOLAS: Yes.
(*PETER and NICHOLAS move away. A.G. returns to his chair.*)
A.G.: If all trumpeters blew such cracked tunes – (*He takes up the prayer-book and begins to read. EMILY and PATIENCE can be heard calling to each other. A.G. listens intently. After a moment PATIENCE enters to stand in the open doorway.*)
PATIENCE: Please, will you –
A.G.: What? Oh, hullo, my dear.
PATIENCE: Hullo. Mrs Doon says to tell you she'll be down in a moment, and –
A.G.: Thank you.
PATIENCE: And if you would like some sherry please to help yourself.
A.G.: Right-o.
PATIENCE: It's in there.
A.G.: Won't you stay and talk to me until Emily comes down.
PATIENCE: I'm sorry. I'm very busy. (*She makes no attempt to move.*)
A.G.: I see. Well, in that case, I mustn't keep you here.
(*PATIENCE remains motionless.*)
You may go. I shall be all right. Quite all right.
(*PATIENCE goes, leaving the door open.*)
PATIENCE: (*Off.*) He's in there.
EMILY: (*Off.*) Thank you. Run and get my gloves from my room. (*EMILY comes in, closing the door behind her.*)
Goodness, A.G. You look very handsome this morning.
A.G.: Do I?
EMILY: Did you have some sherry?
A.G.: No.
EMILY: Well, I'd like some – wouldn't you?

A.G.: If you're having some.

EMILY: It's in there.

(*A.G. takes the sherry and pours out two glasses.*)

Do you know, it's about six years since I went to church.

A.G.: Is it?

EMILY: Yes. Which one are we going to this morning?

A.G.: St John's.

EMILY: (*She takes the sherry.*) Thank you. That's the one –

A.G.: On the corner –

EMILY: I know. Opposite Woolworth's.

A.G.: That's right.

EMILY: We've got time for this, haven't we? (*She holds up her glass.*)

A.G.: Oh, yes. It's just six minutes' walk.

EMILY: How do you know?

A.G.: I – (*He shrugs his shoulders.*)

EMILY: What a precise person you are.

(*There is a pause.*)

I can't remember any prayers, I'm afraid, except – 'From Ghoulies and Ghosties and Long-Leggedy Beasties and things that go Bump in the night, Good Lord deliver us'. Will that do?

A.G.: I should think it will be very suitable.

(*PATIENCE enters with EMILY's gloves.*)

EMILY: Thank you, darling.

(*PATIENCE goes out.*)

What do you mean by 'suitable'? (*Before he can reply.*) I shall want a prayer-book, shan't I? Now where – ?

A.G.: I'd like you to have this one. (*He holds out the ivory-bound prayer-book.*)

EMILY: But that's yours.

A.G.: I have another. (*He takes a small leather-bound book from his pocket and holds out the other to EMILY, who takes it.*)

EMILY: What a beautiful book. (*She opens it at the fly-leaf and reads.*) 'To Helen, on her birthday, from Mummy. September – '

A.G.: Today is her birthday.

(*EMILY stares at him for a moment and then snaps the book shut.*)

EMILY: Dear God! Do you want me to cry? Is that what you want?

A.G.: No!

EMILY: Is all this premeditated?

A.G.: No!

EMILY: Why do you work on my feelings with your dead wife?

A.G.: Please –

EMILY: What is your object, A.G.? You ask me to go to church with you on her birthday. Very well. I'll go to church with you and I'll pray for the peace of her soul. I'll speak of her to you. You may remember her with me. You may tell me again and again of her dreadful death but – to give me, a stranger, this most intimate possession –

A.G.: Stranger?

EMILY: – and expect me to remain unmoved – no, A.G. No!

A.G.: Emily!

EMILY: What is your purpose?

A.G.: It was not to distress you.

EMILY: (*Holding out the prayer-book.*) Why? Why this one?

A.G.: It was my intention that you should keep it. It is a present to you. (*He pauses.*) Apart from its associations you said yourself it is a beautiful book.

EMILY: Do you wish to part with it?

A.G.: To you, yes.

EMILY: Why to me?

(*He does not answer.*)

Why to me?

(*He is silent.*)

Answer me. Why do you give this to me?

A.G.: As to your suggestion that I'd purposely give you cause for tears –

EMILY: A.G.!

A.G.: – and I am shocked by your lack of understanding.

EMILY: Why do you give this to me? (*She pauses.*) Do you love me?

A.G.: No.

EMILY: Well, that's a plain answer to a –

A.G.: Twenty years is not a long time.

EMILY: Meaning – ?

A.G.: Meaning that love for me –

EMILY: Yes?

A.G.: Love for me is –

(*EMILY waits for him to continue.*)

Meaning that love for me is contained within one night.

(*EMILY holds out the prayer-book to him.*)

Keep it. At least for this morning.

(*EMILY retains the book and as A.G. continues to speak she opens it and turns the leaves.*)

The bed, very large, with coarse linen sheets – comfortable though – we had travelled a long way that day, you remember – we washed in the water from the jug – heavy, stone-cold jug – No one had come near us since we entered the room – (*He speaks quietly.*)

EMILY: I can't hear what you're saying.

A.G.: Helen and I were afraid. We laughed but we were afraid. That's why we made love.

EMILY: I don't want to hear about it.

A.G.: But you understand me?

EMILY: Yes.

A.G. : Do you?

EMILY: Yes.

A.G.: Then will you answer me this? Although I love no one must I live without friends? You can't answer that?

EMILY: You're a nice person, A.G., but –

(*A.G., looking at the clock, interrupts.*)

A.G.: We haven't drunk the sherry.

EMILY: Leave it.

A.G.: You're ready?

EMILY: Yes.

A.G.: Come along then.

(*They move towards the door. A.G. takes the large prayer-book.*)

I'll carry that for you. I thought you would like to walk.

EMILY: Yes, I do.

(*A.G. stops.*)

A.G.: When was that painted? That picture of you.

EMILY: Just before Nicholas was born.

A.G.: I see. I can get the car now if you would prefer.

EMILY: No, I'd like to walk.

(*They go out. There is a pause. The front door shuts. After a moment NICHOLAS and PETER enter. They go quickly to the window and look into the street.*)

NICHOLAS: There they go. That strut of A.G.'s is more comic seen from the rear. I want you to observe the angle of his hat – jaunty, I believe, is the term. Notice the swing of the cane – Yes, look! A full circle. Ah! He tips his hat to an acquaintance. (*Mimics.*) 'How d'you do. How d'you do.' (*He pauses.*) And note, please, Peter, Emmy's grace.

(*The church bells cease to be replaced by a single bell.*)

A little quicker. They mustn't be late. It is obviously some kind of occasion. Did you notice the ostentation of the prayer-book? Ivory-bound. I doubt if it contains his single, reiterated prayer – 'Thy kingdom come, Thy will be done on Earth as it is in Helen'.

(*PETER moves from the window.*)

They are crossing the road. Mind the horse dung, A.G. He has offered Emily his arm so neatly crooked at the elbow. (*He laughs.*) She has refused.

(*PETER has taken up the two glasses of wine left by EMILY and A.G. He takes one to NICHOLAS.*)

They are about to turn the corner. (*NICHOLAS takes the wine.*) Thank you. They are gone. (*NICHOLAS stands staring through the window. Quietly.*) That child will be run over. (*He bangs the window with the handle of his stick and shouts.*) Look out, little boy! (*Pause.*) All right. He has fallen. Well, at least he can cry. (*He turns from the window.*) There is a certain pathos in the actions of a person unaware he is observed. Presumably the child in the adult – the child playing a silent, lonely and mysterious game. From what I could see of A.G. whilst he was alone in this room – that keyhole is badly placed; too high – I gathered he spoke a little to himself. He was clumsy, knocking something – I couldn't see what – to the floor. He moved towards that wall and put his hand in a strange gesture towards – would it be that picture of Emily? – and then came the cry of her name. I couldn't be sure what would follow and so I gave the signal to reveal ourselves by laughing.

PETER: And what better way to reveal ourselves?

NICHOLAS: No. No, the fear in A.G. was there at that moment. It was not caused by our laughter. It was there in the call of Emily's name. What was the cause?

PETER: Perhaps he knew he was being watched.

NICHOLAS: I doubt it. Was it the portrait? His outstretched hand on the varnish – cold to the touch –

PETER: (*Laughs.*) No!

NICHOLAS: It doesn't really matter, does it? I mean, the fear is there. The origin doesn't concern us.

PETER: I'm not sure the fellow is frightened. He showed some spirit when he found us listening at the door – I am presuming he knew we were listening. I must practise tolerance and – and, what was it? – Humility?

NICHOLAS: No. Respect. And I must grow up.

PETER: How right he is.

NICHOLAS: How right.

(*They laugh.*)

But the spirit of attack in him at that moment was because of his fear. An animal –

PETER: At bay? Oh, no! I can't have that. No. He's just a dear little lonely old man.

NICHOLAS: The greatest of all his fears is that someone will disclose the fact that he is afraid.

PETER: Absurd!

NICHOLAS: Why have you begun to ridicule me? You said yesterday that – What's the matter?

PETER: Nothing.

NICHOLAS: Oh, come on. Now, come on. There's something wrong this morning. Since Thursday, when you came here, you have been angry and defiant – only too willing to discuss the A.G. affair with me. It's true we made no definite plans but you were loud in your support of anything I might do – anything. You remember you definitely offered me your co-operation. Until last night you were malicious and violent towards A.G. It was only last night you said of A.G., 'It is his innocence we must destroy,' and, you said, 'That cannot be achieved by intimidation,' and then you yawned and went to bed saying we'd discuss it further this morning. Here is this morning and you are taking my conjectures, my attempts at a solution to our problem, my tentative, inexperienced, efforts to put A.G. in his rightful place and you are laughing at them – and, I suppose, at me. I am not a pathetic character. Don't think that. I am strong and I can do without your support.

PETER: I am sure of it. I'll tell you the truth. I had a bad dream last night.

NICHOLAS: Well?

PETER: You must have experienced the dream that comes so near nature that the first waking hours must be spent in disentangling reality from the fantasy.

NICHOLAS: Was the dream about us – this place?

PETER: No.

NICHOLAS: Did you scream in the night? I heard someone. It might have been Emily.

PETER: Possibly it was me.

NICHOLAS: Will you recover?

PETER: Yes.

NICHOLAS: You will recover your feelings towards A.G.?

PETER: There is a change.

NICHOLAS: I know! Why? Because of me?

PETER: Now, listen, Nicholas.

NICHOLAS: Why? Because I have –

PETER: Listen to me. I've explained to you the immediate impact on me of the story of the death of this man's wife. You know the tears he shed in that place at that time attacked my greatest conceit. You know that and you understand.

NICHOLAS: Yes, I understand and sympathize. I'm no artist but I understand.

PETER: But consider: the woman's death was so fantastically comic in its elements. You admit? To hang by the heels, skirts about her head, distraught lover fluttering around in an agony of indecision and dismay while a clown in a circus ring below flew through a hoop and the immense audience howled with laughter. The woman fell, was killed. (*He laughs.*) No, Nicholas, it's too much. I can't take it seriously. Perhaps, after all, A.G.'s tears were tears of laughter.

NICHOLAS: Then you can no longer – ? Do you find it cold in here?

PETER: Not really, no.

NICHOLAS: The sun should warm the room but – (*He moves to the door.*) We must talk about this, Peter. (*He calls.*) Patience!

PETER: I'm quite willing, Nicholas. I want to help you.

NICHOLAS: Patience!

PATIENCE: (*Off.*) Coming! Coming!

NICHOLAS: (*Mimics viciously.*) Coming! Coming!

(*PETER looks up in surprise.*)

PETER: What's that?

NICHOLAS: (*He moves back into the room.*) I want you to listen to me. Patience has – I have been gentle and considerate but her violence to me – No. This is what I wish to say. When you offered me your help you remember I said the only active thing within me was my hatred of A.G.

PETER: I'm trying to understand you, believe me. You say, your wife –

NICHOLAS: No. My – my love for Patience is passive. It is she who takes any initiative in such matters. I don't wish to speak of that.

PETER: Why not?

NICHOLAS: Yet I can speak of it to you.

PETER: Certainly.

NICHOLAS: It is relevant.

PETER: Then tell me, child.

NICHOLAS: The girl has degraded me beyond expectation. (*He turns away from PETER.*) I was prepared as a necessity of marriage to give myself to a degree but she has made me debase myself until – I – don't – sucking at – in the violence of – look at her hands, you look – Before, I'd only limited knowledge – walking home through the park at night I had seen the couples linked on benches, lying among bushes, plucking at each other's clothing in an aimless passion like dying people. Even the sight of this attacked my – my – yes, innocence. Yes! my innocence. Now this girl, my wife, has made me – My bedroom which we share has been my refuge for many years. The shelves still hold my childhood books, the cupboard beside the bed still contains my toys. The decorations and furnishing have remained unchanged within my memory.

(*PATIENCE enters. She stands in the doorway.*)

And it is in that room this girl has made me do such things –

PETER: Here's Patience.

NICHOLAS: (*To her.*) What are you doing now?

PATIENCE: I've just finished making the beds and clearing up.

NICHOLAS: Will you light a fire in here, please.

(*PATIENCE goes out. There is a pause.*)

PETER: What do you want to do, Saint Nicholas?

NICHOLAS: I don't know, Peter, I don't know. (*He is terribly distressed.*) I want some kind of revenge.

PETER: Now we're getting down to elementals. Revenge for what?

NICHOLAS: For my weakness.

PETER: Good. And on whom?

NICHOLAS: A.G.

PETER: I see. But why A.G.?

NICHOLAS: Because he is weaker than I am.

PETER: Should I kill him?

(*NICHOLAS does not answer.*)

Should we dress up as ghosts? He –

NICHOLAS: You have no need to dress up.

PETER: He has a belief in the supernatural.

NICHOLAS: No.

PETER: Pity we're not clever enough to swindle him out of all his money.

NICHOLAS: Yes.

PETER: Let's burn down his house.

NICHOLAS: Too close. Damn it! It's next door. (*He begins to smile.*)

PETER: Let us invent some facts, evidence that his wife was an immoral woman before her marriage.

(*NICHOLAS looks up.*)

I was joking.

NICHOLAS: Were you?

PETER: Yes.

NICHOLAS: Were you?

(*PATIENCE enters with a bucket of coal and firewood. She proceeds to lay and light the fire.*)

PETER: Some kind of practical joke. What do you say to that?

NICHOLAS: Yes. Yes, but no dressing up as ghosts, no physical violence. Something about his wife – ?

PETER: Be careful, Nicholas.

NICHOLAS: Of course. Something about Helen. Of course. (*His excitement grows.*) But there must be some preliminary. His attention must be directed to an unknown that threatens him. Now! What do we know? What do we know of him to his discredit?

PETER: Nothing.

NICHOLAS: Nothing.

PETER: But do we need to know anything?

NICHOLAS: What do you mean?

PETER: There is the old trick.

NICHOLAS: What old trick?

PETER: An anonymous letter.

NICHOLAS: Yes, I see. Explain what you mean by it.

PETER: There is a formula. 'All is discovered – ' or 'All is lost. Flee for your life. A Well-wisher.' Simple. We know nothing. If there is something that letter will explode A.G.'s ingenuousness. If there is nothing – if nothing happens we can – we can send him some poisoned chocolates.

NICHOLAS: We –

PETER: But I forgot. You don't want him dead, do you?

NICHOLAS: This is urgent.

PETER: Perhaps just enough to give him tummy-ache. No?

NICHOLAS: No. Be serious. This letter. We can do it at once. We can deliver it to A.G.'s house now whilst he is at church. He is invited to tea and will probably stay for the rest of the evening – he always does. The rest can come then.

PETER: What is the rest?

NICHOLAS: I know. Really, I know what to do. You. Why shouldn't I profit by the presence of a famous clown?

PETER: By all means do so.

NICHOLAS: Thank you.

PETER: But tell me what you propose to do.

NICHOLAS: Later. Let's get this letter done. (*He moves to the desk, speaking. He continues to speak as he writes.*) Tell me, Peter, were you really amused by A.G.'s defiance at the door just now?

PETER: Not amused. Touched.

NICHOLAS: Do you mean emotionally moved?

PETER: Yes. Children –

NICHOLAS: I know nothing about children.

PETER: No. Well, children have the same quality of defiance. I remember once –

NICHOLAS: Are you defending A.G.?

PETER: No. I remember I –

NICHOLAS: The defiance of children, I should imagine, is always in defence of their integrity.

PETER: It is with child or man. A long time ago now but I remember quite –

NICHOLAS: Some other time, Peter, some other time. There. (*He holds up the letter. PATIENCE goes out.*)

PETER: What have you written?

NICHOLAS: (*Reads.*) 'You are discovered, therefore you are lost. She died in vain. Actum est.'

PETER: (*Smiles.*) Oh, what villains we are.

NICHOLAS: (*With mock ceremony.*) Mr Bembo. Do you sanction this note being sent to A.G.?

PETER: I do. What is more I will carry it myself.

NICHOLAS: Thank you, sir. I will seal it. (*He turns to the desk, puts the letter into an envelope and begins to seal with wax.*) Why did you insist I leave Emily and A.G. alone together this morning? I've never done so before.

PETER: Emily asked me to arrange it.

NICHOLAS: What?

PETER: Emily asked me to arrange it.

NICHOLAS: I see. Now why?

PETER: What are you talking about?

NICHOLAS: Why should Emily want to be left alone with A.G.?

PETER: You think she should have asked you?

NICHOLAS: No, no! She doesn't trust me. She'd never ask me. (*He holds up the sealed letter.*) This must go at once. Peter, I trust you.

PETER: You may do so.

NICHOLAS: I have to go to London tomorrow to have a fitting for a new leg. I shall take Patience with me. I shall go by an early-morning train and I shall be back by night. It is an appointment that is difficult – impossible to break.

PETER: Yes.

NICHOLAS: I shall be back as soon as –

PETER: You needn't hurry.

NICHOLAS: Of course I must hurry back. (*He indicates the letter.*) Is this the way, I wonder? Whether or not it is a beginning. We must have faith in it.

PETER: I have faith. (*He moves to NICHOLAS and nudges him.*) Hey! (*He puts up the index finger and thumb of one hand and makes of them a small 'O'.*) Look through there.

(*NICHOLAS peeps through.*)

That's me. I have faith.

NICHOLAS: I understood you to say your faith had evaporated with your bad dreams.

PETER: You have misunderstood me again.

NICHOLAS: Have I? I am not always bright.

PETER: The dreams destroyed any remaining faith I possessed in my powers to hold affection for – that is, I suppose, at my age, to love – any person. And for that matter to hate any person with an active, destructive abhorrence. All that is finished: done with. But you are young and very brave. Carry on! I will give you all I can even if it is nothing more than my applause. I can give you that. See! (*He begins to clap his hands.*) Bravo! Bravo!

NICHOLAS: Promise me this. Promise me you have considered us. All of us. Myself, my wife, my mother, yourself and A.G.

PETER: All of us. In every way. I have observed A.G. in my mind. I have reconstructed a satisfactory past – one to include the story of his wife – and a suitable present life for him. I have arrogated myself to imagine his weaker moments and debased myself to observe – as at the door – his stronger moments. I have included you in your misery, Emily in her kindness, Patience in her ignorance and myself in my boredom and my conclusion is this: I will entirely endorse any action of yours because you are young and very brave.

NICHOLAS: You can think all this and retain your reason?

PETER: Yes.

NICHOLAS: Good. (*He smiles.*)

PETER: My sanity is secure but I confess to a slight tension of my scalp and neck muscles – excitement, do you think?

NICHOLAS: I should think so. You are an excellent friend. Forgive my doubts.

PETER: I forgive them.

NICHOLAS: But remember, there must be no violence towards A.G.

PETER: Don't be silly! He is younger than I am and he could probably beat me blindfold. Anyway, my last sight of him in his happiness with Emmy moved me so much that I couldn't now harm a hair of his head.

NICHOLAS: There is this to deliver. What's the time?

PETER: About eleven.

NICHOLAS: His house will be empty. I know his habits. Mrs Barton, his woman-help, arrives today at eleven-thirty.

PETER: I'll go with it. (*He takes the letter.*)

NICHOLAS: One more thing.

PETER: Yes?

(*NICHOLAS does not speak.*)

Yes?

NICHOLAS: What do you hope to gain from this?

PETER: Another ten years of life. Come along, you moody fellow, the scheme is under way with this letter. What more do you want?

NICHOLAS: The ending.

PETER: Already?

NICHOLAS: I have been completely honest with you, Peter.

PETER: And do you doubt my honesty?

NICHOLAS: No.

PETER: You do. You think I am unreliable. You think I should do something more than applaud.

NICHOLAS: I do not.

PETER: You lie. But it is understandable, this – defiance. Not only your leg lets you down, eh? By the way, have you forgotten what you told me about your wife?

NICHOLAS: No.

PETER: You have. What has she made you do?

NICHOLAS: Peter, in God's name – !

PETER: Was it done in God's name? (*He winks.*) Why, most certainly. You are married. What did you tell me about your wife? Must I tell you? – Must I?

NICHOLAS: Yes, please.

PETER: How she was brought here as a bride, loved but friendless. Left to her own devices, treated as a servant. Given by necessity a share of your bed in the room containing your toys and fairy-tale books – articles which could only intimidate and terrify her by reason of your unknown past. You condemn her actions directed against the weakness of your body. You are a fool. She is a child and every invitation which you are too weak to resist arises from her love for you. Realize the delicacy of her spirit and imagine the repugnance she forces herself to overcome on seeing you, nightly, minus a leg. A deformed creature. You imply she's not human. Take away that contraption (*He points to NICHOLAS's leg.*) and what becomes of you?

(*There is silence.*)

Now let's hear no more of honesty and trust.

NICHOLAS: What can I do to please you?

PETER: Accept with gratitude all qualities of kisses and demonstrations of love no matter from whom they may come. Be grateful for memory: it is the booby prize for those who have failed or are ruined. (*He holds up the letter.*) Do I drop this through the letter-box?

NICHOLAS: I should think so.

PETER: Yes. The delivery in the normal way of a normal letter. I shall walk on through the town for a while. Is there anything of interest to see?

NICHOLAS: Nothing except a brass band playing in the public gardens.

PETER: How do I get there?

NICHOLAS: Go down past Elliots, the builders, over the way.

PETER: Will you come with me?

NICHOLAS: No.

(*PETER goes out. He returns after a moment carrying his hat and coat.*)

PETER: Shall I send your wife to you?

NICHOLAS: (*After a pause he laughs.*) How very sweet and gentle of you, Peter. But you're wrong. There's been no 'lover's tiff' – there is nothing to 'make up'. We haven't quarrelled. Goodbye.

(*PETER goes out. NICHOLAS sits before the fire. He takes out his notebook and pencil. PATIENCE opens the door.*)

PATIENCE: Can I come in?

NICHOLAS: Of course.

(*She enters carrying a child's teddy-bear which she places on the piano out of NICHOLAS's sight.*)

PATIENCE: Has everyone else gone out?

NICHOLAS: Yes.

(*PATIENCE stands looking out of the window.*)

PATIENCE: Why is Peter going to A.G.'s house?

NICHOLAS: He's taking a letter from me to A.G.

PATIENCE: You've never written a letter to me.

NICHOLAS: Haven't I? But we've always been together.

PATIENCE: Are you cross with me?

(*NICHOLAS does not reply.*)

You haven't spent any money today.

NICHOLAS: No.

PATIENCE: Your book –

NICHOLAS: I do my week's accounts on Sunday mornings. And then on Mondays I pay my bills and collect any debts.

PATIENCE: I see.

NICHOLAS: We shall be starting early in the morning.

PATIENCE: All right. (*She sits on the arm of NICHOLAS's chair.*)

NICHOLAS: Pull your skirt down. And if you want to sit down sit properly in a chair. Don't lounge about on the arms.

(*PATIENCE goes to a chair and sits.*)

Now about tomorrow. As I said we shall be starting early and we'd better arrange – You've finished your work, haven't you?

PATIENCE: Yes. Emily gave me some dresses this morning. I've been putting them away.

NICHOLAS: Are they nice?

PATIENCE: They're old-fashioned. I think, perhaps, if I alter them a bit –

NICHOLAS: You're not to alter them.

PATIENCE: I shall look very funny if I don't.

NICHOLAS: It was very kind of Emily to give them to you, wasn't it?

PATIENCE: Yes.

NICHOLAS: I hope you thanked her for them.

PATIENCE: Yes, I did.

NICHOLAS: And I hope you've put them carefully away.

PATIENCE: Yes, I have. That's what I've been doing. I'd just finished when you asked me to light the fire in here. (*She holds out her hands. The palms are black with coal-dust.*)

NICHOLAS: Haven't you washed your hands?

PATIENCE: Not yet. I cleared out that big cupboard beside our bed for the dresses. It was full of your old toys. I discovered him. (*She points to the toy on the piano.*) He's funny, isn't he?

(*NICHOLAS turns and sees the toy bear.*)

PATIENCE: The rest of the toys and the books I packed carefully away in my trunk. I think we might send them all to the orphanage, don't you? The kids would dearly love them even though they are a bit out of date. (*As she speaks NICHOLAS goes quickly from the room. PATIENCE sits motionless until he returns from the bedroom. He comes back into the room. The girl watches him.*) What did you want to arrange about tomorrow?

NICHOLAS: You didn't know, of course.

PATIENCE: What didn't I know?

NICHOLAS: I can't scold you because you cannot be expected to realize what a wrong thing you have done.

PATIENCE: I've done nothing wrong. Really, Nicholas. I've done nothing.

NICHOLAS: It would have been useless to have attempted an earlier explanation to you.

PATIENCE: An explanation of what?

NICHOLAS: You slut. You'll go upstairs to my room and unpack those toys and books and put them back exactly as you found them.

PATIENCE: I can't remember how they were. What did you call me?

NICHOLAS: You can't remember how they were?

PATIENCE: No, not exactly. I'll put them back if you want me to do that. I didn't know –

NICHOLAS: You can't remember how they were.

PATIENCE: I've told you, no. They were in such a muddle.

NICHOLAS: You have destroyed them.

PATIENCE: Of course I haven't. I told you. I've put them carefully away in my trunk.

NICHOLAS: You have destroyed them. Just as if you had burned them.

PATIENCE: I think you're making an awful fuss.

NICHOLAS: Am I?

PATIENCE: I think so.

NICHOLAS: Have you no regard for other people's property?

PATIENCE: But you are my husband –

NICHOLAS: Yes.

PATIENCE: – and they are your baby toys. But you're not a child now, Nicholas.

NICHOLAS: And my only excuse for you is that you are a child.

PATIENCE: Well, come to that, you're only about five years older than me –

NICHOLAS: Shut up!

PATIENCE: I'll go and put them away, the toys, as nearly as I can remember, in their old places.

NICHOLAS: No, it's finished: done with. Even you with your limited understanding must realize that. It's done with. They can never be put back.
(*There is a pause.*)

PATIENCE: Will you explain to me what I've done wrong? (*She pauses.*) I don't understand. (*She pauses.*) I was very careful with them. Don't you know how delighted I am by the seeing and the touching of the toys that belonged – still belong – to you? Do you think I could destroy them? I suggested they should go to the kids at the orphanage to pass on, continue, the happiness, that was all. I shouldn't send him (*She indicates the toy bear.*) because I think he's funny. I brought him down to ask you if I might keep him for myself. I'll love him as much as you've loved him. When I was taking the toys from the cupboard and the books from the shelves I thought of you as a boy. (*She laughs.*) Come, Nicholas! Tell me what you were like. Were you handsome or ugly? Naughty or good? Noisy or quiet? (*She goes to embrace him.*) Were you ever in love with any little girls then? Who were your friends? What did you think about at nights, alone, in that room before – ?
(*NICHOLAS turns and strikes her across the face. After a pause PATIENCE bursts into howls of pain.*)
You've hurt me!
(*NICHOLAS stands watching her as she cries.*)
Why did you hit me? You've hurt me very much. Why did you hurt me? Have I deserved it? You have never been angry with me before. Never once. What did I say? 'Who were your friends? Were you ever in love? Noisy or naughty or – ' Did I give offence?
(*NICHOLAS goes to her and puts his arms about her. As the girl's sobbing dies a brass band can be heard playing in the distance.*)
God! How you frightened me.
(*NICHOLAS leads her to the door.*)
You want me to go? I will. I'll go and put back the toys and the books in their places. At once. I'll go now. Don't worry. They shall all be put back as they were before. I can remember. (*She goes out. NICHOLAS returns to the room. He sits. After a moment he rises and moves towards the door.*)

NICHOLAS: (*He shouts.*) Patience! Patience!
(*There is a pause.*)
Patience!
PATIENCE: (*Off.*) What is it?
(*NICHOLAS returns from the door. He stands by the toy bear. Suddenly, dropping his stick, he snatches up the toy and holds it to him in an embrace. He is whispering endearments to the toy as PATIENCE calls again.*)
Yes? I'm listening. What is it?

*CURTAIN*

## Scene 2

*The same: late afternoon of the same day. Present are EMILY, PETER, A.G. and PATIENCE. PATIENCE is wearing one of the dresses given to her by EMILY. It is of grey silk and is generally too large for the girl. They are finishing tea. PATIENCE is crossing the room with two cups to place them on the small table before EMILY.*

PETER: Come now. Be cheerful.
A.G.: Be quiet.
PETER: But why? We have cause to be cheerful.
A.G.: Cause?
PETER: Yes.
A.G.: But nothing has happened.
PETER: And isn't that cause enough for us to be happy?
A.G.: Three times in the last half-hour you have said to us, 'Be cheerful'. No one has answered you.
PETER: I didn't expect an answer.
A.G.: Now you tell us we should be happy because nothing of importance has occurred. Did you expect something frightful to happen?
PETER: Oh, yes.
A.G.: What?
EMILY: What, Peter?
PETER: Don't be angry.
A.G.: Take your hand away from your face – let me see you.
(*PETER removes his hand; his expression is innocent enquiry.*)
PETER: Well?

A.G.: What do you mean? – Well.

PETER: I thought you wished to ask me something.

A.G.: Ask you – ?

PETER: Yes. I thought you wanted to ask my advice.

A.G.: This is absurd!

PETER: Not at all.

A.G.: But it is! The conversation is absurd – without reason!

(*A.G. moves across the room to return his teacup to EMILY. He passes before PETER who, sitting, puts out a leg and trips A.G. who falls to the floor, the teacup flying from his hand.*)

PETER: My dear fellow! I'm so sorry! Are you hurt? (*He assists A.G. to his feet. PATIENCE picks up the broken cup.*)

EMILY: Come along, A.G. Sit down. (*She leads A.G. to a chair.*)

PETER: Yes. Come along.

EMILY: What a nasty fall.

PETER: Yes. I can't forgive myself. I must watch what I'm doing. Don't look so reproachful, old man. It wasn't intentional. If you were a child I should be inclined to say, 'Temper! Temper! That's where temper lands you.' (*He laughs.*)

EMILY: Are you all right now, A.G.?

A.G.: Yes.

EMILY: Would you like some water?

A.G.: No.

EMILY: Patience, go and get some water.

A.G.: No! (*He shouts.*) I don't want any water.

EMILY: Very well.

(*A.G. rises from the chair and moves across the room staring at PETER. The others watch him.*)

A.G.: I struck my head.

PETER: Then come and sit down – rest.

A.G.: Yes, rest. Rest and be cheerful.

PETER: (*Smiles.*) Now look. Come and sit down. It wasn't as bad a fall as all that, was it?

A.G.: Bad enough.

EMILY: Would you like to go home, A.G.?

A.G.: No. (*He turns to PATIENCE.*) Why should Mr Bembo wish me to fall?

PATIENCE: I don't know.

PETER: It was an accident.

PATIENCE: It was an accident.

A.G.: (*To PATIENCE.*) Do you know – you live in this house – do you know of any reason why Mr Bembo should wish to hurt me?

PATIENCE: I don't.

A.G.: He must have a reason, mustn't he?

(*The girl does not answer.*)

Mustn't he?

(*PATIENCE moves to the door.*)

Don't go! Please don't go!

(*PATIENCE goes out. A.G. turns to face PETER.*)

She is afraid of you? Or of me?

PETER: She is afraid of neither of us. She is embarrassed, that's all.

A.G.: Embarrassed! Dear God!

PETER: I tell you it was an accident. The girl realizes that. I'm sorry. It merely happened that when you were passing me I stretched out my leg: you tripped and fell. I can assure you I have nothing against you personally – and if I had anything against you I'd not play schoolboy tricks on you. I am not in any way a malicious person. You remember me? I am an old clown. Reverse the positions. Suppose you had accidentally tripped me and it was I who had sprawled on the floor. What would have happened? Everyone in the room, you with them, would have laughed and shouted, 'Bembo! You old fool!' and then laughed again.

A.G.: And you would have stood up in pain and bowed and fixed a smile on your face.

PETER: You understand me?

A.G.: I understand you deliberately tried to harm me.

PETER: I'm sorry you should think that. I can say no more.

A.G.: And if you would do that how else might you threaten me?

PETER: (*In sudden anger.*) I've never threatened anyone in my life. (*To EMILY.*) May I put the lights on?

EMILY: Of course.

(*PETER does so and then crosses to draw the curtains.*)

Come and sit down, A.G.

A.G.: Thank you, my dear.

(*EMILY takes the tea-tray from the room.*)

PETER: (*At the window.*) I wonder when they light the coloured lamps in the public gardens. Those hanging from the trees. (*He pauses.*) I say, I wonder when they –

A.G.: Yes. I heard what you said. On Wednesday.

PETER: What happens on Wednesday?

A.G.: A fête. A children's sports meeting and, at night, dancing in the gardens.

PETER: It would be a brave soul who danced in those gardens from what I saw of them this morning. And all this in aid of – ?

A.G.: The local British Legion.

PETER: Have you ever fought in your life?

(*A.G. does not reply.*)

Tell me. In the gardens there is an engraved stone –

A.G.: With my name – yes.

PETER: You –

A.G.: I presented the building where the public can buy tea and refreshments.

PETER: Ah! Refreshments. Do they?

A.G.: What?

PETER: Buy either?

A.G.: No.

PETER: I'm not surprised. Who would imagine they could be refreshed by that dismal hut?

A.G.: I was not responsible for the design.

PETER: You presented it to the town. Now what did you hope to gain by doing that?

A.G.: What do you mean?

PETER: What did you hope to get out of it?

A.G.: Nothing. It was the gesture of a newcomer to the town. It was given in memory of my wife who played in those gardens as a child. You would have known that if you had troubled to read the words on the stone.

PETER: Have you seen it recently?

A.G.: I –

PETER: The stone is defaced. Your name remains but otherwise new hands, new lovers have been at work. No mention of Helen but there is 'Syd loves Lil' and 'Lil loves Syd' cut deep.

A.G.: They can be prosecuted for that.

PETER: Do you do many – many 'good works'?

A.G.: When I –

PETER: Then let me impress upon you the urgent need to aid the charity for Crippled Children.

A.G.: We have no such local charity.

PETER: Then start one.

A.G.: Why do you smile?

PETER: It is of great importance. Emily will help you. I will help you.

(*EMILY has entered the room.*)

EMILY: What will I help?

PETER: A.G. to start a charity fund for crippled children. I'll start it here. (*He takes a coin from his pocket.*)

A.G.: A halfpenny?

PETER: Don't sneer at it. Four hundred halfpennies may well buy one little wooden leg. Collect, A.G., collect!

EMILY: Yes, I'll help.

(*NICHOLAS and PATIENCE enter. NICHOLAS carries the reading lamp.*)

NICHOLAS: I shall never invent another damned thing for you, A.G. This lamp has caused endless trouble.

A.G.: I'm sorry, Nicholas.

NICHOLAS: What do you do with it when you get it home?

A.G.: Nothing.

NICHOLAS: Well, if it doesn't work now I give it up. Here you are. (*He hands the lamp to A.G.*)

A.G.: Thank you. (*He holds out his hand to PETER.*)

PETER: What is it?

A.G.: Your halfpenny.

PETER: You refuse to do as I ask. I'm sorry – not for my sake but for the children, A.G., the children.

A.G.: Fool!

NICHOLAS: Are you two playing some kind of game?

A.G.: Shove ha'penny.

PETER: Did you make a joke, A.G.?

A.G.: Yes. Do you mind?

PETER: Not a bit. I'm delighted.

(*A.G. speaks to EMILY. PETER watches NICHOLAS and PATIENCE.*)

PATIENCE: Are you all right, Nicholas?

NICHOLAS: Of course I'm all right.

PATIENCE: Why didn't you come down to tea?

NICHOLAS: I've been in my room mending A.G.'s lamp.

PATIENCE: I haven't seen any of you all the afternoon.

NICHOLAS: No.

PATIENCE: I was afraid to come and look for you.

NICHOLAS: Were you now?

PETER: You mustn't be afraid of us.

PATIENCE: Mind your own business.

PETER: I'm sorry.

A.G.: (*To EMILY.*) You don't think he'll mind?

EMILY: Of course not.

NICHOLAS: What won't I mind?

A.G.: What?

NICHOLAS: I presumed you were speaking of me.

A.G.: Yes.

NICHOLAS: Well, then. What won't I mind?

A.G.: I should like – (*He stops.*)

EMILY: A.G. would like –

NICHOLAS: Let me hear him. Let him tell me himself. Yes?

A.G.: I'd like to speak to you.

NICHOLAS: Certainly.

A.G.: Alone.

NICHOLAS: Oh. (*He looks about the room.*) Well, we'd better go outside.

(*NICHOLAS and A.G. go out.*)

EMILY: Did you see much of the town during your walk this morning, Peter?

PETER: What? Oh, yes. The gardens and the town hall and the – the 'Crown', is it?

EMILY: Opposite the town hall?

PETER: Yes.

EMILY: That's right. 'The Crown'. It's the first time you've been out since you've been here, isn't it?

PETER: Yes. (*To PATIENCE.*) Do you like living here? In this town, I mean.

PATIENCE: I've never known another.

PETER: You must show me the sights some time.

EMILY: She can take you to the Farthingale Hill.

PETER: We might go out to tea.

PATIENCE: I'd like to.

(*NICHOLAS enters. He smiles at PETER.*)

EMILY: And what was so secret?

NICHOLAS: Didn't he tell you just now?

EMILY: No. He merely asked if I thought you would mind if he spoke to you alone.

NICHOLAS: (*Laughs.*) And you expect me to tell you?

EMILY: Of course.

NICHOLAS: A.G. wants our help – our advice.

EMILY: What about?

NICHOLAS: (*To EMILY.*) What's the matter?

EMILY: Nothing.

NICHOLAS: Oh, yes, there is. What is it?

EMILY: A.G. –

NICHOLAS: Yes?

EMILY: His behaviour in church this morning was inexcusable.

NICHOLAS: What did he do?

(*EMILY does not answer.*)

Spit on the cross?

(*Pause.*)

He has received an anonymous and, he says, threatening letter.

EMILY: From whom?

NICHOLAS: Don't be silly.

EMILY: You know. You know who sent it.

NICHOLAS: He wants our advice and our – our guesses as to who it is from and why it was sent. I said we would be more than pleased to help him clear up the mystery.

PETER: Of course. We can't have our little friend threatened by outsiders, by strangers. Of course we must help him.

NICHOLAS: He came to me alone. But I think I convinced him of your sincerity and desire to aid. He seemed suspicious of you. He even hinted that you might have written the letter yourself.

PETER: What did you say to that?

NICHOLAS: I said I didn't think you could write.

EMILY: Where is he?

NICHOLAS: He's gone to fetch the letter. He'd left it at his house.

PETER: He wants our advice?

NICHOLAS: Yes.

PETER: And our pity? That's what he's working for, isn't it?

EMILY: Why should he be pitied?

PETER: A frightened man with no understanding of the threats against him – he feels he requires pity.

EMILY: What are the threats against him?

PETER: We shall know.

EMILY: You already –

NICHOLAS: I cannot pity him. I've never pitied anyone in all my life.

PETER: Yourself?

NICHOLAS: No!

PETER: You have never – ?

NICHOLAS: I've sometimes used the word. I am forced to use the common jargon to make myself understood. My meaning has more often been –

(*The front door is closed. There is a pause. A.G. comes into the room. He is carrying the letter. He stands before the others for a moment and then speaks to NICHOLAS.*)

A.G.: You've told them?

NICHOLAS: Yes.

PETER: We are very distressed. No man likes to be threatened. It is most disturbing. You can be sure of our support and, if necessary, our action against this scoundrel. You have come to us. That is good. It is always to friends you must go in the case of fear.

(*There is a pause. A.G. speaks to NICHOLAS and EMILY.*)

A.G.: The circumstances are these. When we returned from church this morning – (*He pauses and then speaks to PETER.*) I am not afraid.

PETER: Liar!

A.G.: What?

PETER: Any man must be afraid when threatened. Listen to me! We can only give you our advice and help in this matter providing you are honest and give us your faith.

A.G.: (*To NICHOLAS and EMILY.*) When we had returned from church this morning and you had left me I went to my house. This letter must have been delivered by hand in my absence. It lay just within the door and on entering I trod on it – you can see the mark of my sole – (*He holds up the letter. PETER shouts with laughter. NICHOLAS goes to take the letter but A.G. refuses him, withdrawing to a corner of the room.*) The paper and envelope are blue and of a good quality.

PETER: (*Taking a sheet of the identical paper from the desk.*) Something like this?

A.G.: Very like that. It's sealed with red wax. (*Pause.*)

EMILY: And what does it say?

A.G.: (*Taking out the letter and reading.*) 'You are discovered, therefore you are lost. She died in vain – ' and then something I can't read.

NICHOLAS: 'Actum est.'

(*There is a pause.*)

A.G.: I must go home. (*A.G. hesitates before running to the door. NICHOLAS has meanwhile moved to stand before the door which he shuts.*)

PETER: (*Speaking immediately.*) But where is the threat in that? I don't understand you. No, I don't understand this at all. You have been misleading us. You gave us to believe you were in some kind of danger.

(*Speaking through these lines of PETER's, NICHOLAS has taken A.G.'s arm, saying,* 'Come and sit down. Dear oh, dear oh, dear!' *and leading him to a chair.*)

You must explain more to us.

NICHOLAS: This has given you a very nasty shake-up I can see.

PETER: Yes. You must rest and recover your senses.

NICHOLAS: You're not well enough to run about like that.

PETER: I take it the reference in the letter is to your wife.

NICHOLAS: Give him time to recover. He has had a bad shock – delayed, you know. Is there anything I can get you, A.G.? A glass of water?

(*A.G. does not answer. NICHOLAS takes the letter from him.*)

Now what can we make out from this?

PETER: May I see?

NICHOLAS: Certainly.

(*They stand together examining the letter.*)

A good-quality paper – yes.

PETER: A man –

NICHOLAS: Or woman –

PETER: – of taste.

NICHOLAS: From the handwriting?

PETER: From the paper.

NICHOLAS: The wax – is that a thumbprint?

PETER: Perhaps.

NICHOLAS: A clue.

PETER: The handwriting –

NICHOLAS: A trace of affectation.

PETER: Indeed, yes.

NICHOLAS: More than a trace.

PETER: There is arrogance.

NICHOLAS: Yes.

PETER: That initial Y.

NICHOLAS: A flourish.

PETER: Dear me, yes.

NICHOLAS: It is obvious we –

PETER: Yes?

NICHOLAS: We have to deal with a dangerous fellow.

PETER: I'm afraid so.

NICHOLAS: But perhaps a trifle careless.

PETER: Why do you say that?

NICHOLAS: The paper was folded –

PETER: – before the ink was dry.

NICHOLAS: Careless.

PETER: Yes.

NICHOLAS: We may catch him in that.

PETER: We may.

NICHOLAS: His meaning. He writes –

PETER: 'You are discovered – '
NICHOLAS: Meaning A.G. is discovered.
PETER: Obviously.
NICHOLAS: ' – therefore you are lost.'
PETER: Meaning A.G. is lost.
NICHOLAS: Quite.
PETER: So far, so good. 'She – '
NICHOLAS: A.G.'s wife.
PETER: Well –
NICHOLAS: You seem doubtful.
PETER: I suppose it must be.
NICHOLAS: Who else?
PETER: We'll take it as being his wife.
NICHOLAS: 'She died in vain.'
PETER: The cause was not enough.
NICHOLAS: No.
PETER: Pity.
NICHOLAS: Unfulfilled.
PETER: 'Actum est.'
NICHOLAS: 'Actum est.'

(*There is a pause.*)

PETER: (*To A.G.*) Better? (*To NICHOLAS.*) He is badly shaken by this. (*Shouting.*) The blackguard! How dare he intimidate helpless men! How dare he play upon the emotion and sensitivity of a man like this! (*He indicates himself.*)
NICHOLAS: Peter! This situation –
PETER: (*To A.G.*) You are in great danger.
NICHOLAS: Yes.
PETER: You must behave naturally, however.
NICHOLAS: We –
PETER: Casually.
NICHOLAS: The situation calls –
PETER: You must not – must *not* betray the slightest anxiety or fear.
NICHOLAS: I agree.
PETER: You must laugh. Be – be –
NICHOLAS: Devil-may-care.

PETER: But I do not.

(*PETER and NICHOLAS laugh.*)

Yes. That is how you must behave.

NICHOLAS: Better?

PETER: Feel better, A.G.?

NICHOLAS: Well enough to discuss our plans? For we have plans to help you. Haven't we, Peter?

PETER: We have.

NICHOLAS: Yes, you look better. Listen to me. Can you hear me? (*To PETER.*) Do you think he can hear me?

PETER: (*Shouting at A.G.*) Can you hear us?

(*A.G. gives no indication.*)

Yes, he can hear us.

NICHOLAS: Right.

PETER: It is obvious from this letter that you are threatened. Oh, yes. I understand the threat. Foolish of me not to realize it from the first instance. Now! Have you any idea who wrote this letter?

NICHOLAS: He can't hear us.

PETER: (*Kneeling by A.G.'s side.*) Yes, he can. Do you know who wrote this letter?

(*In the silence A.G. raises his arm and points at PETER. PETER, purposely misunderstanding, moves to leave A.G.'s finger pointing at EMILY.*)

Emily? Absurd! You didn't send this letter, did you, Emmy?

(*EMILY goes quickly from the room. A.G.'s finger remains pointing until PETER slaps down his hand.*)

Don't point. It's rude.

NICHOLAS: No matter who sent it you can rely on our help.

PETER: You shouldn't have accused Emily like that. Even in fun. I expect you've upset her.

NICHOLAS: We'll help you. You've come to us as your friends and we shan't disgrace you. I promise you dear, dear A.G., we shan't fail you.

PETER: We are extraordinarily capable – hardly used, of course, but capable of dealing with things like this.

NICHOLAS: Our plans are these. Shall I tell him or will you?

PETER: Carry on.

NICHOLAS: We're going to protect you.
PETER: We'll stay with you.
NICHOLAS: So don't worry.
PETER: If you are afraid to be alone –
NICHOLAS: Yes, alone in your house –
PETER: You can come and stay here. Can't he?
NICHOLAS: Of course he can.
PETER: You can move in and close up your own house.
NICHOLAS: And live with us until it is all over.
PETER: We won't desert you.

(*There is a pause.*)

NICHOLAS: This has upset you, of course.
PETER: It would have upset me. But we must be cheerful.
NICHOLAS: You need taking out of yourself for a while. Doesn't he?
PETER: Yes.
NICHOLAS: Have you any suggestions?
PETER: (*Pauses.*) Let's all go and have a drink.
NICHOLAS: Fine. There you are, A.G. What about that, eh? We'll all go and have a drink.
PETER: Then come back here with us and we'll amuse you. Keep your mind occupied until bedtime.
NICHOLAS: Yes. Let's do that, shall we, A.G.?
PETER: Just a moment. Let him recover himself. Give him a few minutes.
NICHOLAS: Yes. Take your time, A.G. We're in no hurry.

(*NICHOLAS and PETER move apart from A.G. and speak quietly together.*)

What a damned thing to do. Attack him through the memory of his wife. We all know how fond he was of her.

PETER: We do. No one who has heard the story of her death could fail to be moved by the gracious memories he has of her last hours.
NICHOLAS: The cruelty of 'She died in vain'.
PETER: Ah, yes.
NICHOLAS: When by her very death she made A.G. what he is now.
PETER: Don't speak of it. (*He fingers beneath his eyeshade.*) Are we ready?

NICHOLAS: Give him a moment longer.

(*They stand in respectful silence.*)

PETER: He is moving.

NICHOLAS: Yes. I think he's all right now.

(*PETER moves to A.G. and, taking his hands, raises him from the chair.*)

PETER: Ups-a-daisy. Has he a hat and coat?

(*NICHOLAS indicates the hallway.*)

Come along then.

(*The three men go out – A.G. between NICHOLAS and PETER. PATIENCE remains still until the front door is heard to close when she moves to the window. She draws back the curtain and stands staring into the street. EMILY comes into the room.*)

PATIENCE: Are they going to murder him?

EMILY: No, of course not.

PATIENCE: Why did they send that letter?

(*EMILY has seated herself at the piano. Looking at PATIENCE she strikes a chord and then speaks.*)

EMILY: What a pretty child you are.

PATIENCE: (*Very pleased.*) Am I?

EMILY: Yes, very pretty.

PATIENCE: Thank you. (*She bobs a little mock curtsey.*)

*CURTAIN*

# ACT THREE

*The same: 9.30 the same evening. EMILY is sitting in an armchair; she is holding a book. PATIENCE is seated on a low stool set at EMILY's feet. EMILY puts down the book, leaving it open. She then puts an arm about PATIENCE's shoulders in a gentle, affectionate gesture.*

EMILY: How charming we must look to anyone who could see us.

PATIENCE: Do you ever think of how you look to other people?

EMILY: Don't you?

PATIENCE: No. I've never really bothered. Nick – Nicholas says –

EMILY: Yes?

PATIENCE: He says I've no pride.

EMILY: Have you?

PATIENCE: No, I don't think so.

EMILY: You are not so aware of yourself as he would like, is that it?

PATIENCE: (*Not understanding.*) I suppose so.

EMILY: When did he say that?

PATIENCE: I don't really – What?

EMILY: When did he say you had no pride?

PATIENCE: Oh, I don't know.

EMILY: Well, how did it come up?

PATIENCE: When I asked him if he'd like to come and watch me have my bath.

(*There is a pause. EMILY then speaks with tenderness.*)

EMILY: Poor Nicholas.

PATIENCE: Will you read some more to me?

EMILY: No more this evening. The men will be back soon.

(*EMILY is tidying PATIENCE's hair.*)

PATIENCE: You have a lovely voice.

EMILY: Thank you.

PATIENCE: You have a lovely face. How old are you?

EMILY: Fifty-eight.

PATIENCE: That's not old, is it?

EMILY: To you, at seventeen, it must be.

PATIENCE: Does anyone flatter you?

EMILY: (*Calling out.*) Who's there?

PATIENCE: What is it?

EMILY: Didn't you hear the door?

PATIENCE: No.

(*They sit listening. There is silence.*)

What's the matter?

EMILY: Nothing. I'm expecting the men, that's all.

PATIENCE: They'll be home soon, won't they?

(*Again they listen.*)

EMILY: One of us must go. (*She goes out of the room. After a moment she returns.*) Nothing. I shall leave the lights on. For their return. (*She closes the door.*)

PATIENCE: (*Picking up the book.*) Who wrote that last thing? You mustn't be afraid.

EMILY: No. John Donne.

(*PATIENCE laughs.*)

PATIENCE: I'm sorry.

EMILY: I don't mind.

PATIENCE: Funny name. Is he dead?

EMILY: Oh, yes.

PATIENCE: All the poets seem to be dead.

EMILY: What did you say?

PATIENCE: I said, all the poets seem to be dead.

EMILY: Nicholas put it another way.

PATIENCE: What?

EMILY: Many years ago, when Nicholas was small – about ten or eleven – I was reading to him. At the end, on his way to bed, he turned at the door (*She indicates the door.*) – it was this room – and asked me if the poet was dead. Yes, I said. Of course, he said, only dead men could write like that.

PATIENCE: That's the only story you've ever told me about Nicholas. He remembers some of the things you read to him.

EMILY: Does he? He never speaks of them to me.

PATIENCE: Did you read these poems to him?

EMILY: I can't remember. Probably.

(*There is a pause as PATIENCE refers to the book.*)

PATIENCE: I didn't know such things were written.
EMILY: What? Things like – ?
PATIENCE: Such as the poems you read to me. About love.
EMILY: What poetry have you known?
PATIENCE: 'Marmion'.
EMILY: (*Smiles.*) What?
PATIENCE: 'Marmion'. I remember that. A long poetry story in a red cover.
EMILY: School? (*PATIENCE nods.*) Did you like it?
PATIENCE: No. But this – (*She indicates the poem.*) – such things as this are thought by men about women but surely most secretly.
EMILY: That poem was probably written most secretly.
PATIENCE: But it is here, in print, for anyone to read. How is that?
EMILY: The man was a poet.
PATIENCE: Teachers! You won't find me being guided by old, dead men.
EMILY: I didn't mean that.
PATIENCE: This girl he writes about – she's dead?
EMILY: Yes. She's dead.
PATIENCE: And all the men whose poems are in this book – they're all dead?
EMILY: All dead.
PATIENCE: 'O my America! my new-found-land.'
EMILY: Don't break the book like that!
PATIENCE: Well, I'm alive. Very much so. Say it again.
EMILY: What?
PATIENCE: That I'm pretty.
EMILY: You're pretty.
PATIENCE: I'm prettiest when – Nobody flatters me, either. Let's talk about such things.

(*EMILY moves away.*)

Nicholas said you'd probably try to educate me. He warned me about it. (*She pauses to study EMILY's reaction to this.*) Did you hear what I said?
EMILY: Yes, I heard you. Should we both have a drink? They must be back soon. (*EMILY moves to pour out the wine.*)

PATIENCE: Nicholas made me drunk on our honeymoon.

EMILY: Did he?

PATIENCE: On whiskey. I could hardly stand.

EMILY: Couldn't you?

PATIENCE: The hotel porter had to carry me to the bedroom.

EMILY: Oh?

PATIENCE: I was sick. I was sick all over the bedroom floor.

EMILY: Poor Patience!

PATIENCE: Have you ever been drunk?

EMILY: Yes.

PATIENCE: Really drunk?

EMILY: Here you are. (*She holds out the glass of wine to PATIENCE.*)

PATIENCE: What's the time?

EMILY: Just after twenty to ten.

PATIENCE: Oh.

(*Pause.*)

EMILY: Where did they say they were going?

PATIENCE: They just said to have a drink. No special place.

EMILY: They can't be far away.

PATIENCE: Why not?

EMILY: Nicholas' leg.

PATIENCE: Of course.

EMILY: He can't –

PATIENCE: No, of course not. He won't – A.G. has the car though and – Ought I to get some food ready for them?

EMILY: There's some cold meat and salad.

PATIENCE: Very well. (*She goes to the door and then turns to EMILY.*) Aren't you coming?

(*EMILY shakes her head. After a moment of indecision, then fear, PATIENCE returns quickly into the room.*)

What? What?

(*EMILY is silent.*)

Well, we can get it when they come in. It won't take long. Meat and salad. (*She takes up her glass of wine.*)

(*Looking at EMILY, PATIENCE sees that in her abstraction her glass is tilted and the liquid spilling.*)

Hey! You're spilling your drink. (*She takes out her handkerchief and wipes the wine from EMILY's* dress.) Clumsy. You mustn't be clumsy. You are always so delicate. (*She laughs and kisses EMILY.*) Mustn't be clumsy.

(*EMILY suddenly takes PATIENCE in a close embrace.*)

What is it? Dear Emily.

(*PATIENCE returns the embrace.*)

Don't look so amazed. (*She laughs again.*) No harm done. I only kissed you. Look at me. I've enjoyed this evening very much. Thank you for it. Did you mean to please me? Because you have. So you see – no harm done. (*She disengages herself from the embrace and puts down the two glasses.*) So. Here, I say! Why do you look at me like that? (*She laughs.*) Have I said something foolish?

(*EMILY shakes her head.*)

What's the matter? You do look unforgiving.

EMILY: Come and sit down again.

PATIENCE: I don't want to sit down.

EMILY: I have something to tell you.

PATIENCE: What?

EMILY: Something I've been asked to tell you.

PATIENCE: By Nicholas?

EMILY: Yes.

PATIENCE: I guessed that. Clever, eh? I seem to have annoyed him. He won't speak to me.

EMILY: I'm sorry.

PATIENCE: Well, come on. What is it?

EMILY: Nicholas –

PATIENCE: Yes?

EMILY: He has suffered great disappointment.

PATIENCE: Yes?

EMILY: It is only human.

PATIENCE: You mustn't talk to me like that. Human. Men and women do this and that. I am myself and I behave as Patience Loratt – Patience Doon. He is Nicholas Doon and as Nicholas Doon he must be expected to behave. I don't need excuses for him. (*She pauses.*) Go on. (*She pauses.*) Go on!

EMILY: He is going to kill himself. (*She goes quickly on.*) Himself. Nicholas. Himself. He says he intends to kill himself. It is part of a plan that I don't understand: to kill himself. Do you believe me? Do you, child?

PATIENCE: Child! I am a child and you make fun of my innocence.

EMILY: No!

PATIENCE: I meant –

EMILY: I'll forget that you're a child. I'll ignore your innocence.

PATIENCE: I meant to say ignorance. I am not innocent. I am foul. (*She wanders to the door and goes out of the room. EMILY, following, stands in the open doorway, calling after her.*)

EMILY: He has had great provocation.

PATIENCE: (*Off.*) What?

EMILY: Don't go. I've more to tell you. It is a defensive act. Don't you understand, the secrecy and the joking are directed against himself. The plot is against himself. (*PATIENCE returns to the room. EMILY stands aside to allow her to enter.*)

EMILY: For any of us to take, at any time, an instrument of suicide is easy. (*She is silent. PATIENCE has moved into the room. She picks up her glass of wine and puts it down again, untouched. She moves about the room. EMILY watches her.*)

PATIENCE: Now, look. You say he's told you this?

EMILY: Yes. It's true. Do you believe it?

PATIENCE: Do you?

EMILY: There's nothing to be done.

PATIENCE: Do you believe it?

EMILY: I don't know.

PATIENCE: It's a joke, isn't it?

EMILY: I don't know.

PATIENCE: Did it seem as if he was joking?

EMILY: Peter laughed.

PATIENCE: And Nicholas?

EMILY: He wasn't laughing. It's something to do with A.G.

PATIENCE: But he's a joke. I mean, they laugh at him. When did they tell you this?

EMILY: This afternoon. They –

PATIENCE: Sit down.

(*EMILY sits.*)

EMILY: Nicholas asked me, just before he went out this evening with Peter and A.G., to tell you. He wanted you to know.

PATIENCE: Forget my innocence! (*She laughs. The two women stare at each other in silence. Into the silence the telephone rings. EMILY remains unmoving and it is PATIENCE who answers it.*) Yes. Yes; Patience. Very well. (*She puts down the receiver.*) Peter. Phoning from a close-by box. They'll be home in a minute, he said.

EMILY: Nicholas –

PATIENCE: They're all together, he said. Did Nicholas say anything about me?

EMILY: Then he's not in the house. (*She moves quickly to the door.*)

PATIENCE: Did he? Did he talk about me? Tell me. It's important.

(*EMILY returns to PATIENCE.*)

EMILY: Give me your hands. (*She takes PATIENCE's hands.*) No, he didn't talk about you. Just asked me to tell you. (*She raises and kisses PATIENCE's hands, laughing.*) Funny! Now I see the mortality in everything. I've not thought of it before. My husband died away from me – miles away. But now I see it as you appear to see it. You talk about your innocence – your ignorance. I am as ignorant of this experience as you. But now, Nicholas – You are young and strong and if it is his intention to – You say it. Go on. You say it.

PATIENCE: Nicholas is going to kill himself.

EMILY: If that is his intention you must exercise your strength and surrender yourself to the lack of comprehension that is the blessing of your youth. By attempting to understand you may, by chance, succeed and that will destroy you.

PATIENCE: What do you mean? You talk like a book.

EMILY: I mean soon Nicholas will kill himself. We must not obstruct his designs or we shall distort the pattern of our lives. You must attempt, therefore, not to understand but to accept.

PATIENCE: But it wouldn't be friendly not to try to save him. Besides, it's against the law.

EMILY: You must know – Rather. How can you tell who are friends and who enemies? That is the basis of Nicholas's suspicion.

PATIENCE: When I married him –

EMILY: Very well, then. Don't believe it. It's not true. It is a joke. But remember, some people see quite clearly –

PATIENCE: They are here.

EMILY: – that a man has no other –

(*The front door is heard to open and the sound of the men's voices is also heard for a moment: the door is heard to close. There is silence. The two women stare at the closed door of the room.*)

PATIENCE: I was lying about my being drunk. I made it up to frighten you.

(*Pause.*)

EMILY: Why don't they come in?

(*After EMILY has spoken there is another pause: the door then opens and PETER, A.G. and NICHOLAS enter. A.G. is in the centre, his arms linked with those of the other two men. All three are in a state of great exultation but, although they have been drinking, they are not drunk. They come fully into the room.*)

A.G.: I have two friends!

NICHOLAS: Hullo, Mother.

A.G.: Emily!<br>EMILY: Hullo, Nicholas. } *Together.*

A.G.: Did you hear me, Emily? I have two friends!<br>PETER: Only just in time. I think it's going to rain. } *Together.*

EMILY: Yes, I hear you, A.G. Have you walked far?

NICHOLAS: We've been to the 'Crown'.<br>A.G.: The three of us have been talking together. } *Together.*

PETER: What's the time?

EMILY: You're not tired, Nicholas?

NICHOLAS: No. (*To PETER.*) Getting on for ten.

(*A.G. is touching EMILY's arm and speaking her name quietly in an attempt to gain her attention.*)

PETER: We should have been home earlier but when we came out of the 'Crown' there was an accident and we couldn't drag A.G. away from the spectacle.

A.G.: (*Laughing.*) I say!

EMILY: What happened?

NICHOLAS: A car ran into a horse drawing a cart.

PETER: We saw it happen and A.G. insisted on staying until they put the beast away.

A.G.: Really, I was – (*Laughs.*)

PETER: And so we stood there – just watching the dying animal.

NICHOLAS: (*Pointing to A.G.*) Is that blood on your shoes?

A.G.: (*Laughing.*) No, no! Of course not. (*He bends down to wipe his shoes.*)

PETER: So that's – (*He smacks A.G.'s behind.*) – why we're late.

A.G.: It was Nicholas who said, 'We may as well wait until the end.' I was quite willing to come away. (*He laughs.*) Good gracious me! You speak as if it were some kind of entertainment.

PETER: Your face was, as they say, 'a study'.

A.G.: (*To EMILY.*) Peter sat by the animal's head and talked to it. Most extraordinary.

EMILY: Are you hungry? I mean, do you want supper now?

NICHOLAS: No, later. You'll stay, won't you, A.G.?

A.G.: I'd like to, Nicholas, I'd like to.

NICHOLAS: Good. Let me take your hat and coat. (*He takes A.G.'s hat from his head and assists him with his coat. NICHOLAS and PETER then go out to remove their own coats.*)

A.G.: Emily, I have something to tell you.

EMILY: What?

A.G.: It's secret.

EMILY: What's that?

A.G.: Not really, I suppose. They've told me. You know it was Nicholas and Peter who sent that letter to me. (*He laughs.*) The rascals!

EMILY: Why?

A.G.: Eh?

EMILY: Why did they send it?

A.G.: Because of Helen. We had a talk about it. They say I am always going on about her and that I bore people – people like you – with my stories of her. I must admit I didn't realize it but now they have mentioned it – been completely honest about it – I believe it must be true. Nicholas says I'm to ask your forgiveness. Will you forgive me, Emily?

EMILY: Of course.

A.G.: I'll take back the prayer-book from you.

EMILY: I hadn't accepted it.

A.G.: No, but – well, I'll take it back. I suppose the memory of her has obsessed me. But there was no one else. You do understand that, don't you? No one. But now – Nicholas. He says he will find me interests to occupy my mind.

EMILY: Good.

A.G.: I have spoken to you about my child.

EMILY: What?

A.G.: The unborn.

EMILY: Oh, yes.

A.G.: May I – ? (*He stops.*)

EMILY: You may do anything you wish so long as you don't make a fuss about it.

A.G.: Nicholas says I can see more of him and he wants me to drive him out in my car. (*To PATIENCE.*) You too, of course, my dear.

EMILY: That's good.

A.G.: Yes, I think it will be good for both of us. You see, Emily, Nicholas' assurance of friendship gives me a future. It is good, isn't it? Forgive me, Emily.

EMILY: Yes, I'm sure it will be very good for you.

A.G.: So, you see, that letter and all the fuss was a joke. (*He pauses.*) A cruel joke. (*He laughs.*) Of course, I had a pretty good idea who sent it. I mean the paper was –

PATIENCE: You have never told me about your wife.

A.G.: (*Unsurely.*) Haven't I?

PATIENCE: Will you?

A.G.: Perhaps: some time. Nicholas says the memory is unhealthy. He says I should not speak or write of her.

She's dead, he says; there must be no more about her. Even the memoirs I am writing – Nicholas says I must put, 'At this time I was married' – 'In this month my wife died'. That is all.

(*NICHOLAS and PETER have entered, unseen by A.G.*)

It won't be easy. I had already written much about her – a pity I have to destroy it. Her name was Helen. (*He moves to PATIENCE, speaking to her.*) She was about your height – her hair was fair though – she had a scar on her arm, just there – (*He touches PATIENCE's left arm.*) – an accident when she was a child playing in the gardens. (*He pauses.*) That dress you are wearing – is it fancy dress?

PATIENCE: It's one of Emily's old frocks. A present from her to me.

A.G.: That explains it. (*He touches the dress.*) Grey silk. That would have been a fine dress to Helen. She loved – She died, you know. She was killed at a circus by falling from – (*PETER has moved to A.G. and now puts an arm around A.G.'s shoulders. A.G. turns to see the two men.*)

Hullo, Nicholas. You were wrong. Here's someone (*He laughs and indicates PATIENCE.*) – who has never heard my stories about Helen.

NICHOLAS: Now, I've warned you. If you keep on about it I've warned you what will happen.

PETER: One of these days, now our curse is upon you, you'll open your mouth, say, 'Helen', and – Puff! – you'll disappear.

A.G.: (*Laughing immoderately.*) Yes, Peter.

NICHOLAS: What have we got for supper?

EMILY: There's some cold meat and salad.

NICHOLAS: Will that suit you, A.G.?

A.G.: Anything will do. I'm not very hungry.

(*PETER still has his arm around A.G.'s shoulders and he is whispering: A.G. giggles.*)

NICHOLAS: I met Gerald Hussey in the town.

EMILY: Oh?

NICHOLAS: He was with some girl. He's just got back from India.

EMILY: It must be years since you saw him.

NICHOLAS: Yes. When we were at school.

(*There is renewed giggling from A.G. NICHOLAS laughs.*) Shut up, you two! Ah! I feel pleasantly tired. I haven't walked so far for a long time. (*He yawns.*) Delightfully tired – and no pains.

PETER: Does your leg ever hurt you?

NICHOLAS: The actual leg, no –

PETER: I –

NICHOLAS: – but I am easily tired. Where is my darling wife? (*He speaks without irony.*)

EMILY: Patience!

NICHOLAS: Come here.

(*PATIENCE moves to him.*)

And what have you been doing since I've been away? (*To EMILY.*) Has she behaved herself?

EMILY: Oh, yes.

NICHOLAS: Have you been talking about me? Has Emily been telling you what a beautiful baby I was – with two fat legs? Did she say I was noisy or quiet? Naughty or good? Did she tell you I was in love with Caddy Jellyby? Well, I wasn't. Nor was the diary I kept –

A.G.: Would you like a game of cards? We could play bridge.

NICHOLAS: Me?

A.G.: Yes.

NICHOLAS: I don't want to play. Emily?

EMILY: No.

NICHOLAS: Peter?

PETER: No.

NICHOLAS: No, A.G. We don't want to play bridge.

A.G.: I don't mind.

NICHOLAS: (*To PATIENCE.*) Those were the things you wanted to know, weren't they?

A.G.: I only thought it would be something to pass the time.

NICHOLAS: Don't mutter, A.G. (*To PATIENCE.*) Caddy Jellyby was –

A.G.: But, of course, we can talk about anything now, can't we? (*He laughs.*) Except one subject.

NICHOLAS: That's right.

(*PETER is turning out the contents of his pockets on to the desk.*)

A.G.: I've told Emily.

NICHOLAS: What? (*To PETER.*) Looking for something?

PETER: Yes. An address.

A.G.: (*Laughs.*) Going to write another letter, Peter?

PETER: That's right.

A.G.: (*To NICHOLAS.*) I told Emily about – the things you said – about my wife – (*He stops.*)

NICHOLAS: And – ?

A.G.: She understands and she has forgiven me.

NICHOLAS: Emily?

A.G.: Yes. You remember you told me to ask her forgiveness?

NICHOLAS: Did I?

A.G.: Yes. Don't you remember?

NICHOLAS: I expect I did. (*He yawns again.*)

A.G.: But surely! You made a great point –

NICHOLAS: Yes, yes, A.G.; that's all right. We'll go out together. You can take me out in your car.

A.G.: I will, yes.

NICHOLAS: There are many places I should like to see again that – I can't walk to them now but you will take me in your car. To the places I want to see again. Farthingale Hill –

A.G.: Yes, Nicholas, we arranged all that.

NICHOLAS: Did we?

A.G.: (*In sudden fear.*) You haven't had too much to drink, have you?

NICHOLAS: No.

A.G.: We arranged all those things. Don't you remember?

(*NICHOLAS nods.*)

I said – You remember I said I admired you?

PETER: Yes. We remember everything you said.

NICHOLAS: (*He is sitting, his eyes closed.*) I'd like my supper.

EMILY: I'll get it.

NICHOLAS: No. Later.

EMILY: Very well.

NICHOLAS: Later. You're staying, A.G.?

A.G.: Well, yes. You asked me to and I said yes.

NICHOLAS: Of course.

(*There is silence. PETER is sitting at the desk writing a note. Suddenly A.G. begins to chatter.*)

A.G.: Farthingale Hill. I haven't been there myself for some time. A famous local beauty spot, Peter. Perhaps you've heard of it? When the rhododendrons that cover the south side are in bloom it's a picture. I didn't see them this summer. As I say I haven't been there for – oh, I don't know – it must be eighteen months. One doesn't, you know.

NICHOLAS: Well, you shall go there again with me.

A.G.: Thank you, Nicholas.

NICHOLAS: Not at all. Thank you, A.G.

A.G.: You can have the car –

NICHOLAS: What?

A.G.: You can have the car without me if you like. I mean, I won't come unless you want me.

NICHOLAS: No, you must come and drive. That's part of the agreement.

A.G.: Say you want me to come with you.

NICHOLAS: I do want you to come with me.

A.G.: I've never understood why you've not borrowed my car before. I've offered it several times. It was Emily who accepted it for your honeymoon. I thought you'd like it then because – well, it's better than going by train, eh?

NICHOLAS: Much better. It was very kind and generous of you to think of it, A.G. You're a very kind person and your generosity is alarming – as alarming as your exaggerated pathos. But I forgive you: Emily forgives you: we all forgive you. Don't worry. We are going to find common interests and exploit them. You know, I've found you suddenly, much as I found Peter here. We're going to be friends, A.G., friends! Think of that!

A.G.: What is it?

NICHOLAS: What? } *Together.*<br>PETER: You can't hope to – }

PATIENCE: (*To A.G.*) Don't!

A.G.: Just a moment, my dear. (*To NICHOLAS.*) What is it?

NICHOLAS: What is what?

PATIENCE: Look here!

A.G.: Ssh!

PETER: What's the matter, A.G.? (*There is a pause.*)

A.G.: There's nothing the matter with me.

PETER: Well, why did you suddenly shout out like that?

A.G.: I'm sorry. I thought you were making a fool of me again. You're not, are you?

PETER: No.

A.G.: I'm speaking to Nicholas. I don't mean the remarks about my kindness and exaggerated pathos – that's a joke, isn't it? I mean, I see that but – you're not making a fool of me again?

PATIENCE: (*To A.G.*) Listen to me!

NICHOLAS: I have a proposal to make.

PATIENCE: Don't listen to him. Go home now. Go home.

NICHOLAS: Peter. (*He turns to PETER who is still seated at the desk.*)

PETER: Yes?

PATIENCE: (*To A.G.*) I'll walk home with you. Come along.

A.G.: I don't want to go home.

NICHOLAS: No, of course he doesn't want to go home.

A.G.: Really I don't, Nicholas. I don't.

NICHOLAS: Of course not. (*To PATIENCE.*) Leave him alone, you silly girl. (*To EMILY.*) Send her to bed.

PATIENCE: No.

(*EMILY moves towards her.*)

No!

(*EMILY stops: there is silence.*

*PATIENCE and A.G. are standing together staring at NICHOLAS. NICHOLAS taps twice on the floor with his stick and then extends the handle towards A.G. who takes it. By this means NICHOLAS guides A.G. to a chair where A.G. sits.*)

NICHOLAS: Don't get excited. Nothing to get excited about. (*PETER comes from the desk carrying the note he has written sealed in an envelope.*)

PETER: You said you had a proposal to make.

NICHOLAS: Yes.

PETER: I can only make a suggestion.

NICHOLAS: Well?

PETER: 'That passion may not harm us, let us act as if we had only eight hours to live.'

NICHOLAS: And how do you do to you. (*He laughs.*) You're old, you know, really quite old.

PETER: Ah! You've mistaken the meaning. (*To PATIENCE.*) Hasn't he?

NICHOLAS: I've told you I'm not very bright at times.

PETER: I shan't tell you the qualification of the suggestion. I'm afraid it would be useless.

NICHOLAS: (*Mocking his solemnity.*) Ah, yes, indeed. Now let me see. See if I can guess. Something about a long life.

PETER: A hundred years, if I remember rightly.

NICHOLAS: Oh, a very long life.

A.G.: (*To PATIENCE.*) What are they talking about? (*To EMILY.*) Emily!

PATIENCE: They're talking about the day Nicholas will die.

A.G.: What a thing to talk about.

NICHOLAS: Yes. And this was going to be a quiet evening with your friends, wasn't it, A.G.?

A.G.: Yes.

NICHOLAS: Well, then, what else can we talk about?

PETER: I must go and post this.

NICHOLAS: The post will have gone.

PETER: Never mind. The box is outside the house, isn't it? I noticed –

NICHOLAS: That's right.

PATIENCE: I'll take it for you.

PETER: No, it's all right.

NICHOLAS: Well, now. What shall we talk about?

PATIENCE: (*To A.G.*) Tell me about your wife.

NICHOLAS: Shall we talk about Emily and Peter many years ago? You don't know about that, A.G. (*He pauses.*) No? What about Patience and myself in the present? (*He pauses.*) No? Come on, what shall we talk about? Sit down, Peter.

PETER: I'm going out.

NICHOLAS: Let Emily read some poetry to us. (*He picks up the book of verse and snaps it shut.*) Not that? (*He pauses.*) Well, come along. Let's have some other suggestions Peter? (*PETER shakes his head.*)

Let's talk about the things A.G. and myself are going to do together.

A.G.: Yes.

PATIENCE: Tell me about your wife.

(*There is a pause.*)

NICHOLAS: Very well. Go on. Tell her. You may as well. (*A.G. is silent.*)

Well? (*He suddenly appears furiously angry.*) Well? How do you begin? Don't sit there like a mute. She is waiting to hear your story. That's what you want to talk about, isn't it? Very well, then, let's have it. How will you begin it? 'Once upon a time – Once upon a time – '. Say it! 'Once upon a time – '

PETER: 'Once upon a time – '

A.G.: 'Once upon a time – '

NICHOLAS: ' – twenty years ago – '

A.G.: ' – twenty years ago – '

NICHOLAS: ' – when I was young and handsome. When I was – '

A.G.: ' – when I was young and handsome.'

NICHOLAS: ' – I was married to a girl named Helen.' Come along, old man. Her name was Helen. Remember?

A.G.: ' – I was married to a girl named Helen.' (*He speaks to PATIENCE.*) Helen Dyson before I married her. Helen –

NICHOLAS: Yes?

A.G.: Helen was ten years younger than me. At the time of which I speak I was forty and we had been married for three years. I had known her for eight years before our marriage. She worked as a cashier in one of our shops. When she came to work for us my father was still alive – we were grocers, you know – and my brother and myself held only minor positions. But in the year my father died – (*NICHOLAS turns to PETER who is still holding the letter. NICHOLAS takes the letter and says,* 'I'll take that.' *PETER says,* 'Very well.' *They smile at each other. NICHOLAS goes out. A.G. continues uninterrupted.*)

I took sole charge of the shops and Helen and I were married. She left the shop then, of course. (*He pauses.*) She was a pretty girl but shy, very shy. (*He smiles.*) Are you shy? We were married for three years. We were happy – lived very quietly – not in this town where she was born but near Bristol – my shops were round there. Very happily, very quietly we lived and we wanted children. Do you want children? Yes, we'd have liked a baby very much but it was then we found we couldn't have one. After being married three years Helen was examined and that's what they told us. No children. You understand how disappointed we were? Helen was very distressed and insisted that she had failed me. That was not so, of course, but she said to me many times, 'I have failed you.'

(*He pauses.*) She died, you know. She died at a circus performance in Spain. A circus with Mr Bembo here as a star performer. Yes, she died. It was very tragic. I'll tell you about it. (*He edges forward on his chair.*) We had travelled to Spain, you see, on a holiday. After the third week of the holiday we came to a town one night and we saw the advertisements for the circus. Mr Bembo's name was in large letters – he was famous then. Helen was very fond of the circus. Are you?

PATIENCE: I've never been to one.

A.G.: Haven't you? Anyway, Helen was very fond of them and that night before going to sleep she said to me, 'Will you take me to the circus tomorrow?' Of course, I did, and the following evening we went to the performance. Now I want you to understand this quite clearly. The stands – set around the ring, you know – those stands had a fault in their construction. I have spoken to Mr Bembo about this. Helen and I were forced – we were late – to sit high in the back row of the stand. We were, I think, quite thirty feet from the ground. I've spoken to Mr Bembo about this also but he says he can't remember. But I should say we were quite thirty feet up from the ground. We had taken our places and Mr Bembo had begun his turn. You must get him to tell you about it some time. I suppose it was very funny. There was a child who came from the audience – to hold a paper hoop – Mr Bembo jumped through the hoop and then there was the laughter: and then Helen turned to me and complained of illness.

(*At this point PETER begins to speak with A.G. He speaks to PATIENCE.*)

Her face was puckered and I thought she was going to cry. I took her hand to lead her away from the place but we could only go singly on the narrow platform. That is why I say to you the stands were badly constructed. You see, she let go my hand and went on before me, alone. Then she fell.

(*PETER's voice accompanying this last passage has become louder. A.G. stops speaking.*)

PETER: He turned to her and, indeed, she seemed ill. He was alarmed. Taking her hand he attempted to lead her away but the way of exit was narrow and it was only possible to go singly. He insists the stands were faulty but I can assure you it was the normal method of construction. She went on alone and then fell. She fell outwards away from A.G. and the other spectators.

(*When A.G. stops speaking PETER pauses and then continues to speak to PATIENCE saying*:)

As A.G. has told you it was very tragic – she was spared nothing for her fall was not direct. No, for the strap of her shoe caught, by some chance, in the structure and she hung, head downwards, her skirts about her head, while A.G. here stood in understandable indecision. You mustn't laugh! You mustn't!

(*PATIENCE shakes her head. She is not laughing.*)

No! (*To A.G.*) She is young. She doesn't understand. (*To PATIENCE.*) The shoe-strap broke and she fell to the ground. She was dead when the soldiers – it was soldiers?

A.G.: Yes.

PETER: – when the soldiers picked her up and A.G. had climbed down to reach her. (*He pauses.*) I was present at that time but I was in ignorance. I was not told of the incident until I met A.G. Now I know. Now all of us here know. I believe today is her birthday?

A.G.: Yes.

PETER: Many happy returns of the day.

EMILY: Where's Nicholas?

PETER: He went out to post a letter for me. (*He again speaks to PATIENCE.*) Which of the many reasons that A.G. has given us made her do such a dreadful thing – that I don't know.

A.G. : Do what?

PETER: Her reasons for –

A.G.: Do what?

PETER: Why, kill herself.

A.G.: It was an accident.

PETER: What's that you say?

A.G.: I say it was an accident.

PETER: Your wife's death?

A.G.: Yes.

PETER: Then you have misled us.

A.G.: No!

PETER: You have always led us to believe your wife was a suicide.

A.G.: Never!

PETER: Oh, yes.

A.G.: No!

PETER: Oh, yes.

A.G.: No!

PETER: But you have implied, if not stated, so many reasons.

A.G.: Not one!

PETER: One: that she was to remain childless. Two: that she regarded herself as a failure in marriage. Three: that she couldn't live with your kindly reproach. Four: that she was afraid to return to England and a life of boredom with you among the sugar and spices. Five: that she was unbearably moved by the sight of the child coming bravely to me from the audience. Six: that my performance that day was so bad that the poor lady went straight off and did away with herself. Which of these reasons was the actual cause I say I don't know. But you've not only given us reasons – there are the various incidents. Her shoe catching and her hanging head downwards: to give her time for the full realization of the act, do you think? The business of love-making on the preceding night: what other motive had you in telling us that, eh? And other things – many other things. For instance –

A.G.: But I didn't mean that.

PETER: Whether you meant it or not –

A.G.: How could you believe such a thing?

PETER: (*He follows NICHOLAS in an appearance of great anger.*) Because we thought it was what you intended us to believe. Our sympathies have been for you because we believed that. Do you mean to say that you didn't know she killed herself? (*He pauses.*) Answer me. Do you really think it was an accident? If so why have you done this to us? We've done you no harm. But you have infected us.

A.G.: But it's not true! What you say is not true!

PETER: We believed you. All of us. (*He appeals to EMILY and PATIENCE.*) Didn't we? We believed him. Do you want further proof? From the person who believed in you most fully? (*He goes to the door and, opening it, calls.*) Nicholas! Nicholas! (*He turns back to A.G.*) Would you like to go and try to find him? No, you wouldn't, would you? Now you're afraid, aren't you? Now you're afraid.

A.G.: Yes!

PETER: Nicholas! Nicholas! (*He goes out of the room and can be heard calling NICHOLAS's name through the house. Then there is silence.*)

EMILY: I don't want to hear again about your wife. Never.

PATIENCE: What is keeping Nicholas? Emily, come here quickly.

(*Exit. PETER returns. He stands in the open doorway.*)

PETER: He's dead or dying.

(*PETER, who is carrying NICHOLAS's stick, stands staring at A.G. A.G. falls forward on to his hands and knees and begins to crawl across the room. PETER comes into the room.*)

PETER: Vile: treacherous: insensate fellow. Evil: unkind: monstrous toad. (*He pushes A.G. with the stick. A.G. rolls over. There is a disturbance from the room upstairs: no voices are heard. PETER goes out leaving A.G. lying on the floor. After a few moments A.G. gets to his feet. For some time he stands apparently trying to rub some stain from the knee of his trousers with his bare hand. Then he goes to the door and switches off the lights. He goes out. In the lit hallway he can be seen putting on his hat and coat. When he is dressed he turns to look up the stairs. He calls. After a pause NICHOLAS's voice is heard to call distinctly.*)

NICHOLAS: Goodnight, A.G., my dear.

A.G.: Goodnight. (*He leaves the house: the front door is heard to close, PETER and NICHOLAS enter. PETER switches on the lights of the room and together he and NICHOLAS go to the window. NICHOLAS pulls aside the curtains and looks into the street.*)

NICHOLAS: There he goes. (*He raps loudly on the window with his stick. Then he and PETER stand in silence watching A.G. returning to his home. EMILY and PATIENCE come into the room together. NICHOLAS releases the curtains and the two men turn back into the room. They suddenly laugh together.*)

PATIENCE: I knew it was a joke. (*She goes to NICHOLAS. She is laughing.*) I knew it was a joke. When Emily told me I said it was a joke. I didn't believe a word of it.

NICHOLAS: Clever girl.

PATIENCE: (*She goes to EMILY.*) How foolish – how foolish of you not to see the joke. When you told me I could have laughed. Really, I could have laughed out loud. What shall we do tomorrow?

(*NICHOLAS shakes his head.*)

PETER: I really thought that's how you would employ your time.

NICHOLAS: I was listening to you.

PETER: You really must grow up.

(*They laugh.*)

I'll go and post it now. It's quite important.

(*PETER goes out.*)

NICHOLAS: (*Calls after him.*) But I tell you the post's gone.

PATIENCE: (*She has been dancing about the room.*) Of course I knew it was a joke.

NICHOLAS: I suppose you must have done.

PATIENCE: (*She has picked up the toy bear.*) May I keep this, now?

NICHOLAS: No, Patience.

PATIENCE: Oh, very well. (*She throws it down. NICHOLAS picks it up.*)

NICHOLAS: What about some supper? (*He looks about the room.*) A.G. seems to have gone home.

(*EMILY begins to move to the door.*)

I'll get it. (*To PATIENCE.*) Come with me.

(*NICHOLAS and PATIENCE go out. EMILY picks up the reading lamp and puts it away. She then pulls out into the room a small table on which to set the supper tray. PETER is coming back into the room.*)

*CURTAIN*

# SAINT'S DAY

# Introduction to SAINT'S DAY

Written in 1947-9, *Saint's Day* was originally intended as a technical exercise, but it is a complex piece of writing, loaded with symbolism that invites interpretation. What matters most, though, is the theatrical experience. The action, the dialogue and the visual imagery produce a series of powerful theatrical effects which all have meaning, even when the disorientation of the characters spreads to the audience, but the play means only what it is in performance.

Paul Southman is the first in a line of uncompromising heroes who prefer death to dishonesty. Later examples will be the general Rupert Forster in *Marching Song*, and the priest, Urbain Grandier, in *The Devils*. Concerned with the individual who rises higher than the rest of humanity, Whiting questions whether he becomes less human in the process. Forster's tragedy is that he does, and finds out too late. The priest cannot fulfil himself as a man, while Paul has exiled himself from humanity in retreating from society.

It soon becomes apparent that Whiting is distancing himself from the conventions of the West End play more wholeheartedly and more creatively than he did in *No More A-Roving* and *Conditions of Agreement.* The popular playwrights of the period, such as Noël Coward, Terence Rattigan, J.B. Priestley and J.M. Bridie, were not above establishing a situation by making characters tell each other what they already knew. The servant in *Saint's Day*, John Winter, is as dissimilar as Willy Yeats in *No More A-Roving* to the butlers and maids who so often supplied information to the audience by holding conversations about goings-on in the household. Whiting knew it was politer to let the audience be temporarily confused than to brief it in an unsubtle way.

But we soon gather that Paul's daughter, Stella, has followed him into exile, and that his relations with the village are symptomatic of his relations with society. Her husband, Charles, an artist, has also cut himself off from society, and, thinking he does not need an audience, he does not share Stella's determination to rehabilitate her father.

As in Beckett's *Waiting for Godot*, which was being written at about the same time, much of the dialogue consists of very short lines, which makes it sound more colloquial than it is. As in *Conditions of Agreement*, the long monologues stand out in clear relief. None of them is written in verse, but the prose verges on the poetic, while there are many hints that we are being pushed towards an area of experience remote from the banalities of everyday life.

Paul is obviously the saint of the title, and the day of the action – 25 January – is the accepted anniversary of St Paul's conversion. The conversion of Robert Procathren, the fashionable young man of letters who arrives with the intention of escorting Paul to a celebratory banquet in London, carries him in the opposite direction from that taken by Saul of Tarsus when he became Paul. Robert loses his faith in Man, while Paul Southman – at least to some extent – regains his. Though hardly a saint, he is not an ordinary man. As in *Marching Song* and *The Devils*, the word "man" recurs frequently, while references to the lowest common multiples of humanity create a perspective for Paul's superiority to his fellow-men, though he is old and frail and frightened. His death will be a kind of martyrdom.

Robert's conversion is hard for the audience to understand intellectually. A priggishly polite young man suddenly becomes rude and ruthlessly destructive. But it is theatrically acceptable after a series of strange and catastrophic events that have sent the play orbiting away from naturalism. After Stella, who is pregnant, appeals for Robert's help in rehabilitating Paul, his ungenerous reaction makes us feel that if he is representative of the literary world, we sympathise with Paul's rejection of it. He and Charles make fun of Robert for not having fought in the war and for being unfamiliar with firearms. When the pistol goes off in his hands, the bullet passes through the closed door and kills Stella.

Before the men find that she is dead, a trumpet call is heard from outside, and Paul, whose sanity is now precarious, makes the mistake of thinking that the soldiers will be his allies in a war against the villagers. They are marauding deserters, but there is no naturalistic motivation for the violence that will give the play its climax. The forces of chaos are taking over, and Robert's grotesque alliance with the soldiers begins when he asks them not to go.

But in the third act, the play begins to lose its coherence and its force. The style of the writing shifts as the parody element gains the upper hand, and Whiting moves from Eliot to his Greek sources. The conventional messenger is replaced by the village postman, who has a long narrative speech, while a chorus of four village women and a child remain onstage throughout the act. The main action has now shifted to the village, where the soldiers are obeying Robert's destructive orders, but we get only second-hand accounts of what is going on. Blooded, like an animal, by his experience of killing, he is taking a savage revenge against the social order to which he had always conformed.

Paul has withdrawn into madness and the other principal characters are no longer in focus. Stella is dead and Robert, though he has taken over the initiative, does not reappear until the play is almost over. When, following his instructions, the soldiers take Paul out to be hanged in the garden, we are not unmoved, but not as moved as we would be if the build-up to the final catastrophe had been better.

One of the main problems we have to face is that Whiting, especially in the third act, was importing into the play a lot of material he had used already, either in his novel or in his stories. The novel contains a reference to old Paul, "a local celebrity who was hung for his lampoons". In 1946, Whiting wrote a radio play called *Paul Southman: An Appreciation for Broadcasting*. This has not been published, but it is described in Eric Salmon's book *The Dark Journey*. (See Bibliography.) Like the Paul of the stage play, the Paul of the radio play has made himself unpopular by writing a scurrilous pamphlet titled *The Abolition of Printing*, and there are several offstage characters common to both plays, including the printer, John Ussleigh, and another man, Andrew Vince, who are cited when Paul ironically describes how he was arraigned for assaulting "the well known and much-loved whore Society".

The conversion of Procathren may also derive partially (and unsatisfactorily) from a change of heart described in the novel. The main character, Timothy Crashaw, who wants to make a gesture against life, recalls the fear he felt after a childhood fall. "I looked up at the sky and was overcome with unreasoning terror... All acts of violence were inexplicable to me... Revenge, premeditated revenge of the bloodiest kind was the answer!" Another character accuses Timothy of "falling in love with death".

Whiting also incorporated into *Saint's Day* motifs that had been important to him. He wrote in a notebook: "If we are normal human beings, we live surrounded by terrors, clowns, dead loves and old fears, represented by, say, a painting on the wall, some reels of photographic negative, a rose garden and a call from another room. The artist, admitting their significance, naturally reaches out for them in the desperate urgency of creation." The reels of photographic negative appear in *Marching Song*, and two of these motifs are worked into *Saint's Day* – the painting on the wall, when Charles uses Stella's corpse as a model, and the call from another room, which is mentioned twice in her apprehensively prophetic monologue which I quoted in the introduction to this volume. One of the ironies is that she does not know the call will be heard within minutes, and the body will be hers.

# Characters

STELLA HEBERDEN
Paul's grand-daughter

CHARLES HEBERDEN
her husband

PAUL SOUTHMAN
an aged poet

JOHN WINTER
his manservant

ROBERT PROCATHREN
an admirer of Paul

GILES ALDUS
a recluse

CHRISTIAN MELROSE, WALTER KILLEEN, HENRY CHATER
three soldiers

HANNAH TREWIN, MARGARET BANT, EDITH TINSON, FLORA BALDON, JUDITH WARDEN, A CHILD, THOMAS COWPER
people of the village

*Saint's Day* was first performed at the Arts Theatre, London on 5th September 1951, with the following cast:

PAUL SOUTHMAN, Michael Hordern

STELLA HEBERDEN, Valerie White

CHARLES HEBERDEN, Robert Urquhart

GILES ALDUS, Donald Pleasance

Director, Stephen Murray

The play is in three acts, and the scene is laid in a room of Paul Southman's house in England on the twenty-fifth day of January.

ACT I Morning.
ACT II Early afternoon.
ACT III Night.

# ACT ONE

*The day is the twenty-fifth day of January: it is morning. The scene is a room in PAUL SOUTHMAN's house. CHARLES and STELLA HEBERDEN are present, motionless. The woman is standing by one of the three large central windows. The source of light behind the drawn curtains of the room is an oil-lamp carried by the man.*

STELLA: Listen!

(*They stand listening to the chimes of a distant church. The chimes end.*)

CHARLES: Half-past.

STELLA: Nine?

CHARLES: Must be.

STELLA: Might be eight.

CHARLES: No.

STELLA: Surely not ten.

CHARLES: No, nine. Half-past nine. Is it raining now?

(*STELLA has moved to set the clock.*)

STELLA: It might be any time, really. No, it's not raining now.

CHARLES: It was earlier this morning. (*He yawns.*)

STELLA: The key's not on the ledge.

CHARLES: Look behind the clock. There?

STELLA: Yes. There wasn't –

CHARLES: It slips down. Can you get it?

STELLA: Yes. There wasn't any trouble in the night, was there?

CHARLES: No. (*STELLA begins to wind and set the clock.*) How long have you been up?

STELLA: Twenty minutes or so.

CHARLES: I didn't hear you.

STELLA: You were asleep. I shan't wind the strike.

CHARLES: No, don't. It's wrong, anyway. (*He calls.*) John Winter! John Winter! (*To STELLA.*) Where is he?

STELLA: I don't know. I haven't seen him this morning.

CHARLES: John Winter! (*CHARLES, wearing a woollen dressing-gown over his shirt – he is without trousers – stands on one leg chafing a bare foot between his hands. He is below a narrow stairway, set within a wall, leading to an upper floor.*) I'm cold.

STELLA: Go and dress.

CHARLES: John Winter!

STELLA: If he could hear you he would've come by now.

CHARLES: He's up, I suppose.

STELLA: Now, Charles – don't shout again.

CHARLES: What?

STELLA: We don't want Paul to wake early. He's going to have a tiring day.

CHARLES: He's already awake. I heard him moving. (*He has opened the only door of the room and calls down the stairs to the kitchen,* 'John Winter!') I heard him moving in his room as I came down. (*From his room above the narrow stairway PAUL SOUTHMAN calls,* 'John Winter!') There he is.

STELLA: Damn! I wanted him to sleep as late as possible this morning, Go up and –

CHARLES: Get John Winter to make a fire when he comes in.

STELLA: All right. Go up and try to persuade Paul to go back to bed for an hour.

CHARLES: He won't.

STELLA: Try to persuade him. I'm worried – (*PAUL SOUTHMAN calls again*: 'John Winter!') All right, Grandpa! (*To CHARLES.*) I'm worried as to whether the journey will tire him. I hope to God they don't give him anything to drink when he gets there. I'm sending John Winter with him – don't you think that's a good idea?

CHARLES: Yes. (*He is at the window drawing aside the curtains.*) It's going to be a fine day.

STELLA: Go up to him, will you, Charles. I don't want him to shout again or he'll start coughing.

CHARLES: All right. (*He takes up a man's bicycle which is lying in the centre of the room and props it against the wall.*) How are you this morning?

STELLA: All right now.

CHARLES: Sickness gone off?

STELLA: Yes. Yes, it goes when I've had a cup of tea and a biscuit.

CHARLES: Have you made some tea already?

STELLA: Yes.

CHARLES: Where is it?

STELLA: In our room. (*CHARLES goes towards the stairs.*) Didn't you see it?

CHARLES: No.

STELLA: Leave the lamp.

CHARLES: Sorry. (*As he goes up the stairs PAUL SOUTHMAN calls again*: 'John Winter!') I'm coming.

PAUL: I want John Winter, not you. I want dressing.

(*CHARLES goes up the stairs. STELLA clears some dirty plates and cups from a central table and puts them on an ornate but filthy tray. She picks up a bicycle pump from the floor and fixes it into place on the bicycle. Going to the windows she draws back the curtains. The room is large: the building of the year 1775. There are three windows opening on to an iron balcony – entrance to the room can be gained by any of these windows. The balcony has iron steps leading down to the garden. There are two other entrances to the room: one, a door opening on to a small landing above stairs which lead to the kitchens and also to the main door of the house – two, a narrow stairway leading to the upper floors. This gives the room an elevation of being above the ground floor and yet below the main first floor. It stands alone, an architectural freak having no ceiling but a roof directly above it. There is an empty fireplace. The furnishing of the room is minimum for habitation: a table, and about it four chairs – two chairs and a low bench before the fireplace. The furnishings together with the various utilitarian objects about the room – the silver tray, the cups and dishes on the table – are of excellent quality but have lost their grace by neglect and misuse. Several hundred books are piled on the floor in a corner of the room. From the right window the wall of the room is curved and on the plaster surface of the wall is an unfinished painting. This painting represents five human figures and a dog – greater than life-size – grouped about an, as yet, unspecified sixth person. Executed in oils, it is harsh in texture, garish in colour. Below the picture stands a small scaffolding with painter's materials: there is also a ladder. The floor of this part of the room before the painting is raised six inches by means of a half-circular rostrum. The curtains withdrawn, STELLA puts out the lamp. It is light and promises to be a fine clear day. The front door is heard to open and close; footsteps sound on the uncarpeted stairs from below. JOHN WINTER enters.*)

STELLA: Good morning, John Winter.

WINTER: Good morning, Miss Stella.

STELLA: You've been out already.

WINTER: Yes.

STELLA: Where?

WINTER: To get stuff for the fire.

STELLA: Surely you keep that in the cellar.

WINTER: You may remember –

STELLA: What? Speak up.

WINTER: I say you may remember I moved it some days ago. I moved it from the cellar to my shed because of the damp – it's mostly wood.

STELLA: I didn't know you'd moved it.

WINTER: Mr Charles will remember. He helped me.

STELLA: Anyway, you've got the stuff for the fire.

WINTER: I've left it at the door. I didn't want to bring it in until the room –

STELLA: Very well.

WINTER: – until the room had been tidied. I've already cleaned the grate.

STELLA: You look frozen.

WINTER: It's very cold out of doors.

STELLA: Well, don't stand there! Grandpa – Mr Southman has been shouting for you. My husband has gone up to him.

WINTER: Should I light the fire first or go up and dress Mr Southman?

STELLA: I don't know. I – (*They stand silent for a moment.*) Oh, go and dress him but try to keep him in his room for a while. I want him to rest this morning. Just a minute! I want to talk to you. This man who is coming to visit us today –

WINTER: Mr Procathren.

STELLA: You know about him?

WINTER: Mr Southman mentioned him to me yesterday.

STELLA: You know today is Mr Southman's birthday?

WINTER: Yes.

STELLA: In fact, you know all about it.

WINTER: That is all I know – that this gentleman is arriving on Mr Southman's birthday. I think I should go up now. (*He looks towards the stairs.*)

STELLA: Wait a minute! You may as well know it all. This Mr Procathren – Robert Procathren – is a famous poet and critic. He is coming here to do honour to my grandfather on his birthday – honour as a poet. Late this afternoon Mr Procathren, Mr Southman and you will drive to London by car. You will go with them, do you understand? You will go with them to London.

WINTER: Yes.

STELLA: Those are the arrangements.

WINTER: Very well.

STELLA: There is to be a dinner in London tonight – Are you listening to me?

WINTER: Yes.

STELLA: You are not! Please pay attention. There is to be a dinner tonight in London in honour of Mr Southman. It will be attended by very famous men and women. You will go with Mr Southman. You won't go in to the dinner, of course, but wait outside. You will stay the night in London and be driven back tomorrow. Have you any better clothes than those?

WINTER: I have a blue suit.

STELLA: Wear it. One more thing – I shall cook the meal today. What food have we got? (*WINTER is silent.*) Have you any food at all in the house?

WINTER: There's some bacon and vegetables.

STELLA: We shall want some meat and something for – is there any fruit? – is there anything? And coffee – is there any coffee?

WINTER: No.

STELLA: Then you had better go down to the village this morning – early – and get these things. Do you understand?

WINTER: Yes.

STELLA: Go as soon as Mr Southman has finished with you.

WINTER: I shall need money.

STELLA: Here you are. (*She takes a ten-shilling note from her pocket and gives it to JOHN WINTER.*) That's all right, then? (*JOHN WINTER does not reply.*) Don't be so sullen, John Winter! You may be the servant but you know the position as to money as well as I do. We cannot pay those bills in the village at present – but we will in time. Promise them that. You can tell them – promise them – you – because they respect you down in the village – yes, they respect you.

WINTER: They hate me.

STELLA: Nonsense.

WINTER: Truth.

STELLA: Hate you?

WINTER: Of course – why not? – despise me – hate me, they do. I say, why not? A beggar – I have to go to them – a little food – say, a little meat – a little bread – later – a little more bread – a little more meat – Please!

STELLA: John Winter!

WINTER: One day they'll stop – or I'll stop – and then what will happen?

STELLA: Are you threatening me? (*He is silent.*) I say, are you threatening me? (*He shakes his head.*) Come now, you wouldn't like to see Mr Southman or his guest go without food, would you? Would you? No, of course, you wouldn't, because you love him as I love him, and we'll fight for him, won't we? We'll put our pride in our pocket and we'll fight for him. We've got to look after him, you know. There's no one else. Just you and me, that's all. Now, go along. (*CHARLES comes down the stairs: he is dressed and carries a cup of tea.*) John Winter. (*STELLA goes to JOHN WINTER and puts her arms about him.*) John Winter, I want you to go with my grandfather today – go with him to London – because I trust you. Remember, he will be among strangers – all his friends have gone – and he may be frightened. And if he is afraid he will appear ridiculous. I want you to see that he is not frightened – that by his age he is great and not ridiculous. That he is Paul Southman.

WINTER: He is a great and famous man.

STELLA: Of course he is. And today we have an opportunity to remind the world of that. Now, go up and get him dressed, but try to keep him in his room.

WINTER: I've put out his best clothes.

STELLA: He's waiting for you.

CHARLES: He's sitting on his bed cleaning a pistol. You'd better be careful, John Winter.

(*JOHN WINTER laughs and goes up the stairs.*)

STELLA: I told you I'm sending John Winter up to London with Paul, didn't I?

CHARLES: Yes. Are you going to light a fire?

STELLA: Later.

CHARLES: I'm so cold.

(*STELLA fetches an oil-stove from a corner of the room. She lights it.*)

STELLA: Sit over this.

CHARLES: Look! (*He points to the ornate pediment over the door.*)

STELLA: What?

CHARLES: There's a bird – above the door. It's hiding there – behind the scroll.

STELLA: They fly in sometimes. They don't come to any harm.

CHARLES: What was all that just now?

STELLA: When?

CHARLES: With John Winter.

STELLA: Oh, a minor revolt – over getting food from the village. He says they hate him down there. I suppose it's true. They hate us all. Is that stove alight?

CHARLES: Yes.

STELLA: They hate us because they don't understand our isolation. They don't understand us and so they fear us. They fear us and so they hate us.

CHARLES: But only passively. They –

STELLA: Not at all. Do you know that three years ago – before you came here – there was a plan among the villagers to attack this house. Everything was arranged, but on the decided night they sat drinking to get up their courage and when the time came they were all too drunk to walk the half-mile to the house. So the attack didn't come off that time. It may some day.

CHARLES: What would they do?

STELLA: Paul says they'd kill us.

CHARLES: It must be hard for John Winter. He has to go down among them – we don't.

STELLA: Well, I've given him some money this morning so he'll be all right.

CHARLES: By the way, I've got this. (*He takes some coins from his pocket.*) You'd better have it.

STELLA: Thank you.

CHARLES: Do you think John Winter could do something for me in London?

STELLA: What?

CHARLES: If he has time.

STELLA: Well, what?

CHARLES: I've got a small canvas I think I can sell – might get ten pounds for it – if John Winter could take it round to the dealers for me tomorrow.

STELLA: Charles! Will you? Will you really try to sell it? Ten pounds would help so much.

CHARLES: It's that small oil I did of you three months ago. You don't want it?

STELLA: If you sell it we shall be able to –

CHARLES: You don't want it?

STELLA: No, I don't want it. We shall be able to –

CHARLES: Very well! (*A pause.*) Then that's settled.

STELLA: Yes. I'll tell John Winter. (*STELLA moves to CHARLES.*) I'm sorry, Charles, but we must have money. (*CHARLES moves away from her.*)

CHARLES: I know.

STELLA: If only Grandpa would begin to write again. Anything! I'm sure they'd take it. Take it on his name alone. People haven't forgotten him.

CHARLES: Of course they have.

STELLA: They haven't! If they've forgotten him why should this man Procathren be coming down today to take him to London?

CHARLES: The whole thing is probably a stunt. Listen, Stella. Who is going to be at that dinner tonight? I'll tell you. Fashionable people. Poets, painters, novelists and critics à la mode. The kind of people who, twenty-five years ago when Paul wrote his pamphlet 'The Abolition of Printing', turned against him and drove him into this exile and silence. Those are the people who will be receiving him, applauding him tonight. (*There is a pause.*) I don't think you understand, Stella. We've had all this so often before. Why can't you leave the old man alone? For him to attempt to begin again – No, I don't think you could understand.

STELLA: Of course I understand.

CHARLES: Let me put it this way. Go to London today and ask a hundred people who know of Paul – ask them about him – and ninety-nine of them will say he died years ago. I tell you even those who haven't forgotten him think he's dead. His name in a newspaper tomorrow would cause nothing but surprise. Let the few eminent people who do remember him enjoy the entertainment tonight. It won't do them or Paul any harm, but don't you build anything from it – useless and unkind.

STELLA: Charles, this is a chance we've never had before. He'll be remembered by this dinner. Now is the time for him to start writing again. We needn't bother about the physical effect on him – I can do the writing if he'll dictate. Anything! Articles, satires – any of the things that made him famous – made him Paul Southman, the pamphleteer and lampoonist, the poet and revolutionary.

CHARLES: He's eighty-three.

STELLA: I know.

CHARLES: All those things – useless – he's an old man – quite out of touch – he has no idea what has happened in the outside world in the last twenty-five years. There have been changes, you know.

STELLA: Then we'll start taking the newspapers again. I'll try to get him out, even if it's only to the village. We'll buy some new books and I'll read to him.

CHARLES: You know he can't concentrate for two minutes either reading or being read to. You know he will never go to the village. You know – you must know he's a very old man and he's finished. Finished! I'm trying to explain in such a way that you can understand. (*Pause.*) It won't work, Stella. (*Pause.*) Let him die in peace. (*Pause.*) Let him alone. (*CHARLES goes to the door.*)

STELLA: Charles, I want to speak to you. Charles! (*He stops at the door.*) I've lied to you.

CHARLES: What?

STELLA: I've lied to you.

CHARLES: What about this time? (*She does not answer.*) Come along, you know you enjoy the confession more than the lie. I suppose you're not going to have a child.

STELLA: No, it's not that. I've lied to you about my age.

CHARLES: Well?

STELLA: I told you I was twenty-eight last birthday. I was really thirty-two.

CHARLES: That makes you twelve years older than me instead of eight. All right.

STELLA: I don't –

CHARLES: Did you think four years would make so much difference?

STELLA: You look so young.

CHARLES: And who is there to see me but you?

STELLA: This morning there will be Robert Procathren. I was going to suggest that we pretend to him that you're my brother – not my husband.

CHARLES: Don't be absurd!

STELLA: Is it absurd? Well, never mind. Go and get yourself some breakfast.

CHARLES: Yes, I will. And Stella –

STELLA: Yes?

CHARLES: Don't try to get the old man back to work.

STELLA: All right. But I think it would be a good thing – not only for us, but for him.

CHARLES: (*In sudden anger.*) It would not! It would not be a good thing. It would not be a good thing for any of us. What is it you're hankering after? You want something from it. You're planning something, aren't you – aren't you?

STELLA: Don't speak to me like that! (*In silence STELLA picks up the tray and goes out of the room and down the stairs to the kitchens below. CHARLES shouts after her.*)

CHARLES: It's only that you don't understand. (*He is unanswered. He goes to the stove and warms his hands: he ties his shoe-laces: he goes to the scaffolding set below the mural painting: he examines the painter's materials set on the scaffolding. STELLA returns to the room. She begins to wipe the table with a damp cloth. CHARLES speaks.*) I've got a pain in my side. (*A pause.*) Had it last night. Worse this morning. (*STELLA does not reply.*) Here. (*He indicates the position of the pain. STELLA ignores this and CHARLES turns back to the painter's material.*) Do you think John Winter could get me some stuff in London?

STELLA: I should think so.

CHARLES: Now, what do I want? I want some –

STELLA: Write it down.

CHARLES: What time is this fellow arriving?

STELLA: No special time. Just this morning.

CHARLES: Procathren – Procathren.

STELLA: What do you say?

CHARLES: Nothing. Have you got Paul anything for his birthday?

STELLA: Yes. A pair of slippers.

CHARLES: Where are they?

STELLA: In the table drawer. Why?

CHARLES: When are you going to give them to him?

STELLA: When he comes down, I suppose.

(*CHARLES has taken a small parcel from the canvas bag hanging on the scaffolding.*)

CHARLES: Will you give him this at the same time?

STELLA: Why don't you give it to him yourself?

CHARLES: No, you. Here you are. It's a scarf – woollen scarf. Take it.

(*STELLA takes the parcel and puts it in the table drawer.*)

STELLA: Where's the pain?

CHARLES: What?

STELLA: The pain you said you had – where is it?

CHARLES: Here.

(*STELLA puts her hand to his side.*)

STELLA: Bad?

CHARLES: Rather. I may have strained myself. I fell from there – (*He indicates the scaffolding.*) – yesterday. I called out for you as I fell – you didn't hear me. Just a minute. You've got a cobweb in your hair. Stand still. (*His hands go to her head.*) No. No, it's your hair. White. Your hair is –

PAUL: They must go. I have decided – (*PAUL SOUTHMAN can be heard speaking to JOHN WINTER as they come down the stairs.*) – we could manage it between us –

CHARLES: Your hair is going white.

PAUL: You think I'm too old, but I could give you a hand.

STELLA: Charles!

PAUL: Away with them. That's what I say – careful! – then we shall have a clear view –

STELLA: Charles!

PAUL: – a clear view if anything threatens.

STELLA: I'm ugly to you, aren't I, Charles?

PAUL: (*Laughing.*) What do I mean by that, eh, John Winter?

STELLA: Charles! Speak to me. I'm ugly to you, aren't I?

PAUL: As it threatens at all times we must be prepared. (*PAUL SOUTHMAN and JOHN WINTER reach the foot of the stairs.*) Good morning.

STELLA: Good morning, Grandpa.

CHARLES: Good morning, Paul.

PAUL: What's the time?

STELLA: About a quarter to ten.

(*JOHN WINTER puts a chair beside the oil-stove. PAUL sits.*)

PAUL: Thank you. I've just been telling John Winter about an idea of mine. A precaution. I'll tell you later. I'll have some breakfast now, John Winter. (*JOHN WINTER goes out.*) Is there no fire?

STELLA: We'll have one lit in a few minutes.

PAUL: Good. It's very cold. I've been very cold in bed all night. (*He looks up at STELLA and CHARLES, smiling.*) It is today I have to play the great man, isn't it?

STELLA: Yes.

PAUL: You notice I'm dressed up?

STELLA: You look very nice.

PAUL: You understand I realize the importance of today?

STELLA: I hope you do.

PAUL: Is the weather going to be fine?

STELLA: I think so.

PAUL: The sun shining?

STELLA: I hope so.

PAUL: The flags hung out in London for me?

STELLA: (*Laughing.*) Perhaps.

PAUL: (*Laughing.*) Excellent.

STELLA: Many happy returns of the day, Grandpa. (*She gives him her present.*)

PAUL: God bless my soul!

STELLA: God bless you, indeed – pretending you didn't expect it.

PAUL: How neatly it's parcelled up – with such a tight little knot. What is it, I wonder? I am supposed to be able to open it, am I? I mean, there is something inside.

STELLA: Let me do it.

PAUL: No, no. I've done it now. (*He has undone the parcel and holds up the pair of slippers.*) For my feet?

STELLA: And this is from Charles.

(*CHARLES turns away.*)

PAUL: What is it, Charles?

(*JOHN WINTER enters carrying a cup of tea and a plate of rusks.*)

CHARLES: A scarf.

STELLA: You mustn't tell him.

CHARLES: Knitted by myself with wool from a pair of my old socks.

PAUL: Excellent! Now I shall be warm at both ends. (*He pauses in undoing the parcel.*) I hope it's not green. I don't like green things. (*He takes out the scarf: it is green.*)

STELLA: Put it on, Grandpa. You look very handsome. Doesn't he, Charles?

PAUL: Do I?

STELLA: Of course you do, darling.

(*JOHN WINTER takes a box of cigarettes from his pocket. He holds it out to PAUL.*)

PAUL: What's this?

WINTER: Birthday present, sir.

PAUL: Thank you, John Winter. I forgot your last birthday, didn't I?

WINTER: Yes, sir.

PAUL: Good of you to remember mine. Cigarettes. Have one?

WINTER: Thank you.

STELLA: Now, Grandpa, you don't want to smoke. Have your breakfast first.

PAUL: Very well. (*He begins to dip the rusks in the tea.*) Stella, John Winter and I have been discussing – Stella!

STELLA: Yes? (*She has been whispering with CHARLES who begins to go from the room.*)

PAUL: John Winter and I have been – Where's Charles going?

CHARLES: I'm going to get some breakfast. Can I pinch one of your cigarettes?

(*After CHARLES has taken a cigarette PAUL puts the box into his pocket. CHARLES goes out.*)

PAUL: John Winter. John Winter, where are you?

WINTER: Here.

PAUL: I saw the dog from my window just before I came down. He was limping. What's the matter with him? You haven't been beating him again, have you?

WINTER: I never beat him.

PAUL: I've told you before – I won't have that dog beaten. Do you understand?

WINTER: Yes.

PAUL: He may misbehave himself but he's getting old and he doesn't know what he's doing. He's getting old and a little simple. I suppose you'll be beating me soon. Now remember –

STELLA: (*To JOHN WINTER.*) You'd better get down to the village. I want those things.

PAUL: Is John Winter going out?

STELLA: Yes. He's going down to the village to get some food. We can't give Mr Procathren bacon.

PAUL: Why not?

STELLA: Go along, John Winter. Meat, bread, dried fruit of some kind and coffee.

(*JOHN WINTER begins to wheel the bicycle from the room. PAUL calls after him.*)

PAUL: O, brave John Winter! Going down among the enemy again. Would you like to take my pistol? Be careful not to break wind in the High Street or they'll be after you. (*JOHN WINTER has left the room.*) One day they will.

STELLA: What?

PAUL: Kill him.

STELLA: No.

PAUL: Why not?

STELLA: Like them, he's a servant; they would never kill one of their own kind. They hate him, perhaps, but –

PAUL: Are you suggesting that John Winter is working with the villagers against us?

STELLA: No, of course not.

PAUL: Such a thing had never occurred to me. Is it likely?

STELLA: No.

PAUL: Is it?

STELLA: No! Don't get such an idea into your head. I didn't mean to suggest it. John Winter is loyal. He loves you dearly.

PAUL: He beats the dog.

STELLA: He denies that.

PAUL: I won't have that dog beaten. I must exert my authority. John Winter is my servant, and he shall obey my orders.

STELLA: Of course. (*A pause.*) What are you thinking?

PAUL: He moves quite freely among the villagers, you know.

STELLA: To spy on them. So that we can be warned of any danger. Now come, Grandpa. Don't be silly. Of course John Winter is loyal to us. Remember the night when they intended to attack the house and John Winter sat with you out there on the balcony waiting for them. He was prepared to fight with you against them – against his own kind. Remember that. (*PAUL is silent.*) What was it you were telling him before you came down?

PAUL: It is absurd of me to doubt him. Absurd! It was cold that night, you know, but he didn't complain. No, he made jokes – very good jokes too – about the villagers. He's brave and he's loyal. It is ridiculous to doubt his honesty.

STELLA: Of course it is ridiculous. What were you telling him as you came down? I'm interested.

PAUL: What? Oh, yes. Yes, Stella. You know the two trees, the elms – that stand in front of the house – ?

STELLA: Tweedledum and Tweedledee – yes?

PAUL: What's that?

STELLA: We used to call them that when I was a child – don't you remember? (*She puts her hands in a defensive boxing attitude.*) Their arms outstretched in constant conflict – remember?

PAUL: Yes, of course. They're dead now.

STELLA: Yes, they're dead now.

PAUL: And I'm going to cut them down.

STELLA: Why?

PAUL: Because they are a danger.

STELLA: To whom?

PAUL: To ourselves. I saw them yesterday as they are – blanched by age – withered, contorted and monstrous. They shouldn't stand before the house. They must be brought down.

STELLA: I played in them when I was a child – with Ellen.

PAUL: You agree they should come down?

STELLA: If you think it's necessary.

PAUL: I believe it is necessary. And it must be done quickly.

STELLA: Very well.

PAUL: That way it will give us less pain. I remember them, too. They were in full leaf the summer morning I arrived here twenty-five years ago. On approach they quite obscured the house and when you were before the door they shadowed you. But now they're dead and must be brought down. I can do it with John Winter.

STELLA: You mustn't do it! Not yourself.

PAUL: With John Winter. You don't think I'm strong enough? I'm quite strong enough. It will have to be carefully done for they must fall away from the house. (*He takes the cigarettes from his pocket.*) I think I might have a cigarette now.

STELLA: Yes.

PAUL: Nice of John Winter. Look! He's written on the box. What does it say?

STELLA: (*She reads.*) 'Many happy returns of the day. Your obedient servant, John Winter.' (*They laugh.*)

PAUL: Absurd of me to suspect him of treachery.

STELLA: Absurd.

PAUL: Have one?

STELLA: Thank you, I will.

PAUL: I suppose John Winter stole them.

STELLA: I suppose so.

PAUL: Sit down.

STELLA: I have a lot to do.

PAUL: For a few minutes. Whilst we smoke our cigarettes. (*STELLA pulls up a stool and sits by him.*) Have you matches?

STELLA: Yes.

PAUL: You remember the trees from your childhood – Tweedledum and Tweedledee?

STELLA: Yes. Is that foolish?

PAUL: I don't think so.

STELLA: Somehow I – Tell me, are they evil now?

PAUL: Not evil – dangerous.

STELLA: They were most benevolent to Ellen and me when we were children. They were almost our only playthings and gave themselves so willingly to masquerading as other places – other worlds.

PAUL: But they're ugly now – ugly and old and dead.

STELLA: Yes.

PAUL: So I shall cut them down.

STELLA: Very well. When did they die?

CHARLES: (*Below in the kitchen, shouts.*) Get out! Get out!

PAUL: What? What's that? What?

STELLA: Charles. (*She goes to the door and calls down the stairs.*) Charles!

CHARLES: (*From below.*) All right. It's the dog.

STELLA: It's the dog.

PAUL: Well, what's he doing to it?

STELLA: I don't know.

PAUL: Why do you all hate that dog so much?

STELLA: We don't.

PAUL: You never seem to give him a moment's peace.

STELLA: He's so large and he will come into the house – and he's begun to smell terribly.

PAUL: Probably I do. I'm getting old. I suppose I shan't be allowed in the house soon.

STELLA: Don't pity yourself.

PAUL: What did you say?

STELLA: Nothing.

PAUL: Stella! What did you say?

STELLA: Charles is really very good to him.

PAUL: Then why does he shout at him? And look – look! What's he doing here? (*They turn to look at the painting.*) What does it mean? What are those monstrous figures? And there's the dog – see? At least I suppose it's my dog. I don't understand such things.

STELLA: He'll say very little about it.

PAUL: Has it a title?

STELLA: I don't know.

PAUL: Things should always be titled. Does he tell you nothing?

STELLA: Very little.

PAUL: I don't understand him. I was nearly sixty when I gave up my work and came to live here – and there was a reason. I was victimized – driven here by my enemies. Charles's work as a painter was recognized when he was – how old?

STELLA: Fifteen.

PAUL: And now he's twenty. There was no attack on him, or on his work. He was acclaimed as a prodigy. Yet he came here, met you, married you – strange, you – and now lives with the old fellow – the poor man. Refuses to show his paintings – except that. What is to go there? (*He indicates the unfinished lower part of the mural.*)

STELLA: There? Oh, another figure – a woman. Charles wants me to model for it but I haven't had time as yet.

PAUL: A woman. Then the other figures – those – will be looking down at her, eh?

STELLA: I suppose so.

PAUL: I don't understand it.

STELLA: Don't –

PAUL: I don't understand it at all.

STELLA: Don't let it worry you. Leave him in peace.

PAUL: Charles? I will. But he mustn't harm the dog. Is that clock right?

STELLA: I think so. I put it right by the village.

PAUL: Procathren should –

STELLA: Oh, Grandpa! (*She laughs.*) I've got something to show you. I found it last night. (*She has taken a page of a magazine from the pocket of her dress and unfolded it.*) It's from a magazine called 'The Tatler' – an old copy – some years ago – look –

PAUL: Who is it?

STELLA: Read it.

PAUL: (*Puts on his spectacles and reads.*) 'The Honourable Robert Procathren, distinguished young poet and critic, photographed last week after his marriage to Miss Amanda Mantess, daughter of Mr and Mrs Sebastian Mantess of – ' it's torn away. What a beautiful young man!

STELLA: Isn't he?

PAUL: Fancy such an elegant and obviously witty person coming to see us.

STELLA: Why not?

PAUL: But, I mean, look at him. Look at his clothes. His hair is trimmed and I'm sure, if you could see them, his fingernails would be spotless. His linen is as crisp as the paper on which he has been writing to me. Oh, dear! He's obviously very famous and very correct. What on earth shall I say to him? Look at those dainty feet in the pointed shoes. (*He stamps in his great black boots.*)

STELLA: Are you making fun of him?

PAUL: Indeed, no. He frightens me.

STELLA: What do you mean?

PAUL: Come, child, you know what is meant by fear. I'm afraid of him –

STELLA: Paul!

PAUL: – his whole appearance is alien to me.

STELLA: His appearance. But, my dear, appearance has never counted with you. Do you mean his clothes? It doesn't matter what he wears, but what he is as a man.

PAUL: About tonight, Stella –

STELLA: He is your admirer – he is coming here to express that admiration. And you can meet him – I give you my word – not as an equal but as his superior. You see – he'll admit that.

PAUL: How you do talk. But, darling, I'm frightened about tonight.

STELLA: You mustn't be.

PAUL: Why don't you try to understand?

STELLA: You mustn't be frightened.

PAUL: I –

STELLA: Look at me. Do you love me?

PAUL: I do.

STELLA: Then if you love me you won't be frightened.

PAUL: So simple? I'm old. Easily frightened.

STELLA: Paul – Paul! (*She grasps his arm.*)

PAUL: You're hurting me.

STELLA: You are greater than any of them. They understand that by these last twenty-five years of exile and mortification you have proved the justice and truth of those opinions expressed in your pamphlets. You have proved your integrity and saintliness and tonight it is that that they will honour. Paul! You're not going before a tribunal.

PAUL: Ha! They will be in judgement on my table manners.

STELLA: It is your poetry they will be remembering.

PAUL: They'll laugh at my fumbling with the knives and forks.

STELLA: They will remember your political writings.

PAUL: A stupid old man! I shan't be able to eat the food they give me. A glass of wine goes to my head and makes me babble like a baby. I shall want to go to the lavatory during their speeches and I shan't be able to go. I shall wet myself again and then you'll be angry with me. O Stella!

(*There is a pause – then STELLA speaks with gentleness.*)

STELLA: There is nothing to fear. I promise you that. I've never promised you anything that has not been perfectly fulfilled, have I? Have I?

PAUL: No.

STELLA: Then you can trust in this promise. You will not be afraid today. (*She gives him her handkerchief.*) Dry your tears.

PAUL: I feel giddy.

STELLA: It's the cigarette. Do you remember what you said when you came downstairs this morning?

PAUL: Within twelve hours –

STELLA: Do you remember what you said? 'It is today I have to play the great man, isn't it?' That's what you said.

PAUL: I was joking, dear Stella.

STELLA: Joking or not – that is what you must do. Play the great man. Now, at this moment, you may tell me of your fears. At this moment, because we are alone and I love you. But from the time of Procathren's coming here you must act the great man. You must meet this elegant and witty young man with your own elegance and wit. Good gracious me! From what Mamma told me you were a great one for acting in your day. (*PAUL laughs.*) Were you? Then remember that when you meet these people.

PAUL: I wish I had some better clothes.

STELLA: You look very well as you are.

PAUL: Newer clothes.

STELLA: And Grandpa –

PAUL: Yes?

STELLA: Also remember – this is a new beginning for you. For twenty-five years – since I was a child, we have been waiting for this moment. Don't fail! Don't fail, now! Go to London today, meet these people, show them that you are yet alive and active and then – then begin to write again. Do this and you won't have to act the great man – you will be the great man.

(*There is a pause.*)

PAUL: And what do you hope to get out of all this, Stella?

(*CHARLES comes into the room from below.*)

STELLA: Nothing – I swear it! Nothing – I believe in you!

PAUL: Take this cigarette from me.

STELLA: Perhaps they have asked you to return because they need you. Perhaps they are in trouble out there and want your wisdom, your advice. Have you thought of that?

PAUL: Why should I give them my advice? They are nothing to me.

CHARLES: Bravo!

PAUL: Hullo, Charles.

STELLA: It is your duty, Grandpa.

CHARLES: Nonsense!

STELLA: (*She turns to CHARLES.*) You, my precious little fellow – and what do you know about it? – you being a stranger here. You, with your paintings stored away unshown – probably unshowable – and your miserable fears of criticism. Well, Paul, does not need to fear criticism. He can go out from here into the world –

unafraid – disarming criticism and censure by his genius. Then how dare you, a stranger –

CHARLES: (*Shouting.*) Stella!

(*There is a pause.*)

STELLA: Yes, Charles?

CHARLES: I want to speak to you. (*He goes up the stairs.*)

STELLA: Yes, Charles.

(*She follows him up the stairs. PAUL left alone, stares at the newspaper cutting in his hand. From the head of the stairs the voices of CHARLES and STELLA rise together.*)

CHARLES: – damnable, damnable things! –

STELLA: – unmeant, unmeant –

CHARLES: – cruel wickedness, most cruel! –

STELLA: – not meant. I never mean to – never mean to –

(*PAUL, staring at the newspaper cutting, suddenly cries out.*)

PAUL: O God! O God!

(*There is silence – then STELLA calls.*)

STELLA: What is it, Grandpa? (*She comes down the stairs.*) What is it?

(*PAUL holds up the newspaper cutting.*)

PAUL: Stella – Stella, look at this man. (*CHARLES comes down the stairs.*)

STELLA: I've seen it, Grandpa. Your nose is running. Wipe it.

CHARLES: Has John Winter gone out?

STELLA: Yes.

CHARLES: I thought he was going to light the fire before he went.

STELLA: It's more important that we should have the food.

CHARLES: I'm so damned cold. Move over, Paul, and let me have a bit of the stove.

PAUL: Charles. I say, Charles, look at this. (*He holds out the cutting.*)

CHARLES: Just a minute, Stella – (*She is combing her hair before a fragment of glass set on the mantelpiece.*) – when will you have time for me to start work on that last figure?

STELLA: I don't know.

PAUL: Charles, look!

CHARLES: Just a moment, Paul. Do you think today, Stella?

STELLA: No, not today. I shan't have a minute to sit today.

CHARLES: Why not, when Paul's gone?

STELLA: Well, I'll see, but I don't know.

CHARLES: I've been asking you for the last three weeks.

STELLA: I know.

CHARLES: Now then – what do you want, Paul?

PAUL: Look at this.

(*CHARLES takes the cutting.*)

CHARLES: Who is it?

PAUL: Read it.

CHARLES: (*He reads.*) 'The Honourable Robert Procathren, distinguished young – ' Oh!

PAUL: Isn't he a grand young fellow?

CHARLES: Indeed, he is. Stella, have you seen this?

STELLA: I gave it to Paul.

CHARLES: Where did you find it?

STELLA: Among some old magazines of yours.

PAUL: Look! Look, Charles, what do they say?

CHARLES: ' – distinguished young poet and critic – '

PAUL: ' – distinguished young poet and critic – '

CHARLES: (*He nudges PAUL.*) Paul, my old one –

PAUL: (*Giggling with anticipation.*) Yes? Yes, sonny, yes?

CHARLES: A splendid young man. Isn't he, Stella? Paul – Paul, tell me –

PAUL: Yes, sonny? Yes, what?

CHARLES: Isn't he the kind of young man Stella admires – very much admires? Clean, upright, bold –

PAUL: Yes? Yes?

CHARLES: – full of a passionate desire – for life. Not like us, my ancient – not like you and me – being, as we are, despised by Stella. No, she'd admire him – this Procathren.

STELLA: (*She turns and shouts.*) I'm not going to quarrel with you!

CHARLES: – admire him very much for what he is and for what he does – the conduct of his life. Yes, Stella would love him – love him dearly –

STELLA: Damn you, Charles! Damn you!

CHARLES: And what is he, Paul, this Procathren?

PAUL: Tell me – tell me!

CHARLES: He is a man. And being a man may we conjecture what he would say to a woman like Stella? I think we may.

PAUL: Yes, I think we may.

CHARLES: He would say that he looks upon life as an adventure, and upon death as an enemy to be fought with desperation. Age as something to be accepted with dignity – women also. A man lacking in pathos but not lacking in attraction. Therefore, a man clean, temperate, respectable, responsible –

STELLA: I shall leave the room!

CHARLES: – restrained, realistic, reasonable –

PAUL: A lovely man!

CHARLES: A fashionable man. His verse turned out as effortlessly as his personal appearance. Smooth thoughts soothing in their catholic simplicity. Love poems – ah, Stella! – a delicious liquidity – casually inspired by the contemplation of his elegant mistress's inner thighs. Not like your – (*He nudges PAUL who giggles.*) – not like your blasphemous, bawdy, scraggy limericks. Yes, Stella, I once knew these beautiful poets. They smell. They smell very nice, but they smell.

STELLA: You're jealous.

CHARLES: Yes, my love.

STELLA: You! You lack attraction but, my God! you don't lack pathos. As you are now – as you are sitting there now – I could weep for you –

CHARLES: There's someone –

STELLA: Weep for you!

CHARLES: There's someone on the stairs.

(*Footsteps can be heard coming up the stairs from below.*)

STELLA: Listen!

CHARLES: It's probably him. (*To PAUL.*) Here he comes to take you away.

STELLA: Behave yourselves! Are you ready?

CHARLES: Ready. (*CHARLES rises, and, standing behind PAUL, whispers.*) Your flies are undone.

(*PAUL looks, finds they are not undone, and laughs.*)

STELLA: Be quiet! (*She is about to move to the door when it is opened from the outside and JOHN WINTER comes into the room. He is carrying parcels of food. CHARLES and PAUL shout with laughter.*)

CHARLES: The distinguished critic!

PAUL: Do I bow, or curtsey, or salute, *or* – (*Laughing, he proceeds to do all these things.*)

STELLA: You make me look a fool, John Winter.

WINTER: I'm sorry.

CHARLES: Blame me, Stella. Blame me.

STELLA: You've got the food. Good. (*She takes the parcels from JOHN WINTER.*) I've told you I'm going to cook today's meal?

WINTER: Yes.

STELLA: I want you to take Mr Southman upstairs to his room now. He is to rest until Mr Procathren arrives.

WINTER: Very well.

STELLA: Do you hear me, Paul?

PAUL: Yes, but I'm all right.

STELLA: Nevertheless, you're going to rest now.

PAUL: See anything of Procathren in the village, John Winter?

WINTER: No, sir. There's been – (*He is interrupted by STELLA. The following conversations between JOHN WINTER – STELLA and PAUL – CHARLES take place simultaneously.*)

S: This is the meat?

W: Yes.

S: What is it?

W: Beef.

S: We have vegetables.

W: Yes.

S: Will you prepare them?

W: Yes. That's the dried fruit.

S: Good. Where's the coffee?

W: I couldn't get any. That's what I –

S: Why not? We've none at all.

W: I know that. If you'll allow me –

C: Probably lost his way.

P: No. He's clever.

C: Perhaps he's changed his mind.

P: Why?

C: Decided not to come and see a dirty old man like you.

P: Charles.

C: Yes?

P: I don't want to go to rest.

C: Tell her.

P: You tell her.

C: It'll do you good.

P: You think I ought to go?

S: I suppose they wouldn't let you have it.
W: There's been trouble in the village.
S: What?

W: There's been trouble in the village.

S: Paul! Charles! Do you hear that?

C: Yes, I think so.
P: All right.
C: You needn't sleep. You can read.
P: Will you come and read to me?
C: John Winter will. I've found a copy of 'Alice' among my stuff? I'll give it to you for an extra birthday present.

CHARLES: What?
STELLA: Something's happened in the village.
CHARLES: Well, what?
STELLA: Come along. John Winter, let's have it.
WINTER: (*He speaks directly to PAUL.*) The reports in the village are confused, sir, but I have been able to gather a little information.
PAUL: Well?
WINTER: Three private soldiers have escaped from a detention camp. They have made their way to the village, and it is believed they slept last night in the village hall. This morning, at an early hour, they broke out of the hall and began marauding and looting the village. Although unarmed they terrorized the villagers. Having obtained food they retired, and are now hiding at some place in the surrounding country.
PAUL: Thank you, John Winter. An excellent and lucid report.
WINTER: Thank you, sir.
STELLA: (*To CHARLES.*) He'll salute in a moment.
PAUL: Let us appreciate the situation.
STELLA: Surely –
PAUL: Be quiet, Stella. Well, John Winter, have you anything to suggest?
WINTER: I can see no immediate danger to yourself, sir, from the situation at present. By their actions the soldiers have automatically allied themselves to us, although ignorant of our aims and even of our existence. Indeed,

by their actions they caused a diversion in the village admirably suited to the day of your visit to London.

PAUL: You think the villagers might have interfered with my going?

WINTER: I had reports to that effect sir.

PAUL: And you said nothing?

WINTER: I was prepared, sir.

PAUL: The idea of an alliance with these soldiers against the villagers must be considered. Perhaps we could offer this house as –

STELLA: Stop playing at being soldiers yourselves for a minute, and listen to me. You are both going to London today for an express purpose. This is no time to indulge in your fancy for campaigning. (*PAUL and JOHN WINTER are silent.*) All right, Captain Winter. Take General Southman to his room.

PAUL: Stella – I –

STELLA: Go along, Grandpa. You can hatch your revolutionary schemes as well up there as you can down here.

(*JOHN WINTER takes PAUL's arm and they begin to move to the stairs.*)

PAUL: Where's that copy of 'Alice', Charles?

CHARLES: I'll bring it to you.

STELLA: You're not to read. You're to rest.

PAUL: Charles said I could read.

STELLA: No, you're to rest. (*PAUL and JOHN WINTER have gone up the stairs.*) Did you hear them? Ridiculous! Two old men with their stupid attempts at military phrases and reports. Did you hear them? 'Situation – immediate danger – diversion – an alliance.'

CHARLES: Yes, I heard them.

STELLA: Absurd!

CHARLES: But I thought – I may have been mistaken – I thought that you appreciated a very real danger from the villagers.

STELLA: I do. It is a very real danger. If the villagers could organize themselves, or could be moved by a moment's rage they would come here and kill us all. At present they suffer from no more than a grievance. And they have cause – they have cause for grievance and for hating us. When Paul came here – when he withdrew himself from the world that attacked him – he chose the village to be his butt. I remember the things he said – (*She has taken two loose cigarettes from the pocket of her dress. She throws one to CHARLES.*) – here – catch! – I remember the things he said about the village when I was a child – unforgivable, beastly and unprovoked. Paul was then no longer in a position to attack his equals and so his abuse, the result of hurt pride, was directed against the villagers. It was unprovoked because he had no quarrel with them but for their sanity and security. Soon they felt – under his attack – they felt their security gone and with it their sanity. The satire that had recently shaken the world was directed against them – against a few miserable peasants in a ramshackle hamlet. They reacted in the way of the world, and as Paul would say, 'declared war on us. That war has continued since my childhood. It has coloured my life – the threat of violence to this tortured family. And so, Charles, I am frightened to hear such nonsense talked by Paul – with encouragement from John Winter – when we need expert and serious conspiracy to save our lives. Reason tells us that we cannot fight the villagers – we cannot do it, and so we must get away – run away if you like. This is what we must do. But how? I can do nothing – you can do nothing – we are useless, helpless and wretched and must appeal to the one man capable of saving us – Procathren. I know! I know he is a poor specimen in your eyes, but we must appeal to him. He may help us. You must admit that we need help, and I have no pride in such matters. I have no pride at all. But try to remember, Charles, that I am a woman – try to be conscious of that at other times than when I am naked. I am a woman and I have a child inside me. Does that explain anything to you? Pregnant women have delusions, they say. Do they? I know nothing about it. Am I deluded, Charles? Am I? I only know that I am possessed by a loneliness hard to bear – a loneliness which I should imagine attends forsaken lovers. (*She stands silent – then:*) Lovers. I am innocent of such things. I have imagined what they do and what they say – these lovers. It seems they find a great delight in music and solicitude, in whispering and smiling, in touching and nakedness, in night. And from these things they make a fabric of memory which will serve them well in their life after death when they will be together but alone. They are wise, for that is the purpose of any memory – of any experience – to give foundation to the state of death. Understand that whatever we do today in this house – this damned house – will provide some of the material for our existence in death and you understand my fear. No one who has lived as I have lived could be happy in death. It is impossible. They speak of us turning in our graves when a slighting word is spoken of us. No, the words were spoken during our lifetime, and it is the memory which causes the unrest. The family – my mother, my father and my sister – out there in the row of graves – what did they store up, I wonder? Dadda who fell from grace in the world when Paul fell and spent the rest of his life living on the charity of the old man – what does he remember? Mamma – magnificent angry Mamma – is she happy in the memory of her justice? Ellen, who died at twenty years, perhaps happy in the memory of my love for her. As for myself, if I die today, my eternal happiness will depend on the tiny memory of you, Charles – you, on your first visit to this place – standing in the doorway – (*She smiles.*) – consciously picaresque – and handing me the flowers from your hat. I thought then that we were to be lovers, but from our marriage you gave me no understanding – no explanation of the mysteries – only a child conceived in violence. Therefore, I must ask a stranger. I can use no female tricks on him. I am not a young girl. I am unused to laughter and my mind is always slow to understand. I can use neither wit nor beauty. I can only appeal to his charity to take me away from this place. Perhaps I can go with him as his servant. (*She pauses.*

*CHARLES is turned away from her. As STELLA begins to speak again there is a single note blown on a trumpet: distant and from the direction of the village.*) Why don't you speak? Now! Why don't you speak, now? You could have released me – you could have freed me from this place if only you could have overcome your fear of the world out there and returned yourself. Even now you could kill my black, desperate, damnable fear of all time being empty if you would tell me – show me how to love. I am human and I am a woman. Tell me. And, O, Charles, Charles, comfort me!

(*He is about to move to her when the trumpet is blown again. It is nearer and blatant, raucous, defiant. CHARLES and STELLA, hearing this, stare at each other.*)

CHARLES: What is it?

STELLA: I don't know.

(*The trumpet is blown again.*)

CHARLES: Listen!

(*PAUL calls from his room upstairs.*)

PAUL: What's that?

STELLA: I don't know, Grandpa. O God! I don't know.

CHARLES: It was nearer.

STELLA: Yes. Nearer.

PAUL: What is it? What is that noise?

(*The trumpet is being blown.*)

*CURTAIN*

# ACT TWO

*The scene is the same. The time: four hours later – early afternoon. A fire has been lit. PAUL and STELLA are sitting at the table; they have just finished a meal. A place is laid for CHARLES who is absent from the room. JOHN WINTER is going about clearing away the remains of the meal. There is silence until PAUL, suddenly turning to STELLA, asks:*

PAUL: What did you say?

STELLA: Some minutes ago I answered your question and said, 'It sounded once more in the distance, then stopped.'

PAUL: What was it?

STELLA: I don't know.

PAUL: It was a trumpet, I know that – but what does it mean? Did you see anything?

STELLA: We didn't look. (*She puts her face in her hands.*)

WINTER: Have you finished with this, sir? (*He indicates PAUL's plate.*)

PAUL: What? Yes. Yes, thank you. (*JOHN WINTER removes the plate.*) Some trick of the villagers, perhaps.

STELLA: They've never dared to come so near to the house before.

PAUL: No. They're getting really mischievous. Did it frighten you?

STELLA: Very much.

PAUL: Mustn't be frightened. (*He stares across the room.*) What's the time?

STELLA: Five and twenty minutes to two.

PAUL: You know, I can't see very well now. It isn't so long ago that I could see that clock from here. Five and twenty minutes to two. (*In silence he takes up a fork and scores deep marks into the tablecloth.*) He's not coming, is he?

STELLA: Procathren?

PAUL: Yes.

STELLA: Of course he is. Don't do that. He's probably been –

PAUL: He's changed his mind as Charles said he would. Decided not to come and see me.

STELLA: It's early yet.

PAUL: No. He's changed his mind.

STELLA: Grandpa – would you care very much if he didn't come?

PAUL: Well, yes. Yes, I should be disappointed.

STELLA: Wipe your mouth, darling.

(*He does so. CHARLES comes running down the stairs into the room. He carries a book which he throws on the table before PAUL.*)

PAUL: Hullo Charles! (*He laughs.*)

CHARLES: That's the copy of 'Alice in Wonderland' I promised you.

PAUL: Thank you, Charles. Stella, can I have something to drink?

STELLA: Water?

PAUL: Yes, please.

STELLA: Get some water, John Winter.

(*JOHN WINTER goes out to the kitchen with the dishes. PAUL sits looking at the book.*)

CHARLES: He's not come yet? (*He stands behind STELLA with his hands on her shoulders. Her hands go up to his.*)

STELLA: No.

CHARLES: I hope he comes.

STELLA: For my sake?

PAUL: What's that?

CHARLES: Nothing, Paul, nothing.

STELLA: He should have been here by now if they're going to get to London.

CHARLES: Yes. You thought he'd be here for this meal?

STELLA: Yes, I did. I don't know why.

PAUL: Has John Winter brought the water yet?

STELLA: No, not yet. Oh, here it is.

(*JOHN WINTER has entered with a jug of water and some glasses.*)

PAUL: I'll pour it out. Have you fed the dog, John Winter?

WINTER: Yes, sir. Some time ago.

PAUL: It must be very cold out of doors. If he wants to come in you are to allow it.

WINTER: He seems to want to stay out.
PAUL: Was he frightened by that noise?
WINTER: I don't know, sir.
CHARLES: Have you heard it again?
STELLA: No. John Winter, will you keep a look-out for Mr Procathren. I suggest from upstairs.
PAUL: He's not coming!
STELLA: Run along, John Winter.

(*JOHN WINTER goes up the stairs.*)

PAUL: (*Chants.*) He's not coming! He's not coming! He's not coming after all, at all.
STELLA: Shut up, Grandpa! And having made so much fuss about the water, why don't you drink it? Charles, I want you to –

(*PAUL, having sipped the water, suddenly reads, from the book.*)

PAUL: 'Once I was a real Turtle.' (*He pantomimes a great sigh: the book falls to the floor.*) Then the world wasn't big enough for me to live in. Every time I raised my voice I banged my head. What a fine, brave, gay little chap I was – the world had never seen my like, it said. (*CHARLES and STELLA are whispering together.*) How I made them laugh – how they loved me. Have you ever heard – felt the roar of applause – like the thunder of blood in your head? But – pity! –

Little Southman's come a cropper
Because he wrote an awful whopper
Telling Kings and Princes too
Just how much they ought to do.
Poor old Paul!
What a fall!
Whoo-ah!

That's what they sang when 'The Abolition of Printing' had been written and I was on my way here. And it was true. What a fall! Whoo-ah!

STELLA: Say something, Charles, and stop him rambling.
CHARLES: Boo!
PAUL: What's that? You, who wouldn't say Boo to a goose dare to say Boo to a Southman? I, who was once a real Turtle – am I now less than a goose?

STELLA: You're an old goose to talk such nonsense, Paul.
PAUL: Quack-quack!
CHARLES: Whither do you wander?
PAUL: Upstairs and downstairs and in my lady's chamber.
CHARLES: Not any longer, you don't.
PAUL: It's my legs – they've gone weak.
CHARLES: Only your legs?
PAUL: I know what you mean, you dirty boy. Blank cartridge. But you'd have been proud of me once, ducky. I was full of the stuff of life when I wrote the 'Abolition'. Then I went neither upstairs nor downstairs but straight into my Lady Society's chamber and lifted the skirts of the old whore. A rough customer – but she kindly displayed her deformities. Then it was whoops with the what-d'you-call-'em – Hullo, Mr So-and-so! – why, bless me, here's the thingamajig – Ssh! – the tiger's gone into the forest – be a man – be a man – deliver the goods. (*He snaps his fingers. ROBERT PROCATHREN has come up the stairs and is standing in the doorway of the room. He is unseen by PAUL, STELLA and CHARLES.*) And when I had performed the obscene gesture what a rush there was to restore the disarray of the filthy old bag. What a-neighing and a-braying to assure her that nothing had been revealed to her detriment. Andrew Vince pulled up the knickers and John Ussleigh pulled down the skirts and Arthur Howell took me, the raper, into custody. The accusation against Paul Frederick Southman! (*He beats on the arm of his chair.*) 'Paul Frederick Southman: you are charged with the assault of the well-known and much-beloved whore, Society, in that you did, with malice and humour, reveal her for what she is and not for what men wish her to be, thereby destroying the illusion of youth and the wisdom of age. Also that you employed the perversion of using for this purpose your pen instead of the recognized organ.' Witnesses called for the prosecution. Andrew Vince: this witness testified the poor old body to be sadly shaken by her experience and vehemently denied the defence's suggestion that he had

rummaged her after finding her crying in an alley. John Ussleigh: this witness, a publisher, stated that he saw the assault but had been under the impression that it was a case of true love. He had known the prisoner for a number of years, etc., etc. An unnamed young man: this witness, called for medical evidence, admitted intercourse with Society on several occasions. When asked by the defence whether he was not repelled by the malformations of Society, he answered, 'I thought all women were like that.' Witnesses called for the defence: none. Sentence: exile. (*He sees ROBERT PROCATHREN. The two men stare at each other across the room. STELLA turns to recognize ROBERT at once.*)

STELLA: Mr Procathren.

ROBERT: That's right.

STELLA: I'm Stella Heberden.

ROBERT: How do you do.

STELLA: How do you do. This is my grandfather, Paul Southman, and my husband, Charles.

ROBERT: How do you do.

STELLA: Won't you come in?

ROBERT: Thank you. I've left my car some distance away. I could find no road to the house.

STELLA: There isn't one.

ROBERT: I suppose the car will be all right.

STELLA: I'm sure it will be.

(*There is a pause and then ROBERT moves towards PAUL, and, smiling at him, says:*)

ROBERT: Well, sir, this is a great occasion for me.

PAUL: How do you do. Stella!

ROBERT: May I say, many happy returns of the day.

PAUL: Thank you very much.

ROBERT: I feel there is no necessity for –

CHARLES: Have you had lunch, Mr Procathren?

ROBERT: What? Yes. Yes, thank you – I have. Surely Mr Southman, there is no necessity for formality between us on this occasion, but there are a few things I should like to say. Have I your permission?

(*PAUL is silent.*)

STELLA: Please go on.

ROBERT: Thank you. I'll be brief. (*He speaks to PAUL.*) What am I doing in coming here today –

PAUL: Did John Winter say he'd fed the dog?

STELLA: Yes, Grandpa. (*To ROBERT.*) You must forgive him.

ROBERT: Of course. I appreciate the honour you do me in allowing me to come here, to this house, today – this house which has been closed to the world for so many years. You withdrew yourself from us, and with yourself your advice and guidance, to punish us for our treatment of you and your ideas. At the time of the attacks on you I was nine years of age and therefore rather too young, actively, to participate in your defence. I have had to wait until today, when I hope – in the following few hours to wipe out the memory of the hatred and violence that was inflicted on you twenty-five years ago by your fellow artists. As a young man my own work was deeply influenced by –

PAUL: What does he say?

ROBERT: No more. I shall say no more. There remains only this: as a material token of our appreciation of your nobility of attitude I have been asked to bring you this book. (*He has taken a leather-bound folio from the brief-case he carries. This book he lays on the table before PAUL who makes no attempt to open it.*) With it may I wish you the best of health and happiness and, again, many happy returns of the day.

(*PAUL nods his head.*)

STELLA: Well, have a look at the book, Grandpa. (*PAUL shakes his head.*) What do you say? Oh, he hasn't got his glasses.

ROBERT: I'm so sorry. I didn't realize that. May I. (*He takes back the book and opens it.*) In this book you will find some sixty-odd appreciations both in prose and verse – they are all, of course, in autograph. Here are Harold Prospect, Richard Lewis Cameron, Helen Newsome, George Reeves and many others writing in honour of Paul Frederick Southman. (*He holds out the book to PAUL.*)

PAUL: I was a real Turtle once, wasn't I? (*He takes the book.*)

STELLA: Don't be silly, Grandpa.

ROBERT: Now, Mrs Heberden –

STELLA: Yes?

ROBERT: I don't want to bother Mr Southman – so may I tell you about the arrangements I have made for today?

STELLA: Certainly.

ROBERT: Well, Mr Southman will have to walk to the car, I'm afraid – that is possible, isn't it?

STELLA: He has a little cart we sometimes pull him around in – he could use that.

ROBERT: Excellent. Now, we should start from here about four-thirty. (*He looks at the clock – then at his watch.*) Surely your clock is exactly an hour fast.

STELLA: Yes. Yes, it is. It's broken.

ROBERT: We should get to London by seven o'clock giving Mr Southman time for a short rest before the dinner.

(*PAUL and CHARLES have been whispering over the book of appreciation. Suddenly PAUL's voice is raised.*)

PAUL: No, no, Charles! A very nice young man.

(*ROBERT smiles at STELLA and continues.*)

ROBERT: The dinner will be a formal affair. Many people wish to meet Mr Southman – I hope it won't tire him – he must say immediately if it does. There will be some speeches – we are hoping that he is going to speak –

STELLA: I think he will – but he's very frightened, you know. (*Very distantly the trumpet sounds.*) It is a fear that he is no longer –

ROBERT: What was that?

STELLA: I heard nothing.

PAUL: There it is again, Stella.

ROBERT: What is it, sir? A barracks?

CHARLES: No. We've no ideas about it, have we, Paul?

(*PAUL and CHARLES grin at each other.*)

ROBERT: A train, perhaps.

CHARLES: There are no trains round here.

(*There is a pause. Then ROBERT laughs, and continues to speak to STELLA.*)

ROBERT: I should tell you, Mrs Heberden, that there will be the presentation of a cheque to Mr Southman tonight. A certain sum of money has been collected by – What did you say?

STELLA: I said I'd like to speak to you about that.

ROBERT: Certainly.

STELLA: Later. You're leaving at half-past four, Grandpa. (*To ROBERT.*) His man, John Winter, will travel with him. That's all right, isn't it?

ROBERT: Quite all right.

STELLA: So you'll be ready, won't you, Grandpa?

PAUL: Stella!

STELLA: Yes? (*She moves to him.*) It's all right, darling! It's all right. (*She puts her arms around him.*) You see, Mr Procathren did come after all. (*To ROBERT.*) He was so frightened – so afraid that you weren't coming. Weren't you, darling? (*She kisses PAUL.*)

ROBERT: (*Going to the mural painting.*) This is your work, Mr Heberden?

CHARLES: Yes.

ROBERT: Interesting. I can't recall seeing anything of yours since the famous show – when was it? – four years ago.

CHARLES: Five.

ROBERT: Five, was it? Anyway, when you were the infant prodigy startling the country with your engravings to the 'Purgatorio'.

CHARLES: That exhibition was a mistake.

ROBERT: For one so young? Perhaps.

CHARLES: I meant otherwise.

ROBERT: If you have any other new work I should be most interested to see it.

CHARLES: For recognition in your literary reviews?

ROBERT: I assure you –

CHARLES: I have nothing. I have ceased to comment upon a society I have forsaken.

ROBERT: But surely, Mr Heberden, the essence –

CHARLES: Did you have a good journey from London, Mr Procathren?

ROBERT: I didn't come from London. I came from Oxford.

CHARLES: I see.

ROBERT: I live there.

STELLA: Did you come through the village?

ROBERT: Yes.

STELLA: It was quiet?

ROBERT: There seemed to be no one about – but I drove through very quickly. Why?

STELLA: No reason.

ROBERT: As a matter of fact, I had intended to start earlier and stop in the village to call on the rector. The Reverend Giles Aldus. Do you know him? (*They are silent.*) He has a library – it has been left in his care – a small collection, but it sounds most interesting. You've heard of it, no doubt.

STELLA: No.

ROBERT: No? I was going to call and ask him if I might see it. They are books of a religious nature – almost legendary as they've never been catalogued. Aldus has never allowed it. I'm told he lives with his mother, and both she and the books he keeps from contact with the world. I'm not particularly interested in his mother, but I'd have liked to have seen the books. However, there was time to see neither. By the way, Mrs Heberden, I must apologize for walking into the house as I did, but I could find no bell or knocker.

CHARLES: We have very few callers.

ROBERT: (*He laughs.*) I nearly fell over a dog in the doorway. I meant to mention this before. There's a –

STELLA: Oh dear! I hope he didn't annoy you.

ROBERT: No, he didn't annoy me.

PAUL: He doesn't annoy people.

ROBERT: How could he? He's dead. (*There is a pause. ROBERT laughs.*) Is that your dog? I didn't know. I thought –

(*PAUL has risen to his feet. He shouts.*)

PAUL: John Winter!

STELLA: Paul – Paul!

PAUL: (*To CHARLES.*) Get John Winter! (*CHARLES is about to move to the stairs when JOHN WINTER comes down into the room.*) John Winter!

WINTER: Yes?

PAUL: John Winter, this man says my dog is dead.

WINTER: Where – ?

PAUL: This man says my dog is dead.

WINTER: Where is it?

ROBERT: In the doorway – down – (*He points.*)

(*JOHN WINTER runs from the room.*)

PAUL: Help me – Charles, you fool – help me!

STELLA: Paul, you're not to –

(*CHARLES has taken PAUL's arm and is assisting him across the room.*)

PAUL: I must go down – I must go down! (*He shouts down the stairs.*) John Winter! Is it true? John Winter, is it true?

(*PAUL and CHARLES go from the room to descend the stairs.*)

STELLA: O God! O dear Christ! (*She has moved to the table and, unseeing, beats down with her fist on the presentation book.*)

ROBERT: Be careful of that book, please!

STELLA: What?

ROBERT: The book. Please be careful. (*He removes the book from under her hand.*) I am most distressed, Mrs Heberden. I had no idea that the dog – you see, I tripped over the carcass and – I thought – well, I really don't know what I thought – the thing was still warm. I must apologize but at the time –

STELLA: – you had something very much more important to think about?

ROBERT: Well, yes.

STELLA: The presentation to Mr Southman.

ROBERT: Exactly.

STELLA: And I agree, Mr Procathren.

ROBERT: What? That –

STELLA: That the presentation was more important than a dead dog.

ROBERT: Thank you.

(*During this conversation between ROBERT and STELLA there is heard from the foot of the stairs at the main door*:)

CHARLES: (*His voice rising to audibility.*) – and we need proof. We don't know anything.

PAUL: Proof! I want no more proof of their intentions. Look at it – look at it – it lies there – dead! Dead!

CHARLES: Paul – Paul! Stop it! (*There is the sound of some heavy object being thrown to the ground.*) Paul – come here! Stop him, John Winter!

(*The main door of the house is thrown open and PAUL can be heard shouting.*)

PAUL: Come out! Come out, you toads! Why do you hide? You were not afraid of an old dog – why be afraid of an old man? Come out and let me see you! (*His last words become a long howl of grief.*)

STELLA: We must hope – we must pray that –

(*There is a pause.*)

STELLA: – that he will go with you this afternoon. I promise he shall go with you. This will make no difference at all. He shall go with you to London, and he will be all right. He will be all right.

ROBERT: We must hope so. Please don't be upset, Mrs Heberden. I can understand this. An old man – an animal beloved of him –

STELLA: But we must get him away from here soon. You said half-past four –

ROBERT: Yes.

STELLA: It must be before that. As soon as possible. At once!

ROBERT: Very well.

STELLA: He'll arrive early in London, but there must be somewhere he can go, surely.

ROBERT: My flat.

STELLA: He can wait there?

ROBERT: With pleasure.

STELLA: Good.

ROBERT: He'll be all right there, I can assure you. He can rest and during that time –

STELLA: Mr Procathren.

ROBERT: Yes.

STELLA: Help me.
ROBERT: How?
STELLA: Help me.
ROBERT: In what way?
STELLA: Please!
ROBERT: In what way can I help you?
STELLA: I had prepared what I was going to say to you.
ROBERT: Then please say it.
STELLA: You will help me?
ROBERT: In any way I can, but –
STELLA: There's very little time.
ROBERT: Before they return? I promise to look after the old gentleman, if that's what you mean.
STELLA: Yes. Yes, of course, you must look after him.
ROBERT: I will.
STELLA: Sir! Sir, our future is in your hands.
ROBERT: You must forgive me, I –
STELLA: Our future is in your most beautiful delicate hands.
ROBERT: You must forgive me but I don't understand you.
STELLA: You are young, you are famous and powerful, you are talented and you can do as I ask.
ROBERT: (*He laughs.*) I am a minor poet – nothing more.
STELLA: Why do you laugh?
ROBERT: I don't know.
STELLA: At this moment – why do you laugh?
ROBERT: Shyness, I suppose. I am shy.
STELLA: I'm sorry but there's no time for the courtesies and formalities as between strangers. You mustn't expect them from me. But please don't withdraw. A moment ago you were willing to help me.
ROBERT: I don't understand what you want.
STELLA: This! This is what I want! I want Paul to be restored to his former greatness. In that way there can be a future for my child.
ROBERT: Your child?
STELLA: I'm pregnant. The child Paul. Innocent, you will admit – in no way responsible. For this child's sake old Paul must be restored to greatness in the world.

ROBERT: But he is a great man now. No restoration is necessary.

STELLA: No, he is not a great man now, but –

ROBERT: I came here today to see a great man.

STELLA: – we can restore him. And this is the way. Listen – this is the way.

ROBERT: There is nothing I can do.

STELLA: Nothing can be done today, certainly. Nothing, beyond our having you take him to London. But in the future we can act. You promised to help me –

ROBERT: Really, I –

STELLA: You promised to help me! And you can help me in this way: until you can get us away from this place keep in touch with me – by letter, in person – I'll get away to London to see you if you wish – but by some means – by any means – we must retain contact.

ROBERT: I can see no point in this.

STELLA: Such a small thing to ask. Be gracious, sir – you have so much – be gracious to the poor. (*There is a pause. ROBERT turns away.*) What can I offer you?

ROBERT: Nothing.

STELLA: You can be godfather to my child.

ROBERT: I am an atheist.

(*Footsteps can be heard coming up the stairs.*)

STELLA: Together we can do so much for Paul. Apart we –

ROBERT: (*He has heard the footsteps.*) All right!

STELLA: You will help me?

ROBERT: Yes.

STELLA: God bless you!

ROBERT: I'll keep in touch with you by letter but you must instruct me. I've no idea what you intend. They're coming back.

STELLA: I will instruct you, as you put it, in our first letters. It is decided then – you and I can go together now. But I must have a token from you.

ROBERT: A token?

STELLA: A material token. That will do. (*She indicates the signet ring ROBERT is wearing.*)

ROBERT: This?

STELLA: Yes. (*She holds out her hand to him. He removes the ring and puts it on a finger of her left hand. As he is doing this PAUL comes in the room from below. He moves quickly and breathlessly across the room to the farther stairs. STELLA calls to him.*) Paul! (*He does not answer but continues up the stairs to the upper floor. STELLA speaks again to ROBERT.*) You mentioned a cheque to be presented.

ROBERT: Yes.

STELLA: It must come to me.

ROBERT: I don't think I can do that.

STELLA: You can contrive some trick.

(*ROBERT still holds STELLA's left hand from the giving of the ring.*)

ROBERT: Some trick. Is that what you're up to, Mrs Heberden?

(*CHARLES enters from below.*)

CHARLES: Where is he?

STELLA: He's gone to his room. Is the dog dead?

CHARLES: Yes.

STELLA: How is he going to take it?

CHARLES: In anger. Listen! (*There is silence.*) I thought I heard him. (*He smiles at ROBERT and STELLA.*) Have you two settled the future?

STELLA: Yes, we have. (*To ROBERT.*) Haven't we?

(*ROBERT, in an agony of embarrassment, moves away from her.*)

CHARLES: Excellent! (*He laughs.*)

STELLA: I'm going to call Paul.

CHARLES: No, Stella – no, let him come down in his own time.

STELLA: You said he was angry. Did you say that?

CHARLES: I did.

STELLA: But why? Why anger?

CHARLES: He's convinced that the villagers poisoned the dog.

STELLA: Did they?

CHARLES: No, I don't think so. It must have died of old age.

STELLA: What a day to choose to die! (*CHARLES is laughing at her.*) It should have waited until tomorrow. (*Suddenly she laughs too, and, continuing to laugh, she speaks.*)

It should have waited until tomorrow, when Paul would have been away. However, we must deal with this – this catastrophe. (*She goes to CHARLES and puts her hand on his shoulders.*) It will take more than the death of a dog to deter me. You see, Charles, I'm no longer alone. I now have an ally who is prepared with me. Mr Procathren has promised to help me.

ROBERT: One moment, Mrs Heberden. I feel I must define the limits of my obligations. They are these: to come here today not only on my own behalf but also on behalf of my committee: to present Mr Southman with the book of appreciations and our congratulations on his birthday: to drive him to London for the dinner tonight and during that time to accept personal responsibility for his safety: to return him to this house tomorrow. Those are the limits of my formal obligations – but – I have promised one thing further – to keep in touch with you by letter in future. I will do that – but it does not mean, Mrs Heberden – (*His voice becomes uncontrolled.*) – it does not mean that I am prepared to become engaged in a partisan way in any family feud or intrigue. What you are attempting to do, and how you are attempting to entangle me – indeed, why – I do not understand. But kindly remember I have stated my obligations and I am not going beyond them.

(*PAUL is coming down the stairs into the room.*)

CHARLES: (*To STELLA.*) As an ally I prefer a dead dog.

(*PAUL comes into the room. Beneath his arm he carries a large automatic pistol; he has removed the clip and is loading it with cartridges. There is a change in his manner. Towards ROBERT he is friendly, almost familiar, and no longer afraid. He speaks with a clear and forceful articulation.*)

PAUL: I must admit that even with my daily care of this weapon I have always looked upon it as being for defence, never for revenge.

STELLA: What are you going to do?

PAUL: You must forgive me, Mr Procathren – Robert – I may call you Robert, may I not? –

ROBERT: Certainly.

PAUL: You must forgive us, Robert, for engaging you in this business. (*He inserts the magazine into the pistol.*) I trust your sympathies are with us.

ROBERT: I know nothing of the circumstances, sir.

STELLA: What are you going to do, Grandpa?

PAUL: Whatever I do it will be with this! (*He lays the pistol down heavily on the table.*) The circumstances, Robert, are these. For many years past now the occupants of this house have suffered victimization by the villagers. The reason has never been clear to me. Perhaps it is based on some delusion with regard to our social standing. Perhaps our being artists – I don't know. But I no longer require reasons. The act – the act of poisoning my dog – is enough.

STELLA: The dog died of old age.

PAUL: Don't be silly, child. This, Robert, is the first direct move they have made. For years the threat has existed – but, although very real, it was no more than a threat. It lasted so long without action that it became a family joke – eh, Charles? – Stella? – but this is an act and must be answered by as direct and cruel an act. Where is John Winter?

STELLA: I want to know what you are intending to do. Are you forgetting that you go to London today?

PAUL: No, I am not forgetting that – and I shall go.

STELLA: You will?

PAUL: Most certainly. Where is John Winter?

STELLA: He hasn't come up yet. And are you going to London?

PAUL: Don't worry, darling – I shall go. At about four o'clock you said, Robert?

ROBERT: Yes, sir. We should start by then.

PAUL: In that case, I must hurry. Now then – we are one – two – three – four men with John Winter and one woman. With the three soldiers we shall be seven men.

STELLA: Soldiers?

PAUL: The soldiers that have escaped from prison. John Winter mentioned them. The soldiers that have anticipated us in their attack on the village. I propose to form an alliance with them. But, first of all, we must find them. I want you, Charles, to do that – and perhaps you, Robert, would care –

ROBERT: I don't wish to be involved in this sir.

(*There is silence. PAUL stares at ROBERT, his hand going out to touch the pistol. He withdraws and turns to CHARLES.*)

PAUL: Then you will go with John Winter, Charles. Bring these soldiers back here. I want to talk to them.

ROBERT: Mr Southman! (*PAUL turns to ROBERT.*) You must understand my position. I cannot – dare not become engaged in something that is of no personal – no personal –

PAUL: Advantage, Mr Procathren?

ROBERT: No, sir! Not advantage, but –

PAUL: I have explained the circumstances to you. You are an intelligent man – you have undoubtedly understood. Will you or will you not help me?

ROBERT: My personal position –

PAUL: I don't understand your doubt and hesitation. With your admiration of myself surely you believe what I have told you to be true.

ROBERT: Of course.

PAUL: We need your help.

ROBERT: I will help you in any indirect way that I can –

PAUL: No qualifications! Will you or will you not help me? I shall not ask again.

(*There is a pause.*)

ROBERT: I will.

STELLA: You are being untrue to me!

ROBERT: What can I do? What else can I do?

STELLA: (*She cries out.*) Then what is going to happen?

(*There is a complete cessation of activity whilst STELLA speaks. She is swept by a sudden storm of foreknowledge, awful in its clarity. The men, silent and unmoving, watch her.*)

Careful! We are approaching the point of deviation. At one moment there is laughter and conversation and a progression: people move and speak smoothly and casually, their breathing is controlled and they know what they do. Then there occurs a call from another room, the realization that a member of the assembly is missing, the sudden shout into the dream and the waking to find the body with the failing heart lying in the corridor – with the twisted limbs at the foot of the stairs – the man hanging from the beam, or the child floating drowned in the garden pool. Careful! Be careful! We are approaching that point. The moment of the call from another room. (*She pauses.*) Give me another of your cigarettes, Paul.

PAUL: What was it, my darling?

STELLA: Give me a cigarette.

(*PAUL takes the box from his pocket and hands it to STELLA.*)

PAUL: We are aware, my dear – stop it! you're trembling – yes, we are aware –

STELLA: Damn! (*She throws away the match with which she is attempting to light her cigarette. ROBERT steps forward and lights it for her as PAUL continues to speak.*)

PAUL: – very much aware of the menace of the point of deviation. We are eagerly awaiting the shout from another room for we know from whom it will come and to whom it will be directed. Also we are aware of the discovery – the destruction of the village – and so we have nothing to fear. All we have to do is to wait a little while – (*JOHN WINTER comes into the room from below.*) – but apparently, not long. Yes, John Winter?

WINTER: There's a gentleman to see you, sir.

PAUL: The whole world is calling on us today. Who is it?

WINTER: From the village.

PAUL: Ah, well?

WINTER: The Reverend Aldus.

PAUL: The holy bookworm, eh? Tell him to come up. (*JOHN WINTER turns and shouts down the stairs,* 'Will you come up, please.') What does this mean? If they think I can't attack clerics they should remember my history. Now for it. (*The REVEREND ALDUS comes into the room. JOHN WINTER goes out.*)

ALDUS: Good afternoon. (*PAUL inclines his head but is silent. The others whisper,* 'Good afternoon.') My name is Aldus.

PAUL: I am Southman. This is my granddaughter, Stella, her husband, Charles Heberden, and a friend and sympathizer, Mr Robert Procathren. (*ALDUS nods to each in turn.*) Please sit down.

ALDUS: Thank you.

PAUL: You will notice, my dears, first of all, the general attitude. That of humility bordering on servility. It is dangerous to the unwary. It has been used by the Church for hundreds of years to gain advantage in a situation such as this. Next, notice the facial expression. A cursory examination and one might take it to be shyness, perhaps idiocy. It is neither. The clothes, notice the clothes. And the posture – neat, precise. If you were to go near him you would smell not sanctity but intrigue. But don't go near him. I forbid it.

(*There is a pause.*)

ALDUS: (*He has a marked impediment in his speech.*) May I speak?

PAUL: Certainly.

ALDUS: You have finished your attack?

PAUL: I have not yet begun.

ALDUS: It is evident, Mr Southman, that I cannot match your fluency in this conversation. I am forced, by my disability to select only certain words for my use.

PAUL: (*He laughs.*) You're doing very well. Carry on.

ALDUS: I have a proposal.

PAUL: Concerning the soldiers?

ALDUS: Yes. You've heard – ?

PAUL: Partly. Tell us – in well-selected words – what has happened – and what you propose.

ALDUS: Late last night these three men came to see me at the Rectory. I was alone. Their leader – (*The trumpet sounds from the middle distance.*) Listen!

PAUL: Yes, we've heard it. Is that the soldiers?

ALDUS: Yes.

PAUL: Apparently we were mistaken. We thought it was your people fooling about.

ALDUS: No, it is the soldiers. I will tell you. These men came to me – they were honest in that they explained the true position – their escape from criminal detention – it was I who practised dishonesty – and by that I have brought –

PAUL: Get on man! There's little time. Certainly no time for self-examination.

ALDUS: Forgive me. Their leader asked one thing of me – shelter for the night. I agreed, and told them that they could sleep in the church hall. They went there. They trusted me. In the early hours of the morning I got up and – moved by some sense of justice outside my province – I – (*He is in tears.*)

PAUL: Come along. What is it?

ALDUS: I say, forgive me. My mother –

PAUL: Never mind your mother now. Tell us about the soldiers.

ALDUS: I got up and went to the hall and locked them in. I locked the soldiers in.

(*Very sharply and suddenly, but shortly PAUL and CHARLES laugh.*)

PAUL: What happened then?

ALDUS: They broke out of the hall just before daylight. One of them had stolen a trumpet from among some band instruments that were stored there. That is the trumpet you can hear. With that they are advertising their presence. (*He has risen from his chair.*) They are marauding through the countryside. The village is terrorised. They attacked the baker –

PAUL: Why the baker?

ALDUS: There seems to be no reason for their acts. They are madmen. I do not understand! I do not understand! (*He is shouting and stammering incoherently.*)

PAUL: Be quiet! (*Then, in silence.*) What do you expect of me?

ALDUS: Come to – come to ask your help, sir.

PAUL: You've what?

ALDUS: Come to ask your help, sir.

PAUL: Against the soldiers?

ALDUS: Yes, sir.

PAUL: I see. How long have you lived in the village, Mr Aldus?

ALDUS: Five years.

PAUL: Five years. Please sit down. Then you know the situation that exists – has always existed between the village and this house?

ALDUS: Yes, sir.

PAUL: You do?

ALDUS: Yes.

PAUL: And yet you come to ask my help?

ALDUS: I know the history of hatred, sir, and yet I appeal to you in my weakness to help us against these men.

PAUL: You turn in your weakness to me, Mr Aldus? You surprise me.

ALDUS: Mr Southman!

PAUL: Telephone for the police.

ALDUS: They destroyed the telephone lines last night.

PAUL: Send one of your young men as a runner.

ALDUS: You know we have no young men among us.

PAUL: And I have two.

ALDUS: Yes.

PAUL: And one of them has a car. Have you tried prayer?

ALDUS: Sir! Sir, we cannot –

PAUL: Have you tried appeasement? Offer them –

ALDUS: We cannot –

PAUL: Have you tried preaching? Appeal to their better natures! (*ALDUS has foundered upon his incoherence. He is silent.*) And so you have come to me. Why?

ALDUS: Because, by reputation, you are a great and powerful man.

PAUL: Thank you.

ALDUS: A man –

PAUL: Would you say a good man, Mr Aldus? (*ALDUS is silent.*) Ah! then you would use evil to combat evil. A strange presumption for one of your ridiculous uniform.

ALDUS: I cannot engage in polemics with you.

PAUL: Very well. You ask me to lead you against these men to achieve – what?

ALDUS: To uphold law and order: to protect the people of my village.

PAUL: Are you not thinking more of your books? Of the danger to your precious books.

ALDUS: No.

PAUL: Are you sure? I heard what Robert said – he didn't think I was listening, but I heard of all your books about God. Think, Mr Aldus! Perhaps you now love the books more than you love God.

ALDUS: No.

PAUL: That would be very wrong, Mr Aldus. Very wrong indeed.

ALDUS: I am thinking of the villagers – of the people. I am thinking –

PAUL: You are? I just thought it might not be so. It is for them you want help?

ALDUS: Yes.

PAUL: Ask me.

ALDUS: What?

PAUL: To help you.

ALDUS: Help us.

PAUL: Properly.

ALDUS: Will you help us?

PAUL: No.

ALDUS: There could only –

PAUL: Again!

ALDUS: What?

PAUL: Ask again.

STELLA: Paul!

PAUL: Shut up! Ask again.

ALDUS: Will you help us?

PAUL: No! (*He has taken up the pistol. He goes to ALDUS and taps him on the chest with the barrel of the weapon.*) No! I will not help you. I shall form an alliance however – oh, yes, I shall do that – but it will be with the soldiers and with them I shall revenge myself upon you and your impudent mob. (*He turns away.*) Go! Leave us! Will someone show Mr Aldus to the door.

(*STELLA moves to ALDUS.*)

CHARLES: I'll go with him.

STELLA: No, I'll go. (*She takes ALDUS by the arm.*) Will you be able to get back all right?

(*ALDUS nods. They reach the door when ALDUS turns.*)

ALDUS: Mr Southman, I will dare to say to you –

(*But PAUL who has been performing a little silent dance, interrupts ALDUS by pointing the pistol at him, squinting along the barrel, and saying:*)

PAUL: Bang! (*ALDUS and STELLA go out. PAUL moves to a position between ROBERT and CHARLES. He puts his arms about them.*) Well, my dear Robert – and my very dear Charles, that pathetic creature has been sent us to represent our enemy. Not very flattering, is it?

CHARLES: (*He is laughing.*) What are you going to do?

PAUL: Charles, no! We must be serious. (*CHARLES is silent.*) We mustn't allow what we've just seen – an awful display of fear, non-comprehension and self-conscious pathos – we mustn't allow that to make us laugh or to make us pity. It is an old trick, and we are human. He wanted to tell us about his mother. She is dead – or dying – or doesn't love him any longer – is angry with him, perhaps, for his part in this business – but I wouldn't allow him to speak of it. It might be that there is really some tragedy, and we cannot allow ourselves to be diverted by sympathy for such things. No, Charles – even though they had sent us the whole circus instead of the solitary clown we must not be amused or allow our emotions to be touched in any way. (*He pauses.*) What am I going to do, you ask? What am I going to do? (*The action becomes centred on ROBERT PROCATHREN – PAUL and CHARLES towards ROBERT. The three men move and speak at extreme speed. PAUL savagely and in great exaltation: CHARLES amusedly and lightly, foreseeing towards what they are moving although not the actual event: ROBERT through fear, attempting to join in the fantastic *jollity as he attempted to join in games and horseplay when a schoolboy.*) Can you fight, Robert?

ROBERT: Well, sir, I –

PAUL: If you can't –

CHARLES: – we haven't much time to teach you.

PAUL: No.

ROBERT: A little boxing when I was at school. (*PAUL and CHARLES laugh with delight.*)

CHARLES: Always the little boys, was it?

PAUL: The boys a little smaller than you –

CHARLES: – but not too obviously smaller.

PAUL: Poor little bastards! I bet you punished them. No, I meant –

CHARLES: I've been told there are rules to that sort of thing. (*He has jumped upon the table and taken up an attitude of defence.*)

PAUL: Shut up, Charles! No, Robert, I meant –

CHARLES: You mustn't kick, must you?

PAUL: I meant, Robert, fighting. With weapons. Such as this. (*He holds up the pistol.*)

ROBERT: No. I've had no experience of such things.

PAUL: Never?

ROBERT: Never.

CHARLES: But surely –

PAUL: Could you learn?

CHARLES: Surely you must have been engaged in some war –

ROBERT: No.

CHARLES: – at your age.

ROBERT: No. I was not fit.

CHARLES: Morally or physically?

ROBERT: Both.

CHARLES: You fought with your pen, eh?

PAUL: Have you never –

CHARLES: Poems of victory!

ROBERT: And defeat.

PAUL: Have you never been moved –

CHARLES: Bravo!

PAUL: – moved by hate or persecution –

CHARLES: Or love?

PAUL: – to contemplate physical violence?

ROBERT: Never.

CHARLES: It has always been unemotional, calm force –

PAUL: – in boxing rings –

CHARLES: – with rules –

PAUL: – and referees –

CHARLES: – against harmless little boys.

PAUL: Do you think you could use this? (*He holds out the pistol to ROBERT.*)

ROBERT: I've never handled one before. (*He takes the pistol from PAUL.*)

PAUL: Will you use it –

CHARLES: It is simple!

PAUL: – with us against the villagers?

CHARLES: Oh, so very simple!

ROBERT: Yes, I'll use it.

PAUL: Against the villagers?

ROBERT: Yes.

PAUL: It's loaded.

(*ROBERT raises the pistol to point at PAUL and CHARLES.*)

CHARLES: Look out!

(*PAUL and CHARLES raise their hands above their heads in mock terror and then shout with laughter.*)

ROBERT: (*Smiling.*) Sorry. (*He turns away.*)

PAUL: There's a catch –

CHARLES: There's a catch in everything, Robert.

PAUL: – at the side of the butt.

CHARLES: Which is the bit you are now holding.

PAUL: You release the catch to fire.

CHARLES: Then slight pressure on the trigger –

PAUL: Face away, dear boy, face away!

CHARLES: That releases the striker which explodes the cap which ignites the powder which, expanding as gas, forces out the bullet –

PAUL: Which brings down the house that Paul built!

CHARLES: Isn't that better –

PAUL: Bang! Bang!

CHARLES: – and simpler –

PAUL: Bang!

CHARLES: – than your boxing with bare fists?

ROBERT: You must explain the method by which – (*The pistol goes off in his hand. PAUL and CHARLES shout with laughter again. ROBERT, dropping the pistol to the floor, stands holding his wrist.*) O God!

PAUL: Oh dear, no, Robert! Not that way at all.

CHARLES: No. You must be conscious of when you fire –

PAUL: – and of the direction in which you fire. Oh, yes, you must be much more careful. It is simple, but not as simple as that. The agency is human, not providential. But at least you can fire it – accuracy will come. (*CHARLES has taken up the pistol from the floor. He removes the clip of remaining cartridges and holds out the pistol to ROBERT.*)

CHARLES: There you are. Now you can play with it.

ROBERT: I don't want it! I don't want it!

PAUL: It's all right now. Unloaded.

CHARLES: Of course it is.

PAUL: Take hold of it and we'll have a little drill.

ROBERT: I don't want it!

CHARLES: But it's perfectly safe now. Look! (*He thrusts the pistol into ROBERT's face and pulls the trigger. The striker clicks: nothing, nothing more. ROBERT after a pause, takes the pistol from CHARLES.*)

PAUL: That's right. Now – (*From almost immediately below the windows, in the garden, there is a great blast blown on the trumpet.*) Listen! They're here – the soldiers! (*He runs to the window.*) Our allies. They're here. They'll know how to use that. (*He is laughing.*)

CHARLES: Can you see them?

PAUL: No. Perhaps my eyes – I can see nobody. (*He opens the window.*) But they're here. (*He shouts.*) Don't be afraid. Come out – come up here. You're welcome. You're welcome!

CHARLES: Can you see them?

PAUL: No. There's nobody. Nobody at all.

CHARLES: Shout again.

PAUL: Don't be afraid. We are friends. We are enemies to the village. Come up – come up!

(*The three men listen in silence and into that silence comes the voice of JOHN WINTER shouting from the foot of the stairs at the main door.*)

WINTER: Mr Southman – Mr Southman, sir!

PAUL: (*Shouting.*) We are friends, I assure you. We wish you well. Bless you, I say, bless oh bless you!

(*Again they listen and again JOHN WINTER shouts: this time from just beyond the door.*)

WINTER: Mr Southman!

PAUL: What is it? What does John Winter want?

CHARLES: I don't know.

WINTER: Mr Southman!

ROBERT: Fools! You fools! Don't you understand? Don't you understand – that is the shout from another room.

PAUL: What?

ROBERT: The shout from another room – that is it. That! Have you forgotten?

CHARLES: Where's Stella?

PAUL: The shout from another room? –

CHARLES: Where's Stella?

ROBERT: Yes. Where is Stella?

CHARLES: She went to show Aldus out.

ROBERT: She should be back, shouldn't she?

CHARLES: Yes.

ROBERT: Well, where is she now? Where is she now?

CHARLES: Stella! (*He runs to the door – for a moment he pauses and then, decided, he begins to open the door. It opens a few inches but that is all: there is some obstruction at the other side.*)

PAUL: (*Shouting to the soldiers.*) Gentlemen, I assure you that we are friends. Come up here and let us talk –

CHARLES: Paul – what is wrong? Why won't the door open? John Winter!

(*PAUL leaves the window and comes back into the room.*)

PAUL: What is it? What are you doing?

CHARLES: Why won't the door open? The door – what is the matter with the door? Help me!

(*But in the moment's pause when neither PAUL nor ROBERT move CHARLES has thrown the full weight of his body against the door. The door opens fully and CHARLES, still within the room, stands looking down at the stairs. He cries out then again, the second time the sound resolving itself into the name,* Stella.)

PAUL: What? What? (*CHARLES runs from the room on to the stairs. PAUL stands plucking at ROBERT's sleeve.*) What is it? What is wrong, Robert? What has gone wrong?

(*ROBERT motionless, does not answer him. CHARLES calls from the stairs.*)

CHARLES: Help me! Help me!

(*PAUL goes from the room on to the stairs. ROBERT left alone, holding the empty pistol, does not move. He does not look towards the door. PAUL, looking down at the stairs, backs into the room. CHARLES and JOHN WINTER come in carrying STELLA: she is dead. For a time the group is still and silent then JOHN WINTER speaks.*)

WINTER: Put her down, sir. (*CHARLES does not move. He stares down into STELLA's face.*) Mr Heberden. Put her down sir. We must see –

PAUL: Stella. Stella. Stella.

WINTER: Put her down, sir.

(*They lay the body on the floor.*)

PAUL: Robert – Stella's hurt.

WINTER: May I – ? Mr Heberden, may I look at her?

(*CHARLES nods his head. He moves quickly to the door. He finds the bullet-hole.*)

PAUL: Or is it a joke? They've played jokes on me before. (*JOHN WINTER opens the bodice of STELLA's dress, exposing her breasts.*) You wouldn't play jokes on me, Robert. That would be cruel. You wouldn't ridicule me. No, she's playing the joke on me. Stella – Stella darling, stop it. It's not a very good joke.

WINTER: There is a bullet wound – here.

PAUL: Stella!

WINTER: It has, I think, passed through her heart.

PAUL: What do you say, John Winter?

WINTER: There is no pulse.

PAUL: John Winter! You dare to enter into this joke?

WINTER: She is dead.

CHARLES: Dead.

PAUL: Dead! You go too far, sir. Leave the room!

CHARLES: John Winter says she is dead. Shot dead.

PAUL: Dead. Dead. The doors are shutting in the empty house. Dead. Dead.

WINTER: Who was it? I heard the shot. (*CHARLES without turning his head, points to ROBERT who, with the empty pistol half-raised has not moved.*) But why? Why?

PAUL: Won't any of you speak to me? I am at fault, I suppose. Listen – I'll confess. You've frightened me. There – I've admitted it. You've frightened me with your joke. Now speak to me.

WINTER: (*To CHARLES.*) Shall we take her upstairs, sir?

PAUL: Speak to me.

WINTER: (*To CHARLES.*) Shall we take her upstairs, sir? Nothing can be done.

PAUL: Nothing can be done. (*CHARLES and JOHN WINTER lift STELLA's body from the floor. They begin to carry her to the stairs leading to the upper floor.*) Nothing can be done. (*PAUL follows CHARLES and JOHN WINTER.*) Don't go, Robert. I'll be down in a minute when I've settled this and then I'll show you how to use the pistol properly. A fine business, indeed. (*CHARLES and JOHN WINTER are going up the stairs.*) Wait for me. Where are you taking my darling? Wait for me.

(*CHARLES and JOHN WINTER, carrying STELLA's body between them, have gone up the stairs from the room. From the foot of the iron steps leading from the balcony to the garden comes a piercing human whistle piping a popular tune. It does not disturb ROBERT who remains motionless, and PAUL has followed CHARLES and JOHN WINTER from the room. There is the sound of heavy boots on the iron steps. On to the balcony and so into the room by the window come three soldiers – WALTER KILLEEN, HENRY CHATER and their leader CHRISTIAN MELROSE. HENRY CHATER carries a trumpet. It is WALTER KILLEEN who is whistling, but he stops as they enter the room to stand a little inside the window. ROBERT, unmoving, has his back to them.*)

MELROSE: Good afternoon. I hear we're welcome in this house. That'll be a change. (*ROBERT does not move. MELROSE raises his voice.*) Good afternoon. (*It is when ROBERT turns that MELROSE sees the pistol in his hand.*) A nice welcome. A very nice welcome, indeed! (*To CHATER and KILLEEN.*) Don't move. (*To ROBERT.*) And what are you going to do with that?

ROBERT: What?

MELROSE: You have a pistol in your hand.

ROBERT: What do you say?

MELROSE: Are you deaf? I said, You have a pistol in your hand.

ROBERT: Oh, yes. It's not loaded – now.

MELROSE: I'm very happy to hear that. Very happy, indeed. (*He takes the pistol from ROBERT, examines it and puts it on the table.*) I thought – just for a minute, you know – I thought we weren't welcome here. (*To KILLEEN and CHATER.*) Come in – sit down – don't fool about. Keep quiet. You can sit there, and you sit there, where I can see you. (*KILLEEN and CHATER come into the room and sit down. MELROSE turns back to ROBERT.*) Who are you? What's your name?

ROBERT: Procathren.

MELROSE: What?

ROBERT: Procathren. Robert Procathren.

MELROSE: Robert, is it? I'll call you Bob – or perhaps Bobby would be better. I'm Melrose – 1535380 Christian – my name not my faith. This is Killeen, and this, Chater. Stand up! (*KILLEEN and CHATER stand up and perform magnificent mock bows to ROBERT.*) That's better. Once upon a time, although you wouldn't think it to look at us, we were soldiers.

ROBERT: Yes, I've heard about you.

MELROSE: Oh, you've heard about us. Then that saves a lot of explaining, doesn't it? About why we're here and –

ROBERT: Yes. You needn't explain.

MELROSE: Thank you very much. But you can explain something to me. Why are you all dressed up?

ROBERT: I was on an errand.

MELROSE: Do you always put on your best clothes to run errands? What's your job?

ROBERT: I'm a poet.

MELROSE: A poet. (*To KILLEEN and CHATER.*) He's a poet. (*MELROSE is about to speak but KILLEEN has risen and recites.*)

KILLEEN: Oh it was down by the river
That I made her quiver
Oh, you should have seen her belly
It was shaking like a jelly
Oh, you should have seen her –

MELROSE: That's enough! (*KILLEEN sits down.*) Give us your professional opinion, Bobby. Isn't that lovely poetry? Well – (*He laughs.*) – never mind. Do you live here?

ROBERT: No.

MELROSE: What are you doing here, then? You don't look right. You don't – (*CHATER blows softly on the trumpet. MELROSE turns on him.*) Listen! I've told you about blowing on it when I'm talking. So shut up or I'll take it away from you. Do you hear? I'll take it right away from you – so shut it! (*To ROBERT.*) Who lives here, then?

ROBERT: The Southman family.

MELROSE: I see. Who was it called to us from the window?

ROBERT: Paul – the old man.

MELROSE: What is he?

ROBERT: A poet.

MELROSE: Birds of a feather, eh?

ROBERT: No!

MELROSE: Well, don't shout. (*He has taken out a packet of cigarettes.*) Have one?

ROBERT: No, thank you.

MELROSE: Well, Bobby, I'm afraid we must be getting on.

ROBERT: No, don't go! Don't go!

MELROSE: What?

KILLEEN: Hey, Christy? (*He has been staring at the painting on the wall.*)

MELROSE: Wait a minute. Why don't you want us to go, Bobby? Come on, tell me – I'm interested. People usually want us to move on as quickly as possible. But you want us to stay. Now, why is that?

KILLEEN: Hey, Christy!

MELROSE: Well, what is it?

KILLEEN: Look! (*He points to the painting.*)

MELROSE: Well, what about it? It's a painting – done with brushes, you know.

KILLEEN: Hey, but Christy – look, look!

MELROSE: I'm looking.

KILLEEN: What is it?

(*MELROSE and KILLEEN move to stand before the painting.*)

MELROSE: Well, what's your guess?

KILLEEN: It's as good as yours. Look! (*He extends a finger.*)

MELROSE: Don't touch!

KILLEEN: All right.

MELROSE: Well, don't touch. It isn't finished. Look – (*He rubs his fingers into the paint.*) – *here.* It isn't finished.

KILLEEN: There's some paint – let's finish it.

MELROSE: No! (*They stand looking up at the painting. Then MELROSE, without turning, asks:*) Are there any women here? (*ROBERT, unaware that he cannot be seen, shakes his head.*) I said, Are there any women here?

ROBERT: There was one.

MELROSE: Oh?

ROBERT: I killed her.

MELROSE: What?

ROBERT: I killed her.

MELROSE: Wasn't that rather a silly thing to do? – when there was only one, I mean.

ROBERT: She was horrible – she was pregnant –

MELROSE: I see.

ROBERT: – but it was an accident.

MELROSE: Is that why you asked us not to go?

ROBERT: Yes. (*There is a silence as the THREE SOLDIERS stare at ROBERT. Then ROBERT, stretching out his hands before him, seems to be about to fall.*) What have they made me do?

(*MELROSE goes to him and holds him.*)

MELROSE: Hold up! Hold up, you're all right. Killeen, get the cure-all. (*KILLEEN goes to a small haversack he has been carrying and takes out a bottle of whisky.*) Now, come along, Bobby, you're all right.

ROBERT: Oh, what have they made me do?

(*MELROSE takes the whisky from KILLEEN.*)

MELROSE: Here – have some of this. Spoils of war.

ROBERT: No.

MELROSE: Oh, don't be an old woman! Go on. (*ROBERT drinks from the bottle.*) Careful! You're dribbling it. Better? Nothing like it, is there? What are you afraid of, Bobby?

ROBERT: Of what is going to happen.

MELROSE: We won't let anything happen to you. Will we? (*He turns to CHATER who, with the trumpet across his knees, is peaceably picking his nose.*) Happy?

(*CHATER grins.*)

ROBERT: You'll help me?

MELROSE: Of course. (*He holds out the bottle of whisky.*) Have some more. We've got another bottle. (*He winks at KILLEEN and CHATER.*)

ROBERT: You will help me?

MELROSE: I've said, yes. Go on, drink up.

ROBERT: Oh, my dear friend, they have made me do dreadful things. But you will help me?

MELROSE: Yes.

ROBERT: Thank God for you!

MELROSE: Yes, indeed.

ROBERT: We must plan what we shall do.

MELROSE: Yes, we will – we will.

ROBERT: Then let us go.

MELROSE: You're going to run away?

ROBERT: No, my friend, I'm going to run towards the event. A thing I have never done before – but now I have the authority. Let us go.

MELROSE: Where to?

ROBERT: First, the village.

MELROSE: All right.

PAUL: (*Calls from an upper room.*) Then nothing can be done! Nothing! And it is no joke – no joke!

ROBERT: (*Whispers.*) No joke.

MELROSE: The old man?

ROBERT: Yes.

MELROSE: With the woman?

ROBERT: Yes.

MELROSE: Should I go up?

ROBERT: No! No!

MELROSE: All right.

ROBERT: You can trust me.

MELROSE: I'm sure I can.

ROBERT: It will all be for the best.

MELROSE: I'm sure it will. (*He looks at KILLEEN and puts his finger to his forehead. They laugh.*)

ROBERT: Let us go.

(*MELROSE picks up the pistol from the table.*)

MELROSE: I'll take this.

ROBERT: (*To CHATER.*) Sound the trumpet! (*CHATER, standing, raises the trumpet smartly and blows a single sustained note. ROBERT looks towards the stairs.*) Ready?

MELROSE: Ready. (*MELROSE, CHATER and KILLEEN move to the window, out on to the balcony and so down into the garden. ROBERT is about to follow them and has reached the window when PAUL comes down the stairs.*)

PAUL: Robert!

ROBERT: I am here.

PAUL: It's no joke.

ROBERT: Indeed, it is no joke. No joke at all. (*He is crouched by the window, one arm outstretched to support himself.*)

PAUL: She's dead.

ROBERT: Yes. Quite, quite dead.

PAUL: You killed her.

ROBERT: I did.

PAUL: Why, Robert?

(*ROBERT is staring at PAUL.*)

ROBERT: Beast-face!

PAUL: Robert!

ROBERT: Beast-face!
PAUL: Robert!
ROBERT: Satisfied? Satisfied by the shift of responsibility, eh?
PAUL: Robert!
ROBERT: Shan't step from under it this time. Surprised, eh?
PAUL: Robert! (*But ROBERT has gone, running down the steps to the garden after the soldiers. PAUL moves to the window.*) Robert, come back! I have forgiven you – I have forgiven you! (*But PAUL can no longer be seen or heard by ROBERT. PAUL turns back into the room.*) I have forgiven him. (*Then, alone and old, he is seized by a terrible paroxysm of grief and fear. His eyes are closed: from his mouth comes a thin sound: his hands go up and tear the scarf from his neck. It is as if he would do himself great physical violence but his strength fails him – he can only stand exhausted.*)

*CURTAIN*

# ACT THREE

*The scene is the same. The time is six hours later: it is night. CHARLES is working on the mural painting. He has gathered the lamps of the room around him and light is so concentrated on his work. His model is the body of STELLA which lies on an improvised bier on the rostrum before the painting. The body is draped but for the face and head. On the floor, at the foot of the bier, lies a collection of human and animal bones. The painting on the wall is almost complete for CHARLES has added the figure of Stella as she lies in death. The other figures now look down at her and the dog stands at her head. At the other side of the room about the fireplace and in darkness but for the firelight are five women and a child. HANNAH TREWIN, MARGARET BANT, EDITH TINSON and FLORA BALDON are old. The other woman, who is young, is JUDITH WARDEN – mother of the CHILD who stands at her side. This CHILD, a girl, is ten years of age. She is dressed, fortuitously, as though for some celebration; although she wears a large pair of boots and a pair of boy's long trousers she also wears a short white embroidered frock of satin. A gay scarf is tied about her head to frame her face and also on her head is a yellow straw hat decorated with tiny artificial flowers. Each of the women in this group carries, wears, or has placed on the floor by her feet some of the surprising objects taken by those flying from a catastrophe. In this case there is a large shining china jug, a gramophone, an oleograph of a scene from 'Romeo and Juliet' and various nondescript bundles. EDITH TINSON has two pairs of shoes slung round her neck by a length of string. MARGARET BANT carries an ornate parasol, and is hung about with an excessive amount of cheap jewellery. HANNAH TREWIN appears to be wearing at least three hats. These things, quite worthless to these people in their present predicament, were snatched up in the last desperate moment. The group is silent and motionless but for the CHILD who bounces a rubber ball against the door. Through the windows the visible expanse of sky is red: the village is burning. It is this fire that JOHN WINTER stands by the window to watch. The tolling of church bells can be heard.*

WINTER: It doesn't look as if he'll be able to sound the bells much longer.

CHARLES: Why?

WINTER: I can see the tower now – very black against the fire – very near – not much longer.

CHARLES: The sooner the better – damned noise.

(*The CHILD is restrained by her MOTHER from bouncing the ball.*)

WINTER: What do they hope to gain by ringing the bells?

CHARLES: Help, I suppose.

WINTER: From God?

CHARLES: God alone knows! (*They smile at each other.*) Where's Paul?

WINTER: Upstairs, sir. Packing.

CHARLES: Packing?

WINTER: Packing his bag.

CHARLES: Does he think he's still expected to go?

WINTER: He seems to have no doubt, sir. I'm afraid he's very ill.

CHARLES: Oh, don't put it like that. Say he's going mad, nuts, bats, potty but not that he's very ill

WINTER: I'm sorry, sir. I tried to explain that he's no longer expected to go to London today and that Procathren may –

CHARLES: What did Procathren say to the old man before he went? That's what I'd like to know.

(*PAUL calls from an upper room:*)

PAUL: The village is burning away. There'll be nothing left as far as I can see – nothing at all.

CHARLES: Why isn't there more light?

WINTER: Shall I get you candles?

CHARLES: No! Don't leave the room. I can see. I can see. (*JOHN WINTER begins to make a rearrangement of the lamps.*) There's someone out there!

WINTER: Where?

CHARLES: Out on the balcony.

(*JOHN WINTER turns to stare out of the window.*)

WINTER: Yes. (*He raps on the window and then, opening it, calls:*) Come along! Come along in here. It's all right – don't be frightened.

CHARLES: Who is it?

WINTER: (*He laughs.*) Old Cowper, the postman. Chk-chk-chk-chk-chk! (*He says as if calling an animal.*) Come on. Come on. *Come on.*

(*THOMAS COWPER appears at the window. He is in the uniform of a country postman and carries his mail delivery bag.*)

COWPER: What do you mean, chk-chk-chk-chk-chk, indeed. Do you think I'm afraid to come in here? If so, let me say I'm as good as any that lives in this damned house and what's more, I'm here in the course of my duty and you are at the moment impeding that duty. Get out of the way! (*JOHN WINTER steps aside and COWPER marches into the room and goes to JUDITH WARDEN holding out a letter to her.*) For you, Mrs Warden, my dear. I've been looking for you all evening – your house has quite gone so I couldn't leave it there. But they told me you'd come this way. It's from your husband, my dear. Well, that's the last one. (*He takes off his cap and turns to CHARLES.*) Now then, young man. Stop that – whatever it is you're doing. I want a few details from you.

CHARLES: Details?

COWPER: Yes. (*He has taken a notebook from his pocket and has a pencil ready.*)

CHARLES: What about?

COWPER: About the disaster, of course.

CHARLES: The fire?

COWPER: Yes. Now leave that dummy alone for a few minutes, there's a good boy.

CHARLES: In what capacity do you want these details? As a postman?

COWPER: As an officer of the law. Police-Constable Pogson is engaged with the fire.

CHARLES: I see.

COWPER: When he heard that I was coming this way he asked me to take any particulars from you. I should like to say that as a civil official I have never taken either side in the quarrel that has gone on between this family and the villagers. You may speak quite freely to me.

CHARLES: Thank you.

COWPER: Not at all.

CHARLES: But I have nothing to say.

COWPER: Haven't you?

CHARLES: No.

*There is a pause.*

COWPER: (*To JOHN WINTER.*) Have you anything to say?

WINTER: No.

COWPER: Oh. (*He puts the notebook and pencil back in his pocket.*) Well, that's all, then. You can carry on with whatever you were doing. (*He speaks to the villagers.*) I don't know what to do with you. I suppose you can stay here tonight. (*He turns to CHARLES.*) Can they – ? What are you laughing at?

CHARLES: You.

COWPER: Is it a laughing matter that the village is destroyed, that the people are wandering homeless, and that the Reverend Mr Aldus is trapped at the top of the church tower and is roasting like a potato?

CHARLES: Is that why he's ringing the bells?

COWPER: I can tell you, young man, this terrible accident is no laughing matter.

CHARLES: Accident? Was it an accident?

COWPER: Of course. You don't think anybody would do such a thing on purpose?

CHARLES: They might.

COWPER: Don't be silly. Of course it was an accident. I should know – I was there when it started. Complete accident, it was. Just after six o'clock – I was delivering the last post – I was late, I'll admit it, I was late. A letter has just gone into Mr Aldus's box, and as I was turning away from the door I saw three soldiers coming to the house. The soldiers – you've heard about them? – bit of trouble from them today – nothing that couldn't have been handled with understanding – old soldier myself – but still – there you are. The soldiers had another man with them – a towny fellow, toffed up like. While they passed I hid in the bushes – didn't want to expose myself to any insults while I was in uniform. Anyway, they went straight into Mr Aldus's house. Just like that – as if they owned it. I could see the four of them talking to Mr

Aldus in his drawing-room – I could see it by the light – by the light of the room. It was the dandy fellow who spoke – talked for about twenty minutes he did and then they came away. I was still hiding as they passed me. The big soldier had his arm around the dandy fellow – and the dandy fellow was talking and talking. I was going to wait until they got from sight before I came out to get on with my round. Then Mr Aldus came to the door of his house and he must have seen me because he called out, 'Cowper, come here.' By the time I'd got to the house he'd gone inside and so I sounded the knocker. He didn't come to the door again, so after a few minutes I went inside. He was in the room with the books and he was carrying armfuls of those books from the shelves and throwing them on the open fire. They were tumbling out from the fireplace into the middle of the room and they were burning, burning away. When I went into the room he stood there for a moment pointing at them and trying to say something, but he couldn't get it out – that stutter of his, you know – and he was crying – crying noisily like a baby. I suppose he wanted me to help him – I don't know really. Anyway, then he went back to carrying more books off the shelves and throwing them on the fire. I was taken aback, I don't mind admitting it. When I'd gathered myself together I ran into the street and began shouting but nobody would come out – they've been hiding from the soldiers all day. I ran through the empty streets but there was no one. When I got back to Mr Aldus's house the place was afire and then I heard the bells – he'd gone into the church and was ringing the bells. The fire spread and nobody would help me – nobody came out – not even P.C. Pogson – until they were forced out by the fire. And now the whole village is destroyed – burned right away. (*He pauses.*) I hope you think I acted for the best, sir.

CHARLES: What? Yes, I'm sure you did.

COWPER: Thank you, sir. (*He puts on his cap and touches the peak to CHARLES.*) But what am I doing? I oughtn't to be here talking. I must get back. Will you let me out, please?

(*JOHN WINTER opens the window and THOMAS COWPER goes out by the way he came. There is a murmuring, a whispering, from the four old women: HANNAH TREWIN, MARGARET BANT, EDITH TINSON and FLORA BALDON.*)

CHARLES: What is it?

EDITH: We saw him.
HANNAH: We know about the man – } *Together.*

EDITH: You speak, my dear.

HANNAH: No. You speak, my dear.

EDITH: Very well. We saw him.

CHARLES: Who?

HANNAH: The man with the soldiers.

MARGARET: The man who talked so much.

HANNAH: Yes, we saw him.

EDITH: We saw him spoil his beautiful clothes by walking through the burning streets.

MARGARET: The soldiers followed him – they were laughing, but he didn't laugh.

EDITH: They came towards us as we ran from the fire.

HANNAH: His white face frightened us.

MARGARET: Yes, it did.

HANNAH: His voice frightened us, too.

MARGARET: Yes.

HANNAH: Long after he'd passed us we could hear it through the sound of the fire.

EDITH: And through the cries of the people.

HANNAH: Even though the bells were ringing. (*There is a pause.*)

FLORA: He spoke to me.

EDITH: No!

HANNAH: Never!

FLORA: Yes, he did.

CHARLES: What did he say? (*She does not answer.*) Well, what did he say?

FLORA: I didn't understand him – I didn't understand what he said – but he spoke to me.

CHARLES: Somewhere here there is a link – (*He strikes his forehead.*) Think, John Winter, think! (*He leaves the painting and moves about the room.*) What did he say to

Paul? What did he say to the old woman? Is it contained in that? I don't know. Perhaps so simple. No, we've missed the moment for discovery. It was when she – (*He points to FLORA BALDON.*) – said, 'He spoke to me.' Gone now. Never mind. Doesn't matter. (*He returns to the painting, but as an afterthought, says:*) But you, John Winter – would you like to get away? You've time. I'll look after the old man.

WINTER: I'll stay.

CHARLES: All right.

(*PAUL has come down the stairs into the room. He is wearing his cloak and carries a hat, a stick and a small case.*)

PAUL: John Winter tells me you have given sanctuary to some women of the village.

CHARLES: Yes.

PAUL: (*To the villagers.*) You are welcome. (*The church bells stop ringing. There is a single bell, then silence. To CHARLES.*) The village is on fire.

CHARLES: Yes.

PAUL: I've been watching the fire from my room.

CHARLES: Have you?

PAUL: It's burning right up – right up into the sky.

CHARLES: Yes.

PAUL: Who is responsible?

CHARLES: It was an accident.

PAUL: There is always the responsibility – it must rest with someone.

WINTER: Mr Aldus, sir.

PAUL: I remember him.

WINTER: He was burning his books –

PAUL: What's the time?

CHARLES: We don't know. The clock has stopped.

PAUL: I must go soon. I'll wait here. (*He sits down.*) Have you got the cigarettes, John Winter?

WINTER: No, sir. Aren't they in your pocket?

PAUL: I haven't looked. (*He makes no move to do so.*) I just thought I'd like a cigarette whilst I'm waiting. Have you finished the picture, Charles?

CHARLES: Not yet.

PAUL: How long will you be?

CHARLES: I shall work until the last moment.

PAUL: What?

CHARLES: Nothing. I shan't be long.

WINTER: Do you want a cigarette, Mr Southman?

PAUL: It doesn't matter, John Winter, it doesn't matter. I just thought it would pass the time until I go.

CHARLES: Paul, my dear, listen to me. You must try to remember. You're not going now. Stella is dead –

PAUL: Poor Stella.

CHARLES: – yes, poor Stella – and Procathren has run away and so you are not going to London after all.

PAUL: An excellent statement on the situation, sonny. Very good.

CHARLES: Well you must try to help John Winter and me by remembering these things.

PAUL: I will.

CHARLES: Good. (*He looks down at STELLA.*) Why is her face all sunken? She looks monstrous. Give me that lamp, John Winter.

PAUL: Is it dark out tonight?

WINTER: There's the fire.

PAUL: Of course, the fire. Good. Go and get the axe, John Winter. Also a saw, spades and some rope – we shall want some rope.

WINTER: What are you going to do?

PAUL: Cut down those two trees. Those in front of the house. I told you about them.

WINTER: Yes, you told me, but –

PAUL: What did she call them? She had pet names for them. What were they? I've forgotten. Never mind. We'll have them down – down they shall come. It'll give me something to do – something to occupy me whilst I'm waiting. You think I'm not strong enough. Is that what you think? (*He stands up and strikes JOHN WINTER across the face.*) Am I strong enough? Am I? I think so. Get the tools.

CHARLES: Yes, go along, John Winter.

PAUL: Yes, go along. And remember you're a servant. The rope must be strong.

(*JOHN WINTER goes out.*)

CHARLES: You'd be better employed digging a grave.

PAUL: That's a very unkind thing to say, Charles. Very unkind, indeed. She must be buried, but surely you can't expect a man of my age to go out at night and dig a grave. You must do it with John Winter. I can't do it. You can't expect me to do it – not at my age.

CHARLES: I meant a grave for the dog.

PAUL: Anyway, she can't be buried until you've finished with her. (*He is staring at STELLA.*) Is that blood on her face?

CHARLES: What? No. Paint.

PAUL: Wipe it away.

CHARLES: We mustn't touch her.

PAUL: It disfigures her.

CHARLES: It is the death that disfigures her.

PAUL: She would have been glad to know I still intend to go tonight. It was her wish – she was most insistent.

CHARLES: Listen!

PAUL: I'd want to please her, poor dead thing.

CHARLES: Listen to me!

PAUL: I'm going, Stella, just as you wished. (*He laughs.*) Shame on me! Talking to the dead.

CHARLES: Listen to me, Paul.

PAUL: Yes, sonny.

CHARLES: You're not going.

PAUL: No?

CHARLES: Do you hear me? You're not going.

PAUL: Am I not?

CHARLES: No. Procathren's run away. The dinner in your honour has all been eaten up and the guests gone home by now. Whilst they chatted and wondered why you were absent – do you remember what you did?

PAUL: What did I do?

CHARLES: You wandered about this house, a crazy old man, talking of your hey-day.

PAUL: Did I really?

CHARLES: Yes. So you can take off your cloak and put away your hat – you are too late now. It is never going to be.

PAUL: How you run on. Get along with your painting, sonny. (*He calls to the CHILD.*) Come here, little girl. Or are you a little boy? (*The CHILD goes slowly to him.*) And what are you called?

CHARLES: Damn you, Paul! God damn you for the beastliness – the selfishness of shutting yourself up in your tower of senility and lunacy at this moment – at this moment!

PAUL: Hush, Charles! You'll frighten the child.

CHARLES: If only I could take refuge in madness as you have done. If only I could convince myself, as you have done, that I am an artist, that the world waited to honour me, that the fires out there were a display for a victory, that these brushes I hold were sceptres and these people princes. Then I might face the future! You have the belief and the refuge – but it is not for me. I cannot go so far. I am not mad. I am not mad. God help me! I can touch the reality and know that I am nothing, that the world censures me, that the fires burn without reason, that these brushes are instruments of torture and these people miserable, frightened clods!

PAUL: Charles, I command you to be quiet! You're frightening this child. (*CHARLES stands quite humbled before the CHILD's penetrating stare.*) Get on with your painting.

CHARLES: Well, try to remember. If you love me, try to remember. Don't pretend. (*CHARLES returns to the painting. PAUL speaks to the CHILD.*)

PAUL: Don't let him frighten you. He's afraid – always has been. Poor Charles! Now then – are you going to talk to me for a little while before I go? What shall we talk about? You can talk, can't you? Well, come along, say something to me. Say, 'Hullo.' Say my name. Say 'Paul'. No? Very well, then, you tell me your name. Haven't you a name? You must have a name. Everyone has a name. Tell it to me for a penny. For twopence, then. Won't you talk to me? Not even for a little while? It can only be for a little while because, you see, I'm going away. Look! I've got my hat – and a stick because I'm very old, and a little case packed with all the things I shall need. Perhaps I should be going now or I shall be late. I wonder what the time is? Ah! you have a watch. What does it say? Let me see. But it has no hands on the face – it's no use at all. Pretty, though. Is that why you wear it? Because it's pretty? I expect so. We don't have pretty things here. I'm sorry. I'd like pretty things and children around me again. Darling, there is one thing I must tell you: I have forgiven you – I have forgiven you. I'm not sad – not really. I'm happy – quite happy. O darling, darling Stella, it's a very great day for me this birthday of mine, There you are – there's something for you to say. Say, 'Many happy returns of the day.' (*After a pause the CHILD says with great clarity,* Many happy returns of the day.) There! I knew you could speak. Well done! 'Many happy returns of the day', you said. And that is what they will say when I arrive – the great and famous people receiving me – they will say – (*And the little crowd speaking together, say,* Many happy returns of the day – *and then, possessed by quite a tiny fever of excitement they cry out separately,* Happy birthday – God bless you – Much happiness to you *and* Good men are rewarded. *PAUL standing and holding the hand of the CHILD at his side speaks to her.*) Can you sing? Can you dance? Dance for me! Dance for me in your lovely gay clothes – as a birthday gift. Not much to ask. Don't be shy. Look at me. I'm very old – oh, very old but I can dance and sing. (*And he does so as the VILLAGERS laugh and clap their hands. CHRISTIAN MELROSE has come up the stairs and stands inside the doorway. PAUL, turning and looking beyond the CHILD, sees MELROSE and stops his singing and dancing: the VILLAGERS stop their laughter and clapping.*) Have you come for me?

MELROSE: That's right.

PAUL: I'm ready. Look, I'm quite ready.

MELROSE: Were you expecting me?

PAUL: Oh yes. (*To the CHILD.*) No more dancing now.

(*MELROSE comes fully into the room. The group of women give a short scream in unison and gather even closer together. The CHILD runs to her MOTHER. After MELROSE has entered KILLEEN and CHATER come in.*)

MELROSE: How did you know?

PAUL: I knew.

MELROSE: Who told you I was coming here?

CHARLES: Don't take any notice of him.

MELROSE: Oh, hullo, over there. And why shouldn't I take any notice of him?

CHARLES: Because he's mad – lunatic.

MELROSE: Is he?

CHARLES: Yes.

MELROSE: Well, mad or not, he's got hold of the right end of the stick.

CHARLES: About going away?

MELROSE: (*Yawning.*) Yes. God! I'm tired.

CHARLES: Who are you?

MELROSE: That doesn't matter. (*KILLEEN and CHATER are clowning and fighting in the doorway. MELROSE turns on them.*) Stop that! You're Charles Heberden.

CHARLES: Yes.

MELROSE: And that. That's your late, lamented wife?

CHARLES: Yes.

MELROSE: I see. Where's the servant?

CHARLES: Downstairs.

MELROSE: Call him.

CHARLES: I refuse.

MELROSE: Oh, all right. (*To KILLEEN.*) Call him. His name's Winter. (*KILLEEN goes to the door and calls down the stairs in a mincing and effeminate way,* Oh, Winter; Winter, come up, please. Your master wants you.) What are these? (*He indicates the crowd of villagers.*)

CHARLES: They're from the village. From the fire. We've given them shelter.

MELROSE: Quite right, too. I'd better not make a mistake. This is Paul Southman, isn't it?

CHARLES: Yes.

MELROSE: I shouldn't think there could be two of him.

(*JOHN WINTER comes into the room from below. He is carrying a coil of rope.*) Ah! Winter?

WINTER: Yes.

MELROSE: Come in. What have you got there?

WINTER: Rope.

MELROSE: I see. Rope.

WINTER: Mr Southman asked for it.

MELROSE: Asked for it, eh? Chater – Chater, wake up! Take that. You know what we want. (*CHATER takes the rope from JOHN WINTER and squatting on the floor begins his work. To CHARLES.*) We thought we'd have to look for rope. (*He calls to JOHN WINTER who is about to go from the room.*) Hey, you! Winter! Stay here. (*And to PAUL.*) And you sit down, old man. You're not going yet.

PAUL: Not yet?

MELROSE: No, not for a little while. (*PAUL hesitant, sits – his hat on his head, and the small bag clutched on his knees.*) Now, Mr Heberden –

PAUL: May I talk to the child?

MELROSE: What child? Yes, if you want to. (*He calls to the CHILD.*) Come here, you, and talk to the old man.

(*The CHILD comes forward to stand beside PAUL.*)

PAUL: I'm not going yet.

(*MELROSE has moved to before the painting on the wall.*)

MELROSE: Your work, Mr Heberden?

CHARLES: Yes.

PAUL: (*To the CHILD.*) Won't you talk to me?

MELROSE: It's very beautiful. I suppose I can call it that, can I?

CHARLES: Certainly.

PAUL: (*To the CHILD.*) Shall we play a game?

MELROSE: Very beautiful.

PAUL: Shall we?

MELROSE: Should be in a church.

CHARLES: (*He laughs.*) Thank you.

MELROSE: What does that mean? Laughing, like that.

CHARLES: Nothing.

PAUL: Crocodiles. (*He has taken his spectacles case from his pocket and, removing the spectacles, begins snapping the case at the CHILD's nose.*)

MELROSE: Is it finished?

CHARLES: No.

MELROSE: Pity.

CHARLES: Yes.

MELROSE: Because it'll never be finished, now, will it?

CHARLES: I suppose not.

MELROSE: Why not?

CHARLES: There won't be time, will there?

MELROSE: That's better – much better! You're beginning to understand. Now we can talk. (*To CHATER.*) How long will you be? (*CHATER stopping his work for a moment, holds up his hand with spread fingers.*) Five minutes? Right. If you'd rather spend those five minutes on your painting, Mr Heberden –

CHARLES: It doesn't matter.

MELROSE: Sure? O.K.

CHARLES: I should need more than five minutes.

MELROSE: Sorry. Can't give you longer than that. Bobby Procathren should be here by then. I don't know where he's got to. Sit down, Mr Heberden. (*CHARLES and MELROSE sit on the edge of the rostrum: the VILLAGERS are grouped together: PAUL plays with the CHILD: CHATER, sitting cross-legged on the floor, the trumpet at his side, is cutting the rope into lengths: WINTER and KILLEEN stand alone.*) Have a cigarette.

CHARLES: Thank you, I will. (*They light cigarettes.*)

PAUL: And it comes along – along – along and snap!

MELROSE: And have some of this. (*He brings out a bottle of whisky.*)

CHARLES: No, thank you.

MELROSE: No? Oh, well – (*He drinks from the bottle throughout the following conversation with CHARLES.*) Are you afraid?

CHARLES: Of course.

MELROSE: You're very young to die. How old are you?

CHARLES: Nearly twenty-one.

MELROSE: I'm thirty-three – but I look older, don't I?

CHARLES: Yes.

MELROSE: I do. I know I do. (*He sees KILLEEN among the VILLAGERS.*) Killeen – what are you doing there?

KILLEEN: Nothing! Nothing at all.

MELROSE: Well, come out of it, there's a good boy.

KILLEEN: I wanted to know if they'd got anything to eat.

MELROSE: You can't be hungry. You can't possibly be hungry! You've just had a bloody great meal. (*To CHARLES.*) I don't know, really. Like animals. (*He laughs.*) Perhaps I shouldn't say that. Your cigarette's gone out. Here – let me light it.

CHARLES: Thank you.

PAUL: (*To the CHILD.*) I was a real Turtle once.

CHARLES: Why are you going to kill us?

MELROSE: Ssh! Keep your voice down. There's no need to frighten the old boy.

CHARLES: You won't do that now. Why are you – you, especially, of all people – going to kill us?

MELROSE: Don't you think I'm capable.

CHARLES: Certainly. I should think so, anyway.

MELROSE: You do?

CHARLES: Yes.

MELROSE: Good. Bobby doesn't think I'm capable. He's dared me to do it. (*He stands up, smiling.*) That's a silly thing to do, isn't it? What does he think I am? What does he think I shall feel? You're nothing to me – neither's the old man. Nobody's anything to me – because there is nobody – hasn't been for years. I care for nothing. They put it right when they said I was an 'incorrigible'. Look at me. What do you see?

CHARLES: A monster.

MELROSE: That's through your eyes – and quite natural. I don't take offence. But Bobby can't see me that way. And why? Because he's lived in the world where people – well, where they behave. Where they do this and that for this and that reason – and they do this and that for this and that reason because they have a life to live – a life to plan – and they've got to be careful. That's how he's judging me – that's how he judged you. Silly, isn't it? (*He laughs.*)

What am I doing standing up talking like this? I must look a perfect fool! (*He sits down again beside CHARLES.*)

CHARLES: Why should he judge me – or Paul – at all? The fool!

MELROSE: You shouldn't have done it, you know. You've brought this on yourselves. People like us shouldn't do such things to people like that – people who live away out there with women and music. You've struck him very deep. He's talked to me about it and my God! can't he talk. He told me about it, all right. I didn't understand one word in ten about his guilt and the way you've destroyed his innocence – but I understood a little. Poor Bobby!

CHARLES: Why?

MELROSE: He's afraid. Afraid of – what do they call it out there in the world? – hell! it's called by a short, sweet name – I know it as well as my own name – what do they call it? –

CHARLES: I don't know.

MELROSE: Got it! They call it 'death'. That's what they call it – death. And that's what he's afraid of.

CHARLES: So that's the corruption beneath the splendour: the maggot in the peacock.

MELROSE: He told Aldus – you know, the clergyman down in the village.

CHARLES: Of course. You went to see Aldus.

MELROSE: (*He laughs.*) Yes, we saw him. Then he began to burn all his books.

CHARLES: Why?

MELROSE: What?

CHARLES: I asked why he began to burn his books.

MELROSE: Because of what Bobby said to him, I suppose – I don't know.

CHARLES: What did he say?

MELROSE: I've told you – I couldn't understand a blind word. He talked nineteen to the dozen, though. Not only in English but in foreign languages. He took down books and read things out of them. Whatever he said must have been very convincing because he made the padre cry – sat there crying like a baby, he did. I don't wonder.

Bobby talked to me – talked until I was drunk with it. I'm so bloody tired as well – we've been on the run for eight days. (*MELROSE sees that the door from below is slowly opening. He calls.*) Who's there? Oh, it's you, Bobby. Come in. We've been waiting for you. (*The door opens fully and ROBERT PROCATHREN stands there. His clothes are filthy and torn, his face and hands blackened by the fire.*) Come in. (*ROBERT steps into the room.*) What's the matter? Did you get lost?

ROBERT: I've been sick.

MELROSE: I should say you have. Look, it's all over your coat. Have you eaten too much –

ROBERT: Probably.

MELROSE: – or is it the exercise? Killeen, have you got a handkerchief? Wipe him down.

KILLEEN: I'm a nursemaid – that's what I am.

MELROSE: (*To CHARLES.*) Bit of a change in him, isn't there? (*MELROSE is exultant, excited by ROBERT's appearance, his degradation.*) Not so beautiful as he was – as we remember him, eh? (*To ROBERT.*) Better now?

ROBERT: Yes. All right, now.

MELROSE: Oh, he's lost that beautiful tie. You've lost your tie, Bobby.

KILLEEN: He gave it to me. (*KILLEEN is wearing the tie loosely round the neck of his uniform.*)

MELROSE: He gave it to you?

KILLEEN: Yes.

MELROSE: Gave it to you?

KILLEEN: Yes!

MELROSE: (*Laughing.*) All right – I'll believe you.

KILLEEN: Well, it's true.

ROBERT: Yes, I gave it to him – as a token.

MELROSE: It's your business.

ROBERT: Melrose.

MELROSE: Yes?

ROBERT: You're not – not 'putting it off', as they say, are you?

MELROSE: No, Bobby, I'm not 'putting it off'.

ROBERT: Don't 'put it off', Melrose.

(*MELROSE goes to ROBERT and takes ROBERT's face in his hands.*)

MELROSE: You think I won't do it, I know. But I'm going to do it.

ROBERT: And what is it you're going to do? Tell me.

MELROSE: You tell me. Ha! It's like a kid's game, isn't it? Who tells who, eh? No, but seriously, Bobby, you tell me. You're the boss from now, you know. You can't get away from it now. If you want to order people like me around you've got to take the responsibility – you've got to. It's always been like that. But it makes me laugh sometimes. 'Melrose do such-and-such!' 'Yes, sir!' – and then I look down and see their eyes and their eyes are asking me, 'Melrose you think that decision is right, don't you? If you think I'm wrong for God's sake don't do it.' But I do whatever I think – if I can be bothered to think. What is it I can do for you, Bobby?

ROBERT: Kill the old man and the boy for me.

MELROSE: Just for you. (*There is a pause and then EDITH TINSON begins to give short repeated screams.*) What are you doing there, Killeen?

KILLEEN: I'm not doing a thing. I'm not near her. It's not me – it's what he said.

MELROSE: Well, shut her up!

(*KILLEEN goes to the woman and her screams stop. It is then a human voice can be heard humming a polite little tune. It is CHATER singing as he works. Now it is apparent what he is doing: from the rope he is constructing two nooses.*)

ROBERT: How long?

MELROSE: Not long. (*He grips ROBERT by the shoulder: his voice is strong and clear but without anger.*) What have I got to lose in this? Tell me that. Nothing! You're a fool to doubt me, Bobby – a fool! (*Turning, he runs into KILLEEN.*) Get out of the way!

KILLEEN: Hey!

MELROSE: What?

KILLEEN: Do you think there's any food in the place?

MELROSE: For God's sake! –

KILLEEN: Well, some biscuits or something.

MELROSE: There must be something the matter with you.

KILLEEN: I'm thirsty too.

(*ROBERT has moved to stand before PAUL. He speaks to him.*)

ROBERT: Southman – Southman, can you hear? You're not asleep – you're pretending. Come alone, look up. Look up!

MELROSE: Listen! He's beginning to talk to the old man. Quiet, everyone!

ROBERT: Please let me speak.

MELROSE: Carry on, Bobby. Let anyone try to stop you.

ROBERT: You must look at me, Southman.

(*PAUL turns his head. ROBERT is now crouched beside him and PAUL looks into his face without recognition, without comprehension.*)

CHARLES: Leave him alone.

MELROSE: (*Shouting.*) Quiet!

ROBERT: Southman – I thought the power invested was for good. I believed we were here to do well by each other. It isn't so. We are here – all of us – to die. Nothing more than that. We live for that alone. You've known all along, haven't you? Why didn't you tell me – why did you have to teach me in such a dreadful way? For now – (*He cries out.*) – I have wasted my inheritance! All these years trying to learn how to live leaving myself such a little time to learn how to die. (*He turns to speak to the CHILD.*) Afraid of the dark? But it is more than the dark. It is that which lies beyond, not within, the dark – the fear of the revelation by light. We are told by our fairy-tale books that we should not fear but the darkness is around us, and our fear is that the unknown hand is already at the switch. I tell you, do not fear, for there is no light and the way is from darkness to darkness to darkness. (*PAUL takes ROBERT's hand and holds fast to it. ROBERT again speaks to him.*) You old rascal! Knowing it is not a question of finding but of losing the pieties, the allegiances, the loves. You should tell. I've been talking to Aldus. Told him I lost faith in God years ago and never felt its passing. But man – oh, take faith in man from me and the meaning becomes clear by the agony we suffer. What a cost it is. Clear – not for all immediately – no, Aldus is out there at the moment chasing his lost God like a rat down a culvert. But for myself – I am well. (*He moves from PAUL.*) Perhaps I should have understood before coming here. There are many signs out in the world offering themselves for man's comprehension. The flowers in the sky, the sound of their blossoming too acute for our ears leaving us to hear nothing but the clamour of voices protesting, crying out against the end – 'It's not fair!' – as they fasten to the walls of life – and the storm is of their own making – it is the howling appeal for tenderness, for love. Only now I see the thing's played out and compassion – arid as an hour-glass – run through. Such matters need not concern us here in this – (*For a moment he is silent.*) – in this place. For we have our own flowers to give us understanding. (*He points to STELLA.*) The rose she wears beneath her heart. There, released, is the flower within us all – the bloom that will leap from the breast or drop from the mouth. It shall be my conceit that a flower is our last passport. Who wears it shall go free. Free, Southman!

(*There is a shrill whistle from CHATER. He has finished his work and points to two nooses lying coiled on the floor before him. MELROSE leaps forward and snatches up the ropes.*)

PAUL: John Winter!

ROBERT: Wait!

MELROSE: Ready!

ROBERT: Wait!

PAUL: Let us go.

MELROSE: Yes, come along, old man.

PAUL: I intend to cut down the trees –

ROBERT: Wait!

PAUL: – that stand before the house. They are a danger.

MELROSE: Quite right.

PAUL: You'll help me?

MELROSE: Yes.

PAUL: Are the tools there, John Winter?

MELROSE: Let him believe it. Come on, let him believe it!

WINTER: The tools are at the door, sir.

PAUL: I see you have the rope.

MELROSE: Yes, I have the rope.

PAUL: Good.

MELROSE: Killeen, take Mr Southman down.

KILLEEN: Right-o.

PAUL: Thank you. (*PAUL and KILLEEN go out and down the stairs.*)

MELROSE: Chater, bring Mr Heberden. (*CHATER takes CHARLES's arm.*) Oh, by the way, you're not a religious man or anything?

CHARLES: No.

MELROSE: What I mean is, do you want to say goodbye to your wife?

CHARLES: No.

MELROSE: Go along, then. (*CHATER and CHARLES go out and down the stairs.*) What are you going to do, Winter?

WINTER: I don't know.

MELROSE: Any ideas?

WINTER: Go away, I suppose.

MELROSE: Have you anywhere to go?

WINTER: No.

(*MELROSE takes some banknotes from his pocket. He separates several and holds them out to JOHN WINTER.*)

MELROSE: Here, take this.

WINTER: Oh, thank you, sir. Thank you.

MELROSE: That's all right. (*JOHN WINTER takes the money and hurries away by the stairs to the upper part of the house. ROBERT moves to STELLA's body and stands looking down at her. There is silence. Suddenly MELROSE speaks.*) Ready?

ROBERT: (*Immediately.*) Ready.

(*MELROSE and ROBERT go out and down the stairs. When they have gone there is a pause and then the CHILD, detaching herself from the group of VILLAGERS, moves across the room to where STELLA's body lies. The CHILD stares from above at the dead face and, extending a finger, touches for a moment the closed eyes. It is then the MOTHER calls to the CHILD.*)

JUDITH: Stella! (*Startled by the call the CHILD stumbles among the bones and so moves from the body. In doing so she accidentally knocks against the table and cries out in pain.*)

Stella, dear child! (*But the CHILD moves on and seeing the green scarf, CHARLES's present to PAUL, lying on the floor, she picks it up and puts it around her neck.*) Stella! We are strangers here, Stella.

(*The CHILD takes up the copy of 'Alice in Wonderland' from the table. The trumpet suddenly sounds from the garden: a raucous tune. The CHILD, with the book in her hand, performs a grave dance to the music. As abruptly as it began the trumpet stops. The CHILD's dance continues for a little but she hesitates, listening. There is no sound. Dropping the book to the floor she runs to her MOTHER and hides her face in the woman's lap. There is no sound and everything is still: quite still.*)

*CURTAIN*

# A PENNY FOR A SONG

## Introduction to
## A PENNY FOR A SONG

In an English garden during the invasion scare of 1940, John Whiting was struck by the contrast between the peacefulness of his surroundings and the pandemonium of preparations being made in case German troops arrived on the coast. Absurd precautions were taken at sleepy seaside towns. Piers were blown up, barbed wire entanglements installed and concrete pillboxes erected on the beaches. As he says in his introduction to the 1957 collection of his plays, "It is rarely necessary to embroider the finer lunacies of the English at war," and though *A Penny for a Song* may look like an extravaganza, the behaviour of the characters is mostly based on factual accounts of English reactions to an earlier invasion scare.

A researcher who was given access to some of his private papers* found manuscript notes that show his main source was Carola Oman's book *Britain against Napoleon.* Rich landowners recruited their own forces. There were "Fencibles" like the St Pancras and Marylebone Volunteers, and the price of the invasion posters in the play is historically correct.

The book reports on a rumour that Napoleon "had under construction a monster bridge, by which his troops were to pass from Calais to Dover, directed by skilled officers in air balloons, and a Channel Tunnel, engineered by a mining expert. The most dramatic tale was that the Emperor, disguised as a British tar, was aboard a south east fishing smack." These rumours are neatly restructured in Sir Timothy Bellboys's madcap scheme to defeat the invasion single-handed by teaching himself French from a phrase book, disguising himself as Napoleon, crawling through a tunnel to come out behind the invading army, and ordering it to retreat.

The play was given only thirty-six performances at the Haymarket in March 1951. Directed by Peter Brook, with designs by the *Punch* cartoonist Rowland Emmett, it failed to

*Gabrielle Scott Robinson: see Acknowledgments.

amuse the critics or the audiences. Whiting lost faith in it, and for the Royal Shakespeare Company's revival of it in August 1962 at the Aldwych, he did some drastic rewriting.

In the original version – the one printed here – the ex-soldier, Edward Sterne, has been blinded during the fighting. This makes him dependent on the small boy, Jonathan, who acts as his guide on their journey to London – Edward thinks he can stop the war by showing himself to the King. Refusing to drop the idea, even when he is told out that King George III is mad, Edward is just as wrong-headed as the other characters. The only one to behave reasonably is the beautiful young girl, Dorcas, who is just seventeen, and the experience of love takes her through the painful process of "putting off childish ways".

The play is unfailingly charming and unflappably good-tempered. Not only does Whiting distil a perfect English summer's day into stage action, he pokes gentle fun at our national blend of sportsmanship, pedantry, lunacy, pomposity and propriety.

His later version of the play may be less literary and less wordy, but it is also less touching, less amusing and more irritable. He should have ignored any criticism he may have received for letting the dandyish house-guest, Hallam, philosophise too much, and for lapsing occasionally into whimsicality and sentimentality during the love scenes between Edward and Dorcas. Rewriting the play as if he had been advised to bring Edward into line with the angry young men being featured in plays at the Royal Court, Whiting makes him into an irascible spokesman for radical ideas based partly on his experiences in France and partly on Tom Paine's book *The Rights of Man.*

We do not need a yardstick for measuring the eccentricity of our insular cloud-cuckooland, and, no longer blind, either literally or metaphorically, the revised Edward is a bull in the china world of the Bellboys. He no longer falls in love with Dorcas, though he takes over some of the lines that had originally been assigned to her, while she takes over some of his. Nearly all these changes are for the worse.

The play ends, as it should, with a dying fall. Hallam and Dorcas are left alone together – the brave and beautiful girl, desolated and abandoned together with the philosophising clown. A song, a spinet inside the house and Hallam picking up the melody on his recorder. But in 1962 the recorder was cut.

Hey, nonny no!
Men are fools that wish to die!
Is't not fine to dance and sing
When the bells of death do ring?

*Anonymous*

For oure tyme is a very shadow that passeth away, and after our ende there is no returnynge, for it is fast sealed, so that no man commeth agayne. Come on therefore, let us enjoye the pleasures that there are, and let us soone use the creature like as in youth.... Let us leave some token of oure pleasure in every place, for that is oure porcion, els gett we nothinge.

*The Boke of Wysdome*

All things can tempt me from this craft of verse:
One time it was a woman's face, or worse –
The seeming needs of my fool-driven land;
Now nothing but comes readier to the hand
Than this accustomed toil. When I was young,
I had not given a penny for a song
Did not the poet sing it with such airs
That one believed he had a sword upstairs;
Yet would be now, could I but have my wish,
Colder and dumber and deafer than a fish.

*W B Yeats*

# Characters

SIR TIMOTHY BELLBOYS

HALLAM MATTHEWS

EDWARD STERNE

JONATHAN WATKINS

LAMPRETT BELLBOYS

GEORGE SELINCOURT

WILLIAM HUMPAGE

SAMUEL BREEZE

JOSEPH BROTHERHOOD

JAMES GIDDY

RUFUS PIGGOTT

DORCAS BELLBOYS

HESTER BELLBOYS

A MAIDSERVANT

*A Penny for a Song* was first performed at the Haymarket Theatre, London in March 1951 with the following cast:

SIR TIMOTHY BELLBOYS, Alan Webb

HALLAM MATTHEWS, Ronald Squire

HESTER BELLBOYS, Marie Lohr

DORCAS BELLBOYS, Virginia McKenna

EDWARD STERNE, Ronald Howard

GEORGE SELINCOURT, Basil Radford

Director, Peter Brook

The scene is the garden before Sir Timothy Bellboys's house in Dorset, on a summer's day in 1804.

ACT I Morning.
ACT II Later in the Day.

# ACT ONE

*The scene is the garden before Sir Timothy Bellboys's house in Dorset. The time is morning of a day in the summer of the year 1804. The garden is bounded on one side by the house: on a second side by a low wall in which there is a gate leading to an orchard and on the third side it is open to the sea and sky. At the moment the curtains of the house are drawn but when, later in the day, they are withdrawn a view is given into a parlour and a dining-room on the ground floor and of three bedrooms on the first floor. There is a front door surmounted by an elegant fanlight. Set about the lawn are various articles of garden furniture. A little apart there is an alcove – a small retreat. This place is cloistered, self-contained – out of sight of the house and garden. There is a well: it is fully equipped with windlass and bucket. The door of the house is closed and the garden is empty but for WILLIAM HUMPAGE who reclines at a point of vantage in a tree above the orchard wall. He is asleep and the sun shines down on his ugly and scarlet face reflecting also in the metal buttons of his strange uniform: satin knee-breeches with worsted stockings and boots all surmounted by a gay tunic which is, perhaps, of some long-forgotten militia. A brass telescope hangs from his hand and about his wrist is tied a silver whistle. He is surrounded by an apparatus the purpose of which is not immediately apparent. It consists of two large wooden flaps or signals – one red, one green and both movable – the green flap being prominently displayed at the moment. Also to hand is a great brass bell very highly polished. It is a fine morning and the sky promises a clear, hot day. Suddenly the curtains of a room on the first floor are torn apart and the window is thrown open. SIR TIMOTHY BELLBOYS, in a state of partial undress, leans out. After a racking yawn he surveys the garden and beyond with interest. Then, in a frightening voice, he shouts:*

TIMOTHY: Humpage!

(*HUMPAGE awakes with a start scattering several small cakes and the remains of an alfresco meal to the ground. He raises the telescope, in reverse, and putting it to his eye begins to scan seawards with an alarming intensity. TIMOTHY calls again.*)

Humpage!

HUMPAGE: Sir!

TIMOTHY: Anything to report?
HUMPAGE: No, sir.
TIMOTHY: Nothing in sight?
HUMPAGE: No, sir.
TIMOTHY: No ships?
HUMPAGE: No, sir.
TIMOTHY: No troops?
HUMPAGE: No, sir.
TIMOTHY: Nothing suspicious?
HUMPAGE: No, sir.

(*TIMOTHY is about to withdraw.*)

TIMOTHY: Were you asleep?
HUMPAGE: No, sir.

(*TIMOTHY withdraws to the bedroom and closes the window but does not draw the curtains. He can be seen moving about the room. By this time SAMUEL BREEZE has entered the garden. He is a servant, neatly dressed: a Londoner by birth. He looks up at HUMPAGE who by this time has relaxed.*)

BREEZE: 'Morning.
HUMPAGE: 'Morning.
BREEZE: Now this isn't right. I can't seem to find my way around this place at all. I'm looking for the outhouses. (*HUMPAGE points to the back of the house.*) But I've just come that way.
HUMPAGE: Then you must have passed them.
BREEZE: If you say so. I'm a stranger here. However – (*BREEZE turns to go back by the way he came and meets LAMPRETT BELLBOYS.*) Good morning, sir.
LAMPRETT: Good morning. (*BREEZE goes out. At the sight of LAMPRETT, HUMPAGE is again galvanized into action. He snatches up the telescope and views the countryside. LAMPRETT speaks to him.*) Humpage!
HUMPAGE: Sir?
LAMPRETT: Attention! Anything to report?
HUMPAGE: No, sir.
LAMPRETT: Nothing in the night?
HUMPAGE: No, sir.
LAMPRETT: No smoke?
HUMPAGE: No sir.

LAMPRETT: Oh. (*After a pause.*) Not even a gorse bush?

HUMPAGE: No sir.

LAMPRETT: Very well, Humpage. Keep your eyes open. Good morning, my love. (*He speaks to his wife, HESTER, who is now standing in the open doorway of the house. She is dressed in clothes of a former period.*)

HESTER: Good morning, Lamprett. Have you seen our daughter?

LAMPRETT: No, my dear, I have not.

HESTER: (*Calls.*) Dorcas!

LAMPRETT: Humpage!

HUMPAGE: Sir?

LAMPRETT: Any sight of Miss Bellboys? (*HUMPAGE views about.*)

HUMPAGE: No sir.

HESTER: Tiresome child. Lamprett!

LAMPRETT: My dear?

HESTER: You have on odd shoes. Change them. (*He goes into the house. LAMPRETT sits, removes his shoes and stares at them.*)

HUMPAGE: Report, sir!

LAMPRETT: (*Leaping up.*) What's that?

HUMPAGE: Miss Bellboys approaching, sir.

LAMPRETT: Oh. (*He sits again. DORCAS BELLBOYS, his daughter, runs into the garden.*) Your mother is looking for you, Dorcas.

DORCAS: Why?

LAMPRETT: I don't know. Where have you been?

DORCAS: Swimming.

LAMPRETT: Absurd habit. Your mother tells me my shoes are odd, but I cannot see it. Can you? (*Together they examine the shoes.*)

DORCAS: They seem to be a pair.

LAMPRETT: I think so. However, I'd better change them – you never know. (*He goes into the house. DORCAS, who is barefoot, sits and begins to rub the dry sand from her feet with a handful of grass. Suddenly and simultaneously two bedroom windows are thrown up and TIMOTHY and HESTER appear.*)

HESTER: Dorcas!

TIMOTHY: Humpage!

HESTER: Good morning, Timothy.

TIMOTHY: Good morning, Hester. One moment, please, Humpage!

HUMPAGE: Sir?

TIMOTHY: Which way does the wind blow? (*HUMPAGE produces a small portable wind-vane which he holds in the air. TIMOTHY observes this.*) That's bad. (*He withdraws.*)

DORCAS: What is it, Mama?

HESTER: How old are you?

DORCAS: Seventeen last birthday.

(*TIMOTHY again appears at his window.*)

TIMOTHY: Humpage, according to my calculations the wind cannot be blowing from that direction today. (*For answer HUMPAGE again dumbly holds up the vane.*) I see. Then we can expect some excitement. (*He withdraws.*)

HESTER: Seventeen. It has occurred to me that now is the time to put off your childish ways.

DORCAS: Yes, Mama.

HESTER: We must all grow up.

DORCAS: Yes, Mama.

HESTER: Good girl.

(*HALLAM MATTHEWS has come from the house. HALLAM, a giant of a man, is an exquisite, a dandy par excellence. His clothes are magnificent in their sobriety.*)

HALLAM: May I wish you a very good day, Hester?

HESTER: Good morning, Hallam. You're up from your bed, I see.

HALLAM: Indeed, yes. Some time ago.

HESTER: You're recovered from your journey?

HALLAM: Fully. You must forgive my petulance on arrival last night.

HESTER: You must forgive our complete ignorance of your visit. Timothy forgot to tell anyone that you were expected. Have you seen him yet?

HALLAM: I've seen no one but you. Even my man, Breeze, has quite disappeared. Perhaps it had better be known at once – I require peace here but not complete indifference to my welfare. There was a touch of asperity in that remark, wasn't there? Please forget it.

HESTER: I've done so.

HALLAM: For today I feel that nothing shall deter me from fully enjoying this charming occupation known as life.

HESTER: How is London?

HALLAM: In uproar. This invitation was god-sent. I asked myself, 'Shall it be a few days in the country with my old friends?' and a few days in the country it is. I shall return to London well able to withstand all assaults on my character and reputation. Only two things could have saved me after the past few weeks' activity – death or a visit. I've chosen this visit.

HESTER: Rightly, I'm sure.

HALLAM: But I'm keeping you from some important duty with my chatter.

HESTER: Good gracious! So you are. (*HESTER goes into the house. HALLAM looks about him with appreciation. He sees HUMPAGE and decides*:)

HALLAM: I think it best, in the circumstances, to ignore you. (*And so, speaks to DORCAS.*) And who are you?

DORCAS: My name is Dorcas.

HALLAM: Ah, yes. The daughter of the house.

DORCAS: Yes.

HALLAM: Charming!

(*BREEZE in a confused state, has wandered into the garden.*)

BREEZE: Oh, there you are, Mr Matthews.

HALLAM: Oh, there you are, Sam. I think I'm a little angry with you.

BREEZE: Why, sir?

HALLAM: Recall: you left me over an hour ago. In that time I have risen, shaved myself, dressed myself and breakfasted. All this without your usual assistance. Is it right, Sam, is it right?

BREEZE: No, sir. Forgive me.

HALLAM: What have you been doing?

BREEZE: Getting very lost.

HALLAM: Why? The place is simplicity itself – there is the charm.

BREEZE: Have you been that way? (*He indicates the way he has come.*)

HALLAM: Not yet.

BREEZE: I beg of you, sir – don't go that way.

HALLAM: You must not expect every thoroughfare to be as straight as St James's Street. The way about here may be tortuous but the occupants are innocent, honest and homely. Let us absorb these unusual qualities and begin the day. What have you for me this morning?

(*BREEZE takes a book from his pocket.*)

BREEZE: Mr William Wordsworth, sir.

HALLAM: Oh, dear! Not a happy choice perhaps, but we must persevere, must we not? And better to have him today in the sunshine than to have him when it is raining. Where shall we take him?

BREEZE: I wouldn't dare to advise you, sir.

HALLAM: In that case we must consult a native of the place. (*He turns to DORCAS.*) Tell me, Dorcas, do you know of a secluded place in the vicinity of this house to which I can retire for a while?

DORCAS: For what purpose?

HALLAM: For the purpose of performing my usual literary chores of the day: which is to have Samuel here read to me from contemporary works. Your expression leads me to understand that you are not fully in sympathy with such an occupation. However, do you know of a suitable place?

DORCAS: I'm trying to think.

HALLAM: Thank you.

DORCAS: There is a ruined cottage on the cliffs.

HALLAM: Excellent! I'd contemplated a field. I'd not dared to hope for a roof.

DORCAS: It has no roof.

HALLAM: No roof. Well, four walls –

DORCAS: Three walls. (*She laughs.*)

HALLAM: I think you are a very nasty little girl. Come, Samuel.

(*TIMOTHY appears at the bedroom window.*)

TIMOTHY: Hallam! There you are.

HALLAM: Yes, Timothy. Here I am.

TIMOTHY: I shall be down soon to greet you.

HALLAM: That will be very pleasant.

TIMOTHY: Your visit here is secret. (*He puts a finger to his lips.*) Ssh! (*HALLAM replies in the same way.*) Where are you going now?

HALLAM: Just a very little way off, Timothy, for a very little while. Samuel is going to read something new by Mr – what's the fellow's name?

BREEZE: Wordsworth, sir.

HALLAM: By Mr Wordsworth – and I didn't wish to alarm or distress anyone in the house.

TIMOTHY: Well, don't be long. I want to talk to you. (*He is about to withdraw, when:*) Keep your eyes to the south!

HALLAM: I will, indeed. (*TIMOTHY disappears.*) Come, Sam. (*HALLAM goes from the garden followed by BREEZE. A diminutive MAIDSERVANT can be seen going about within the house withdrawing the curtains of various rooms. LAMPRETT comes from the house.*)

LAMPRETT: Who was that?

DORCAS: Old Matthews and his servant, Sammy.

LAMPRETT: Don't be familiar.

DORCAS: Sorry, Papa.

LAMPRETT: Mr Matthews is a guest here. (*He looks down at his shoes.*) I've changed them.

DORCAS: Have you?

LAMPRETT: Yes. They look better, don't they? This is the uncomfortable pair. Oh, well – to work! Don't dream away the day.

(*LAMPRETT hobbles out. DORCAS is now lying full length on the grass. HUMPAGE has gone to sleep again. From within the house HESTER calls sharply,* Lamprett – Lamprett! *From her recumbent position DORCAS slowly raises her legs before her. She regards her feet, flexing her toes, and then, continuing the movement proceeds to perform a slow backward somersault. This brings her to an inverted view of the orchard gate where now stand a man and a small boy.*)

EDWARD: There's someone here, I think. (*JONATHAN pulls at his hand, and bending down, EDWARD listens to the boy's whispering.*) Jonathan tells me that we are in a garden speaking to a young lady.

DORCAS: That is true.

EDWARD: We have broken our journey for a moment to ask if we might have a drink of water.

DORCAS: Of course. (*She moves towards the house, and then turns.*) There's milk if you prefer it.

EDWARD: Jonathan?

(*The BOY nods his head.*)

DORCAS: It shall be milk then. Something to eat? (*The BOY shakes his head.*) Please sit down.

(*DORCAS goes into the house. JONATHAN leads EDWARD to a chair and he sits. The BOY squats on the ground beside him. TIMOTHY's bedroom window is thrown up and TIMOTHY leans out.*)

TIMOTHY: Humpage!

HUMPAGE: (*Awakened.*) Sir?

TIMOTHY: The portents are ominous. (*HUMPAGE crosses himself.*) Keep your eyes to the south!

HUMPAGE: Yes sir.

TIMOTHY: Always to the south. (*He notices EDWARD and JONATHAN.*) Good morning to you.

EDWARD: Good morning.

TIMOTHY: A fine morning.

EDWARD: Yes.

TIMOTHY: For a battle, I mean. (*He withdraws, closing the window.*)

(*DORCAS comes from the house carrying a tray with two tankards of milk and some apples. For a moment she stands silent before EDWARD. Then, very quietly, she speaks:*)

DORCAS: I am here.

EDWARD: Yes.

DORCAS: I didn't wish to startle you.

EDWARD: Thank you.

DORCAS: Because you are blind.

EDWARD: What's that?

DORCAS: Because you are blind. Why, what's the matter? It's true, is it not? Now I've startled you – why?

EDWARD: To hear it spoken in that way. Blind! Without pity, as you did. Never, since I returned –

DORCAS: I'm sorry.

EDWARD: No, indeed. Let it be spoken in such a way. (*DORCAS puts the tankard of milk into his hand.*) This was meant for the boy – it was he who was thirsty.

DORCAS: There's one for him. He has it.

EDWARD: Then, thank you. (*He takes the milk.*)

DORCAS: And I thought you would like these.

EDWARD: What are they?

DORCAS: Apples.

EDWARD: For the journey. Thank you.

(*DORCAS gives the apples to JONATHAN, who stores them away in various pockets. DORCAS sits on the ground beside EDWARD. JONATHAN respectfully rises.*)

DORCAS: Sit down, please – Jonathan, isn't it?

EDWARD: Yes. My name is Edward Sterne.

DORCAS: I am Dorcas Bellboys.

EDWARD: How do you do.

DORCAS: How do you do. (*And they laugh at themselves.*) You say you are on a journey.

EDWARD: Yes. I am going to London. And Jonathan, here – Jonathan Watkins – is on his way to a distant village in a holy land. (*He pauses, drinking the milk. JONATHAN, who has drunk his milk at a draught, has taken from his pocket a length of twine and formed upon his hands a cat's cradle.*) We may yet turn back.

DORCAS: Why do you go to London?

EDWARD: I'm going to see the King.

DORCAS: King George?

EDWARD: Yes. I have a request to make of him. (*He pauses.*) I'm going to ask him to stop this war. You're laughing at me.

DORCAS: No!

EDWARD: You may if you wish. (*JONATHAN holds out the cat's cradle to EDWARD, who feeling his hands, takes it and by touch converts it.*) But you must not laugh at my friend here. That I cannot allow. My friend who is on his way to Bethlehem. (*The BOY takes back the cat's cradle.*) You think us absurd?

DORCAS: Why should I? My uncle Timothy believes he can defeat the entire French fleet and army single-handed.

EDWARD: (*He laughs.*) A man after my own heart. He lives here.

DORCAS: Oh, yes. This is his house.

EDWARD: Was it he who called to me a moment ago? Saying it was a fine day for a battle.

DORCAS: That would be him.

EDWARD: And how is he going to defeat the French army – to say nothing of the fleet?

DORCAS: Perhaps in the way that you are going to convince the King that it is necessary to end the war. How are you going to do that?

EDWARD: Show myself to him.

(*There is a pause. DORCAS puts her hand out to EDWARD's arm, hesitates, and withdraws without touching him. TIMOTHY appears at his window.*)

TIMOTHY: Dorcas!

DORCAS: Yes?

TIMOTHY: Is Mr Matthews back?

DORCAS: No.

TIMOTHY: Request him to come up to me when he returns.

DORCAS: Very well.

TIMOTHY: And remember –

DORCAS: To keep my eyes to the south.

TIMOTHY: That's right. (*To EDWARD.*) And you, sir – all eyes to the south.

(*TIMOTHY withdraws. EDWARD turns his blind eyes towards DORCAS. She immediately takes his hand, saying:*)

DORCAS: Please! He doesn't know! Please!

EDWARD: Why to the south?

DORCAS: Because it is from that way Bonaparte will come. They say he will come with his armies any day now. He has been preparing for months and – well, look at the weather.

EDWARD: I can feel the heat of the sun. Yes, I should say it is a very good day for a battle, although from my experience almost any kind of day will do. Are you an orphan?

DORCAS: No. Why?

EDWARD: I thought – living here alone with your uncle –

DORCAS: I don't live here alone with him. Good gracious no! There is Mama and Papa. Mama orders the house for Uncle Timothy and Papa – well, Papa looks after his fire engine and –

(*LAMPRETT appears from behind the house.*)

LAMPRETT: Dorcas.

DORCAS: Yes, Papa?

LAMPRETT: I beg your pardon. Do I disturb you? Good morning.

EDWARD: Good morning, sir.

LAMPRETT: (*Seeing JONATHAN.*) Ah! Little boy. You'll do. Come with me.

(*JONATHAN hesitates.*)

DORCAS: Go with him. He won't harm you. He is my father.

(*JONATHAN rises and slowly crosses the garden to LAMPRETT, who takes him by the arm: together they go out.*)

EDWARD: Did he hesitate?

DORCAS: Jonathan? For a moment.

EDWARD: He doesn't fully understand about fathers and mothers: he is an orphan.

DORCAS: How did you come together?

EDWARD: Four days ago a warm dry hand was placed in mine. It has guided me since.

DORCAS: You were travelling –

EDWARD: – alone. Alone. Hoping to find and make my way by charity. I was singing for my supper outside an empty house when Jonathan came to me. I told him I was on my way to see the King and he explained that he could take me there incidental to his own journey.

DORCAS: Why is he going to Bethlehem?

EDWARD: Last Christmas he was told the story of the birth of a child in Bethlehem. From that story Jonathan recognized his brother. But the story ended and the storyteller forgot to say that the birth was over eighteen hundred years ago, and that the boy has long since been dead. (*HUMPAGE stirs in his sleep.*) Aren't we alone – now – at this moment.

DORCAS: It's no one. And you – Edward – where do you come from?

EDWARD: I was sent home – (*He raises his hands to his useless eyes.*) – three months ago. They landed us at Plymouth and then, to return, took on a cargo of men with arms and legs, with eyes and honest minds. I have been alone since I returned. Now I am going to see the King to ask him to stop the war. Do you understand or do you think I am mad? (*He rises.*) Where are you? You have moved from me?

DORCAS: I am here.

EDWARD: Then tell me: Jonathan goes to Bethlehem not knowing that Christ is dead – do I go to London not knowing – not knowing that –

(*DORCAS has risen to stand by EDWARD's side; she takes his hand. HESTER within the house, calls:* Dorcas – Dorcas. *The girl, looking up into EDWARD's face, says:*)

DORCAS: I did not know that blind eyes could cry. Come away! It is my mother calling me. Come. (*She leads EDWARD out to the orchard. Immediately HESTER comes from the house. She looks about the garden and then calls.*)

HESTER: Lamprett!

(*HUMPAGE awakes and views the horizon through his telescope. LAMPRETT comes into the garden.*)

LAMPRETT: I've changed them, my dear.

HESTER: Changed what?

LAMPRETT: My shoes.

HESTER: Never mind that now. What are you doing?

LAMPRETT: Cleaning the engine.

HESTER: Again?

LAMPRETT: Well, my dear –

HESTER: You cleaned it only yesterday.

LAMPRETT: We must be prepared.

HESTER: Ridiculous! (*LAMPRETT prepares to go.*) Lamprett!

LAMPRETT: My dear?

HESTER: Do I bully you?

LAMPRETT: (*He smiles.*) A little.

HESTER: (*She smiles.*) Forgive me. I must a little or belie my appearance.

LAMPRETT: Of course.

HESTER: Have you seen Dorcas?

LAMPRETT: A moment ago.

HESTER: Where?

LAMPRETT: I really can't remember.

HESTER: She's growing up, Lamprett.

LAMPRETT: Yes, with a young man.

HESTER: What's that?

LAMPRETT: I saw her with a young man.

HESTER: You see! (*She turns to go into the house.*)

LAMPRETT: Hester –

HESTER: Yes?

LAMPRETT: Did you wish to speak to me?

HESTER: I don't think so.

LAMPRETT: You called me as if you wished to speak to me.

HESTER: Then what can I say? (*She pauses.*) God bless you. (*She goes into the house.*)

LAMPRETT: Humpage!

HUMPAGE: Sir!

LAMPRETT: If this fellow, Napoleon Bonaparte, does come over with an army I expect there will be work to do. The battle is sure to start a few fires. Murder, rapine, looting – that sort of thing, you know.

HUMPAGE: Yes, sir.

LAMPRETT: It will, however – (*As LAMPRETT continues to speak, JONATHAN comes in to hand him a polishing rag.*) – be more difficult than usual – thank you, my dear – (*JONATHAN returns to his duties.*) – considerably more difficult. For while we must extinguish our own fires we must be careful to foster those of the enemy.

HUMPAGE: That's right, sir.

LAMPRETT: There our duty as Englishmen must precede our duty as firemen. But knowing how against the grain it will be to foster – indeed, positively encourage! – any fire, friend's or enemy's, I've been considering the advisability of using some combustible mixture in certain hoses. Have you anything to suggest?

HUMPAGE: Brandy.

LAMPRETT: Well, yes –

(*HALLAM MATTHEWS, followed by BREEZE, enters the garden.*)

HALLAM: Take those things to my room, Samuel. I shall sit here for a while. (*BREEZE goes into the house. HALLAM sits down, fanning himself.*) Good morning, Lamprett.

LAMPRETT: Good morning, Hallam.

HALLAM: Inflammatory weather.

LAMPRETT: Yes, thank God. Have you been walking?

HALLAM: Yes. Your daughter –

(*BREEZE re-enters the garden. He carries a small jewelled box which he hands to HALLAM.*)

BREEZE: Your lozenges, sir.

HALLAM: Oh, thank you, Sam. (*BREEZE goes back into the house.*) For my voice, you know. Have one – delicious.

LAMPRETT: No thank you. Been walking, have you?

HALLAM: Yes. Your daughter advised me of a secluded place to which I could retire for the purpose of reading.

LAMPRETT: Excellent!

HALLAM: It was far from excellent. The premises themselves had little to commend them other than an overpowering smell of decaying seaweed, a complete exposure to the sky, and the fact that they were situated on a sheer precipice of several hundred feet. You must know, my dear Lamprett, that nothing is so necessary to a reading of Mr Wordsworth's work than a sense of security.

LAMPRETT: Reading that fellow, eh?

HALLAM: It was my intention. I must attempt to know something of the forces that are conspiring the destruction of my kind.

LAMPRETT: Where was this place?

HALLAM: A ruined cottage – in that direction.

LAMPRETT: Oh, that place.

HALLAM: You know it?

LAMPRETT: Yes. It was burnt out two years ago – a magnificent conflagration! – the only occasion on which my brigade became sea-borne. An unfortunate legend credits me with firing the place – it was the first time my brigade was called out under my captaincy – but I can assure you it is nothing more than a legend. (*He points to HUMPAGE.*) He used to live there.

HALLAM: Now he lives up there?

LAMPRETT: Yes. He's the look-out.

HALLAM: And what does he look out for?

LAMPRETT: Fires. Any spark, flash, flame or cloud of smoke as small as a man's hand and I am instantly informed. The engine stands ready – the signals and bell are summons to the members of my brigade. We should proceed within seconds.

HALLAM: Excellent!

LAMPRETT: I believe Timothy also employs Humpage as a look-out for any sign of this threatened invasion but that is a secondary consideration. Have you seen Timothy yet?

HALLAM: For a moment. He called to me from his window.

LAMPRETT: I think I should tell you, Hallam, that you will find him strange – very strange. God forbid that I should speak ill of my brother –

HALLAM: God forbid!

LAMPRETT: – but this threatened invasion by Bonaparte seems to have unhinged him completely. His behaviour has become eccentric in the extreme. (*HUMPAGE, in his active viewing of the surrounding countryside, turns and lightly strikes the brass bell with the telescope. LAMPRETT leaps to his feet.*) Action!

HUMPAGE: An accident, sir. It was an accident. (*He demonstrates.*) I was viewing about as is my duty, and the bell being in this position – here – my arm raised – so – I accidentally struck the bell – so! (*He does so.*) An accident, sir. See? If my arm is raised – so – and I am viewing – so – I am able – (*He again strikes the bell. Then there is silence. At last LAMPRETT speaks.*)

LAMPRETT: A false alarm.

HUMPAGE: Yes, sir.

LAMPRETT: No fire.

HUMPAGE: No, sir.

LAMPRETT: No smoke.

HUMPAGE: No, sir.

LAMPRETT: In fact, nothing.

HUMPAGE: Nothing, sir.

LAMPRETT: (*Shouting.*) That is no excuse for relaxation! Attention! (*HUMPAGE again takes up the telescope and begins to view with an insane concentration.*) You were saying, Hallam? –

HALLAM: I wasn't saying anything. You were speaking of Timothy.

LAMPRETT: Of course. Quite unhinged, poor fellow. Given to the most extraordinary outbursts and madcap schemes. Very sad to see a man of his capabilities with his reason overthrown. My brother – very sad.

HALLAM: Yes, indeed. But the cause surely is not –

LAMPRETT: Nothing more than this absurd invasion by the French. He has no trust in the official precautions in hand against Bonaparte.

HALLAM: By that he shows his sanity.

LAMPRETT: You mean –

HALLAM: I mean that any system of national defence is non-existent.

LAMPRETT: God bless my soul!

HALLAM: However, what is Timothy proposing to do?

LAMPRETT: I thought you must know. I had imagined you were in his confidence.

HALLAM: I know nothing more than this: that I am arrived from London by Timothy's wish and bring him a box of clothes and a French phrase book.

LAMPRETT: A box of clothes and a French phrase book! My God, what can he be up to?

HALLAM: We shall just have to wait and see, my dear Lamprett, just wait and see.

LAMPRETT: That is a notion to which I have never subscribed. I find out, my dear Hallam, I find out!

HALLAM: Then pray tell me – what have you found out?

LAMPRETT: Nothing.

HALLAM: Nothing. I see.

LAMPRETT: Except that his room is hung with maps and reports of the weather – that he has set four mantraps in the orchard – that I was awakened three nights ago by his calling out words of command in a foreign language – except for these things I know nothing.

(*At this moment TIMOTHY appears in the doorway of the house. He is now fully dressed and carries a pistol. This he raises and aims at the brass bell. He fires and the bell chimes under the impact of the bullet.*)

TIMOTHY: Good shot, sir! Sit down, Lamprett. (*He exhibits the pistol.*) Hit a penny at ten paces last night. Pretended it was Boney's belly-button. Good morning, Hallam.

HALLAM: Good morning, Timothy.

TIMOTHY: A brisk and beautiful day!

HALLAM: Indeed, yes.

TIMOTHY: Have a good journey?

HALLAM: Very fair.

TIMOTHY: Sorry I was not available to welcome you. What time did you arrive?

HALLAM: A little past midnight.

TIMOTHY: Sleep well?

HALLAM: Thank you, yes.

TIMOTHY: Breakfasted?

HALLAM: Yes.

TIMOTHY: Well, that's done.

HALLAM: What, pray, is done?

TIMOTHY: The conventional enquiries as to your general welfare. Tedious, eh? Now, I want to talk to you. Off with you, Lamprett.

LAMPRETT: What's that?

TIMOTHY: I say, off with you. I want to speak to Hallam privately.

LAMPRETT: Oh, very well.

TIMOTHY: Now, Hallam, I wish to tell you about a little plan. That is, when Lamprett has had the decency to absent himself. (*He glares at LAMPRETT who is hanging about the house.*)

LAMPRETT: Timothy.

TIMOTHY: Yes.

LAMPRETT: Where can I go? What can I do?

TIMOTHY: God bless my soul! Our very existence is threatened by Napoleon Bonaparte, and the man asks where he can go and what he can do. Prepare, my dear brother, prepare for the worst in whatever way you please – but prepare.

LAMPRETT: I think you are a very foolish fellow, Tim. (*He leaves the garden with a certain dignity. TIMOTHY stares after him.*)

TIMOTHY: I am being made to understand with increasing force the impossibility of expecting Lamprett to take his life with the smallest degree of seriousness. He has, I'm afraid, an incontrovertibly frivolous nature. Father, had he lived, would have found an even deeper dissatisfaction with his younger son, I feel. During his lifetime he found Lamprett a sore trial. We cannot deny that the affair of Hester whilst Lamprett was at Oxford –

HALLAM: Hester! His wife!

TIMOTHY: Oh, yes, he married her. Father insisted upon it – and quite rightly – after the disgraceful business of the warden's breeches. Hester was his niece, you know.

HALLAM: I didn't know.

TIMOTHY: Lamprett, of course, has lived in complete retirement ever since. His passions must be controlled.

HALLAM: Lamprett's passions!

TIMOTHY: No, no! You misunderstand me. I mean, of course, his passion for lost causes. That is how the disgrace came upon us. Instead of attending to his studies when he was at Oxford he became convinced that women should be admitted to the colleges. To prove their worth he prevailed upon Hester – with whom he was friendly, both of them playing the bass fiddle – to dress in her uncle's second-best ceremonial breeches and coat. So dressed, she attended lectures for three weeks and might never have been discovered had not Lamprett then insisted that to complete the illusion she should begin to smoke. One evening, in his rooms, with Horace Walpole as his guest, Hester was standing before the fire, pipe in hand, when the breeches caught alight. She would have been burnt to the ground had not Lamprett extinguished the fire manually. (*He demonstrates.*) So, of course, he married her, and he's been fighting fires ever since. As for the present – I can only enjoin you to the greatest secrecy.

HALLAM: We are not alone. (*He indicates HUMPAGE.*)

TIMOTHY: Very true. Humpage!

HUMPAGE: Sir!

TIMOTHY: You are not to listen to my conversation for the next few minutes. Do you understand?

HUMPAGE: Very good, sir. (*He covers his ears with his hands.*)

TIMOTHY: No, no, no! You must keep your ears open for other sounds! The approach of danger may be heralded by nothing more than a whisper, the advance of an army may be borne on the gentlest breeze. Take down your hands! (*HUMPAGE remains covering his ears: he grins.*) Take down your hands! (*HUMPAGE does not move.*) God grant me patience! (*TIMOTHY shouts.*) Listen, you blockhead! Listen! (*He then stands silent and at a complete loss until, in a moment of inspiration, he snatches off his hat and throws it to HUMPAGE who, with an automatic reaction, catches it. TIMOTHY seizes the opportunity.*) Listen! You are to keep your eyes open for other sounds, but you are not to listen to me. Do you understand?

HUMPAGE: Yes, sir.

TIMOTHY: Keep your eyes to the south – and give me back my hat. (*HUMPAGE does so. To HALLAM.*) Sorry about that. To continue, I must as I say, enjoin you to the greatest secrecy. It is a well-known fact that this part of the coast is alive with French spies and Bonaparte's personal agents. Now, have I your solemn word that you will not tell a single living soul?

HALLAM: I can give you my word on that with the greatest assurance.

TIMOTHY: Thank you. You have brought me some things from London.

HALLAM: Yes.

TIMOTHY: What are they?

HALLAM: A large black box which you asked me to collect from Drury Lane Theatre –

TIMOTHY: Where is it?

HALLAM: Upstairs in my room.

TIMOTHY: Hidden?

HALLAM: Under the bed.

TIMOTHY: Locked?

HALLAM: Locked.

TIMOTHY: And the second article?

HALLAM: This book – (*He takes it from his pocket.*) – which appears to be –

TIMOTHY: Excellent! (*He takes the book from HALLAM and reads in execrable French.*) 'Sautons à bas du lit, j'entends la bonne qui monte.' Dear me! I'm not sure this is the sort of thing I want at all. (*He turns a few pages.*) Ah! this is better. (*He reads.*) 'Retirez! Je connais le dessous des cartes!'

HALLAM: What does that mean?

(*TIMOTHY consults the book.*)

TIMOTHY: 'Retreat! I know what's what!' Oh, yes – I think I shall find what I want in here. It will repay a few hours quiet study. Good. (*He puts the book away in his pocket.*) Now, Hallam. The situation is roughly this: myself, versus one hundred and seventy-five thousand Frenchmen.

HALLAM: An epic situation, no less. Go on.

TIMOTHY: That is the popular estimate of the number of Bonaparte's troops assembled on the French coast at this moment, and preparing for the final assault. They will make the crossing in two thousand Shallops, despatch boats, caiques, bomb-ships, praams –

HALLAM: Praams?

TIMOTHY: – yes, praams and transports. That crossing may be made at any moment now. What is to be done?

HALLAM: What, indeed?

TIMOTHY: I'll tell you in a moment. But first let us consider the arrangements made by the country as a whole to deal with this menace. Are they daring, brilliant and worthy of the English in such a situation? Are they?

HALLAM: I should say, no.

TIMOTHY: And you would be right. Shall I tell you why they are not daring, brilliant and worthy of the English?

HALLAM: If you please.

TIMOTHY: Because they do not exist. No arrangements for dealing with this menace exist.

HALLAM: Astounding!

TIMOTHY: Disgraceful! A national disgrace! But you will agree that something must be done.

HALLAM: I should think so.

TIMOTHY: Well, what?

HALLAM: You are aching to tell me, Timothy.

TIMOTHY: My first plan was to raise a private army under my command. I actually put this plan into action. Two months ago I raised a force of one hundred and twenty-seven men – eight children: the Bellboys Fencibles. All was prepared, the corps was in being, when I received a communication from some central office in Dorchester informing me that the raising of an army for a private purpose – my God! a private purpose – was illegal. More than that. I was also informed that owing to the national emergency my corps – the Bellboys Fencibles – would be taken over intact. I applied, very naturally, for their command. It was refused. Can you credit that?

HALLAM: With difficulty.

TIMOTHY: Yes, refused. But – and this will strain your credulity to breaking point – I was informed that an officer was being sent from Taunton to take up the command and that they wished me – my God! I can hardly tell you – they wished me to give him any advice and information on the corps and local terrain that he desired.

HALLAM: Which you have undoubtedly done.

TIMOTHY: Nothing of the kind. I refused even to meet the fellow. I withdrew my support and every material object associating me with the corps – including the banners bearing the corps inscription – 'Tintinabulum pueri'. I washed my hands of them.

HALLAM: Understandably.

TIMOTHY: This Taunton fellow – what's his name? – George Selincourt has had them in training now for almost two months, and if you should chance upon a ragged band of scruffy, drunken, ill-disciplined, noisy louts rampaging the countryside you will be viewing our sole defence against Bonaparte.

HALLAM: Alarming!

TIMOTHY: Something, however, must be done. You agree?

HALLAM: Yes.

TIMOTHY: It will be done. Never fear.

HALLAM: You have a plan.

TIMOTHY: I have. (*He smiles in anticipation.*) You will understand that in such a situation a gesture of defiance is useless. The odds are great.

HALLAM: One hundred and seventy-five thousand to one, you said.

TIMOTHY: Yes.

HALLAM: I think those odds may be considered as lunatic.

TIMOTHY: Quite. Therefore, as I say, a direct conflict must be avoided. Yet I contemplate engaging the French single-handed using but a single weapon.

HALLAM: The jawbone of an ass, I presume.

(*TIMOTHY rises to stand a little apart from HALLAM. He pulls a lock of hair down over his forehead and stands squeezing his cheek with his right hand.*)

TIMOTHY: I am a certain person making a grand decision of policy?

HALLAM: How many guesses am I allowed?

TIMOTHY: Oh, come, come! Only one should be necessary. (*HALLAM is silent.*) I'll give you a clue. (*He then says, in his very individual French.*) Mettez bas les armes! Vive la France!

HALLAM: Comme vous écorchez cette lange!

TIMOTHY: I beg your pardon?

HALLAM: Nothing.

TIMOTHY: You understand who I am?

HALLAM: You know, I'm very much afraid that I do. But I don't see –

TIMOTHY: You must see! The resemblance is remarkable, you will admit. I can look very like Napoleon Bonaparte, and there lies the basis of my scheme of defeat for the French. At the moment the likeness is possibly remote but when I am dressed –

HALLAM: Dressed?

TIMOTHY: Exactly! The box that you have brought for me contains a uniform of the French National Guard.

HALLAM: My God!

TIMOTHY: And here is my plan. (*Very quietly he asks.*) Humpage, are you listening?

HUMPAGE: No, sir.

TIMOTHY: Now, Hallam, this is my plan. I shall be informed of the approach of the French fleet, the moment of imminent invasion. At that moment I shall do nothing – nothing! I shall allow the army to disembark, to land on the coast out there. I shall not make the slightest effort to prevent them from doing so. When their landing is almost complete I shall dress in the National Guard uniform and assume my impersonation of Bonaparte. I shall then descend the well. I shall have to be lowered in the bucket. Perhaps you would be so good as to oblige me – (*HALLAM inclines his head in assent.*) I shall then make my way along the tunnel at the bottom of the well which leads to the cliffs, and I shall make an appearance behind – mark this! – I shall come up in the rear of the French army. They will, of course, recognize me as their Emperor and consent to be led by me.

HALLAM: And where, pray, do you intend to lead them?

TIMOTHY: To confusion and ultimate damnation!

HALLAM: How?

TIMOTHY: I shall give orders. Inform them that all is lost: that there is nothing but retreat.

HALLAM: In their own language?

TIMOTHY: Certainly. That is why I required this little book. (*He pats his pocket.*) I know a certain amount, of course. Je suis l'avant coureur! Je suis l'Empereur! – and that sort of thing. (*For a moment he regards HALLAM with a smile – then:*) Well, what do you think of it?

HALLAM: I am really at a loss for words to express my admiration or my –

TIMOTHY: The charm – the essential charm of the plan is its simplicity, eh?

HALLAM: Yes – yes.

TIMOTHY: I will admit to you, Hallam, that I am more than a little nervous – I might also say frightened – of what I am about to do. It is, after all, no small thing.

HALLAM: Timothy – (*He appears to be suffering from some difficulty in expressing himself.*) Timothy, I – (*His head bowed and the words scarcely audible.*) – God bless you! (*Turning away from TIMOTHY, he is shaken by laughter. TIMOTHY, unaware of this, and deeply moved, puts a hand on HALLAM's shoulder.*)

TIMOTHY: Thank you, Hallam, thank you. But you must not distress yourself. (*A pause.*) Can I have the key to the box of clothes?

HALLAM: In my room, on the dressing-table.

TIMOTHY: Thank you. (*He turns to go into the house.*) May I say that your deep emotion proves to be the complete justification of my scheme. I may fail – but what of that? It is what we attempt that matters. I know by your sympathetic reception that I am right at least in the attempt. I can even forgive the desperate foolishness of my fellow-countrymen. Alas! They cannot comprehend what is almost upon them. But I will stand for them. I will be England. (*He again turns to go into the house.*)

HALLAM: Timothy!

TIMOTHY: Yes?

HALLAM: Forgive me.

TIMOTHY: (*Very puzzled.*) Of course, my dear fellow, of course. I shall now retire for a while. A little study, you know. (*He puts the book in his pocket, laughs, and then goes into the house. HALLAM turns to DORCAS and EDWARD, who are now standing at the gateway of the orchard.*)

HALLAM: Hullo, horrid child.

DORCAS: Mr Matthews. (*A deep curtsey.*)

HALLAM: I wish I could rid myself of the feeling that you are making mock of me.

DORCAS: May I introduce Mr Edward Sterne to your acquaintance. Mr Hallam Matthews.

EDWARD: How do you do, sir.

HALLAM: Can I give you my arm to a chair?

EDWARD: Thank you.

(*HALLAM sits beside EDWARD.*)

HALLAM: Travelling, Mr Sterne?

EDWARD: Yes, Mr Matthews. I'm on my way to London. Miss Bellboys kindly provided me and my companion with refreshment, and has also pleasurably detained me with her conversation.

HALLAM: Tell me, does she make fun of you?

EDWARD: (*He laughs.*) I've not noticed it.

HALLAM: She does of me. I'm sure of it. Not directly, you understand. If it was direct I should be justified in spanking her.

(*DORCAS, who for a moment has stepped into the house, puts her head round the doorway.*)

DORCAS: Are you talking about me?

HALLAM: Bless my soul. Why should we talk about you?

DORCAS: I thought you might have nothing better to do.

HALLAM: Nothing better to do. (*To EDWARD.*) You see? Or is it that I am too sensitive. I don't know. (*To DORCAS.*) Come here. (*The girl moves to HALLAM.*) Now sit down. (*She does so.*) You, in your youth, regard us as your clowns, do you not? The world, spinning about the centre of your untouched heart, somersaults for your amusement. Very well, but you must remember –

DORCAS: Mr Matthews –

HALLAM: Don't interrupt! But you must remember that there are some days when the clowns must sit together in the sun and talk of clownish things. (*EDWARD laughs.*) Even if they sit together for no other reason than to think up new ways of distracting you, eh, Mr Sterne. And so, sir, to continue our conversation. I was about to say –

DORCAS: Nothing – nothing – nothing – nothing! (*She rolls on to her back on the grass and, laughing, says:*) Isn't it a lovely day? Too fine and sweet for fighting. Look up, Mr Matthews, look up! (*HALLAM stares doubtfully at the sky.*) Do they look as though they are about to fall?

HALLAM: What?

DORCAS: The heavens. That is what they tell us, you know. That is what they tell innocent people – simple people – like you and me –

HALLAM: Eh?

DORCAS: That the heavens are about to fall. Mr Matthews, you wished to be serious. Then answer me this. Why do men fight each other?

(*There is a long pause.*)

HALLAM: Any suggestions, Mr Sterne?

EDWARD: Where are you, Dorcas?

DORCAS: Here! (*She kneels before him.*)

EDWARD: Why do men fight each other?

DORCAS: That is what I asked.

EDWARD: Perhaps because there is a long-wished-for home they seek, and they are too frail to take upon themselves the responsibility for the journey. Did you never, when you were a baby, know of something you desired but of which – oh, so humanly – you were ashamed? And did you not, perhaps – shall we say – engineer that thing to come about – oh, so sinfully – through the fault of another? (*He smiles.*) You see, my life-loving darling, the dark journey to the dark home is sometimes sweeter than the summer's day.

DORCAS: I think you must be a very serious and unhappy man to speak like that.

EDWARD: Not unhappy, no. A journeying man, that's what I am.

HALLAM: Don't, please, talk of such things. I feel, somehow, as if the sun has gone in.

DORCAS: Why not talk?

HALLAM: Has it?

DORCAS: The sun has gone in for him for all time!

EDWARD: No! You mustn't say such things, Dorcas. Forgive her, sir. I comprehend your distress. We will talk of other things.

HALLAM: Thank you.

DORCAS: (*In a sudden rage.*) I wish to talk! I want to know – to understand – why men do such terrible things to each other. I want to know!

EDWARD: Then come away. (*He rises.*) Mr Matthews will forgive us.

HALLAM: Certainly. I don't wish you to think – (*He pauses.*)

EDWARD: Yes?

HALLAM: I don't wish you to think that I – how shall I put it? Odd, very odd – you two creatures take every word – and God knows there are many – from my head.

EDWARD: I'm sorry, sir. You have lived a sheltered life?

HALLAM: I like to think I have. But you break into my idyll like a swordthrust.

DORCAS: Come along, Edward. (*She takes his hand.*) Can you find something to amuse you, Mr Matthews?

HALLAM: Don't make fun of me at the moment, please. You have a most unfair advantage.

DORCAS: What's that?

HALLAM: Your age. You are young. You have no past.

DORCAS: One day – alas! –

HALLAM: Yes! Try then to reconcile the ambitions and pure designs of youth with the failures and confusions of middle age: the morning, sweet as a nut, with the early evening, sad as a mustard pot: reconcile the loves of boyhood with the friendships and harsh passions of *nel mezzo del cammin di nostra vita.* (*He pauses.*) I think I'm going to cry.

DORCAS: We distress you, Mr Matthews. Shall we go away.

HALLAM: If you please.

DORCAS: Come along, Edward. (*DORCAS and EDWARD go leaving HALLAM staring after them. HESTER comes from the house.*)

HESTER: (*To HALLAM.*) Don't sit in the sun. (*HESTER returns to the house passing BREEZE who is coming out into the garden. HALLAM sees BREEZE.*)

HALLAM: Ah, Sam.

BREEZE: You seem very relieved to see me, sir. Anything the matter?

HALLAM: I'm a little upset, Sam, a little upset. You're happy, I see. Enjoying yourself?

BREEZE: Very much, thank you, sir. Nothing like a few days in the country, is there?

HALLAM: Nothing like it in the whole wide world, I should think.

BREEZE: You are in a state.

HALLAM: Thank you. I couldn't have put it better myself. I am, quite decidedly, 'in a state'.

BREEZE: I don't like to see you in such a way. I leave you contentedly talking about yourself. I come back to find you in a state. From past experience I'd say that people here are either paying too much attention to you, or too little. Has someone suggested that you're either too young or too old? Tell me, sir, is that the way they've been getting at you?

HALLAM: You must teach me your vocabulary, Sam. You express everything so much more accurately than I am able. 'Getting at you'! Oh, yes – yes indeed! The young people speak, and I am revealed – a magnificent ruin.

BREEZE: Then if I may say so, sir, it's not going to do you any good walking up and down like that.

HALLAM: Am I walking up and down? Good gracious me! (*He sinks into a chair.*)

BREEZE: I think we can find you something more comfortable than that, Mr Matthews. (*He looks around the garden and sees the alcove.*) Ah! What about this? (*He goes into the alcove.*) It feels to be dry and warm. You need not necessarily sleep, sir. Will you go in?

HALLAM: I am tempted, I confess. (*Suddenly they smile at each other.*)

BREEZE: Come along, sir. (*HALLAM goes into the alcove.*) Put your feet up. (*HALLAM sitting, does so.*) I think it would be wise to remove your hat. Ah! This is useful. (*He has discovered a shawl.*) Put it round your shoulders. (*HALLAM drapes himself.*) Is the light going to bother you? It's rather strong. (*HALLAM looks doubtful.*) Cover your face, sir. (*He takes HALLAM's handkerchief and puts it over his face.*)

HALLAM: Is it necessary?

BREEZE: Let it be a little curtain between you and the world. Out here, vulgar mankind – behind there, Boodles. How's that? Now you can forget your troubles, can't you? (*He begins to tiptoe away.*)

HALLAM: Where are you going?

BREEZE: To the orchard, sir.

HALLAM: What have you got in that orchard?

BREEZE: Some apples –

HALLAM: Yes?

BREEZE: A pint of cider –

HALLAM: Yes?

BREEZE: And a young woman named Chastity Meadows.

HALLAM: Off you go.

BREEZE: Thank you, sir. (*He goes out to the orchard. HALLAM turns restlessly beneath the handkerchief and shawl. HUMPAGE has again fallen asleep. LAMPRETT and JONATHAN enter in earnest conversation. JONATHAN carries a large home-made firework of complicated design.*)

LAMPRETT: – and I cannot impress upon you enough the vital necessity of placing that apparatus under – mark that! under – the object. The reason for this is the blow-back which might – and this is no exaggeration – decapitate you. (*He crouches beside JONATHAN over the firework.*) My experiments with firefighting by explosives are in a primitive state as yet, but we progress. This is the fuse with which I set it off – this is a linstock. Both technical terms you will learn in due course. Now – ready? When I have lit it we will retire to a safe distance. (*He applies the fuse to the firework and then cries:*) Right! (*He and the BOY rush from the garden. For a time there is stillness, then the firework goes off. It is dazzling, but quite silent. JONATHAN and LAMPRETT return. LAMPRETT explains.*) I am putting the sound in it later. In my opinion, the only way of extinguishing a fire is to blow up – well, everything that is burning if necessary. The loss of life would probably be considerable, but we must keep in mind the main object – and that is, to put out the fire. (*LAMPRETT and JONATHAN go out to the orchard. GEORGE SELINCOURT enters with considerable energy. He is a little upset at finding the garden apparently deserted. Suddenly, from within a room on the first floor of the house, TIMOTHY shouts.*)

TIMOTHY: Bravo! Cours, cours et cours encore!

SELINCOURT: Foreigners!

HUMPAGE: (*He is asleep.*) Yes.

SELINCOURT: Bless me! (*Looking up at HUMPAGE, he moves across the garden until he comes to rest, at a complete loss, just above the alcove where HALLAM MATTHEWS lies. After a moment, HALLAM speaks.*)

HALLAM: Are you by any chance a French spy?

SELINCOURT: Good God! (*He discovers HALLAM.*) What did you say?

HALLAM: I asked if, by any chance, you were a French spy?

SELINCOURT: Certainly not!

HALLAM: Not?

SELINCOURT: No. (*During the following conversation HALLAM does not move or take the handkerchief from his face.*) Excuse me –

HALLAM: Yes?

SELINCOURT: Would you be Sir Timothy Bellboys?

HALLAM: My dear sir, I wouldn't be Sir Timothy Bellboys for all the tea in China.

SELINCOURT: No, no! You misunderstand me. I mean, of course, are you Sir Timothy Bellboys?

HALLAM: No.

SELINCOURT: Not?

HALLAM: No.

SELINCOURT: That is a pity.

HALLAM: On the contrary, sir, it is a stroke of fortune for which I have never ceased to thank Providence.

SELINCOURT: My name is George Selincourt. (*There is silence.*) Selincourt. (*He spells it.*)

HALLAM: Matthews. (*He spells it.*)

SELINCOURT: I've come to advise you not to be alarmed.

HALLAM: Extremely civil of you.

SELINCOURT: The conflict you will hear and see in a few minutes is merely an exercise, a mock battle, a prank of my own, designed to introduce my local defence Volunteers to the conditions they must expect in the forthcoming engagement with the Beast of the Apocalypse.

HALLAM: I beg your pardon?

SELINCOURT: The Fiend of the Bottomless Pit.

HALLAM: I still don't quite –

SELINCOURT: The Serpent of Corsica.

HALLAM: Oh, you mean –

SELINCOURT: Napoleon Bonaparte.

HALLAM: The heat – I think it must be the heat. Very hot today, is it not?

SELINCOURT: More than warm – more than warm.

HALLAM: Then that is undoubtedly the reason for my incapacity to make head or tail of anything that is said to me today. Your name, you say, is –

SELINCOURT: Selincourt. I am commander of the local forces – alas! so small – ranged against Bonaparte.

HALLAM: Yes, yes! I remember. I am with you. Continue.

SELINCOURT: It is my intention to begin a mock battle on, if I may put it so – (*He giggles.*) – your doorstep. The noise may be considerable, not to say alarming. I have walked up to advise you of this. Would you be so kind as to warn Sir Timothy and other members of this household?

HALLAM: Delighted.

SELINCOURT: Thank you. Well, well! I must be off to see to the final disposal of my forces. Are you concerned with military matters, sir? But, of course, you must be.

HALLAM: Why?

SELINCOURT: Everyone must be in this hour of England's peril. Rather interesting: I have retained one-third of my forces under my command. The remaining two-thirds I am using as the enemy – a larger proportion, you notice, as will be the case. This 'enemy' will land from the sea – we have commandeered the local fishing fleet for the occasion – and I shall repulse them. Care to come along and watch?

HALLAM: No, thank you.

SELINCOURT: Ah! Conserving your energy for the real thing, eh?

HALLAM: Yes.

SELINCOURT: What will be your precise duties when the great moment comes? Have you any special qualifications?

HALLAM: I can run very fast.

SELINCOURT: (*Delighted.*) Can you really? Then you may be the very man I'm looking for. My word, this is lucky!

HALLAM: In what way?

SELINCOURT: Well, as a commander of the local forces it is one of my responsibilities to arrange that at the moment of invasion someone runs through the countryside putting up, at certain points, a poster bearing the information. This must be done quickly and efficiently. Perhaps, for the sake of your country, you would care to take on the job. I have a specimen poster here. (*He takes out the poster which he proceeds to unfold. It bears the single word, in large, staring type, 'INVASION'.*) The price is twopence each, one and eight the dozen, or one hundred for twelve shillings.

HALLAM: Am I expected to pay for them?

SELINCOURT: That's very good of you. Then I should advise you to purchase them by the hundred. The simplest arithmetic will show that you save four and eightpence on each hundred bought. No need to make up your mind immediately. Think it over. I'll leave this with you so that you can keep it in mind. (*He pins the poster on the alcove beside HALLAM.*) I've also borrowed a balloon from the local fair to give a further touch of reality to the proceedings. That goes up in half an hour. Now I really must be off. Goodbye.

HALLAM: Goodbye.

(*SELINCOURT goes as DORCAS and EDWARD come into the garden.*)

EDWARD: That's what laughter is, nothing more –

DORCAS: Nothing more than that? Good gracious!

EDWARD: Anyone here?

(*DORCAS looks about the garden, but does not see HALLAM reclining in the alcove.*)

DORCAS: No. No one here. Let's sit down.

EDWARD: There now – I've told you about war, and I've told you about laughter. Anything else?

DORCAS: Yes.

EDWARD: Well?

DORCAS: Love. Tell me –

EDWARD: What?

DORCAS: Tell me – can you love if you cannot see?

EDWARD: I can. (*He laughs.*) Bless me –

DORCAS: No! No, wait a moment and I'll explain what I mean. I can see – (*She pauses.*)

EDWARD: Yes?

DORCAS: I can see – oh, a thing or a person – and seeing I can say I love. But you –

EDWARD: You think that when I lost my sight I lost the power to love.

DORCAS: Yes. No! No, I don't think that. But I cannot understand how you can love anything new – unseen. Something that you didn't love before. How can you fall in love? As I have with you.

(*There is a pause.*)

EDWARD: What did you say?

DORCAS: That I love you, Edward. (*There is a pause then she says quickly.*) I don't seem to be able to help it. I don't want to help it, anyway.

EDWARD: You love me?

DORCAS: Yes.

EDWARD: I love you, Dorcas.

DORCAS: Edward.

EDWARD: Dorcas. Where does your name come from, Dorcas?

DORCAS: I don't know. Timothy does. He sometimes calls me Tabitha. He says it's the same name but I hate it. But, Edward – no, stop laughing! – Edward, listen – I can *see you.* How can you love me when you don't know what I look like? I might be very ugly – I'm not! – but I might be.

EDWARD: (*He laughs.*) I know you're not.

DORCAS: But you can't know, Edward – you can't!

EDWARD: It is now the one thing in the whole world that I do know surely. That you are beautiful and I love you. (*He pauses.*) You don't love me.

DORCAS: I do!

EDWARD: Would you love me had you never seen me?

DORCAS: I think I've always loved you, Edward.

EDWARD: You see!

DORCAS: (*She is laughing.*) Yes, I see.

EDWARD: That is all you need. You don't need to know things like – well, where my nose is. Tell me, is your nose in the right place?

DORCAS: What do you mean?

EDWARD: In the middle of your face.

DORCAS: Of course.

(*EDWARD stretches out and takes her nose between his finger and thumb.*)

EDWARD: So it is.

DORCAS: You're laughing at me!

EDWARD: Just a little. Mind you, it's very nice to know these things. What colour are your eyes?

DORCAS: Now, that's rather difficult to say. Let me think about it for a moment for I don't want to mislead you. (*She sits in silence.*) Hazel. Do you know the colour?

EDWARD: Yes. I remember what hazel looks like.

DORCAS: I should like to kiss you, Edward. (*EDWARD moves to her and very gently they kiss each other on the mouth.*) Oh, you look happy! You look –

EDWARD: I am happy. I love you.

DORCAS: I love you so I expect I look happy too. (*She kisses him.*) Are you going away from here?

EDWARD: Yes. To London, as I told you.

DORCAS: I don't think I want you to go away from here now. Will you return to me? I want you to return to me. Of course you must go.

EDWARD: You understand that?

DORCAS: Oh, yes – but come back. (*She pauses.*) Now I feel sad, is that love?

EDWARD: Yes.

(*Very faintly there is a bugle call from the beaches. HESTER comes from the house.*)

HESTER: Ah, Dorcas. I never seem to be able to find you. What have you been doing?

DORCAS: Putting off childish ways.

HESTER: I see. (*To EDWARD.*) I'm Dorcas's mother. Don't be frightened. It is only my looks that are against me. Ask Dorcas. I'm afraid I'm not so imposing as I look, Mr...

EDWARD: Sterne.

HESTER: Mr Sterne. Nature endowed me with the appearance of a frigate, so what you see you must necessarily admire if not immediately love.

DORCAS: Mr Sterne is blind, Mama.

HESTER: I'm sorry to hear that. Sit down, Mr Sterne. Is Dorcas making you happy?

EDWARD: Very happy, thank you.

DORCAS: I've something to tell you, Mama.

HESTER: And I've something to tell you. Is your news important?

DORCAS: Yes.

HESTER: So is mine. Now listen carefully. I have just heard from Lady Jerningham. She wants me to go and join the Amazon Corps she is forming in East Anglia. I am to command a platoon. This means that – (*LAMPRETT and JONATHAN have wandered in from the orchard.*) Ah! Lamprett –

LAMPRETT: My dear?

HESTER: I am telling Dorcas – (*TIMOTHY comes from the house.*) – that I have heard from Lady Jerningham.

LAMPRETT: Such a pleasant woman.

HESTER: She wishes me to go up to East Anglia to command a platoon in what she calls her Amazon Corps. It is being formed so that the women of England may exercise their natural power of command. I am to be a Sergeant-Major. Stand up straight, Lamprett.

LAMPRETT: Sorry, my dear.

HESTER: I shall be leaving almost immediately, this evening at the latest. I understand that there are recruits to be disciplined. Dorcas will look after the house in my absence. You understand, Dorcas?

DORCAS: Yes, Mama.

TIMOTHY: Are you going to wear uniform?

HESTER: Certainly.

TIMOTHY: Breeches, I suppose! Eh, Lamprett? (*He is seized by quite immoderate laughter.*)

HESTER: I understand that Lady Jerningham has designed the undress uniform herself. An undergarment in the shade of *fumée de Londres* with a cloak and cap of *grisantique*. In action, of course, we shall wear something very different.

LAMPRETT: And I'm sure you'll look very handsome.

(*BREEZE comes in from the orchard.*)

TIMOTHY: I wish something would happen. It distresses me to see everyone standing about like this when we might be getting on with the job of throwing the French into the sea. (*LAMPRETT is examining the poster bearing the stark word 'INVASION'.*) What's that? Another cattle sale?

LAMPRETT: No.

(*TIMOTHY comes to beside LAMPRETT and sees the wording of the poster.*)

TIMOTHY: Lamprett! (*He turns from the poster: then, spinning round, again transfixes it.*) It remains! Lamprett, can I believe my eyes?

LAMPRETT: You can.

TIMOTHY: But that's it, man!

LAMPRETT: Yes.

TIMOTHY: What I've been waiting for.

LAMPRETT: Yes.

TIMOTHY: The official instructions – I remember them well. Part Four, Section VIII: At the landing of enemy troops runners will pass through the countryside liberally distributing bills bearing the single word, INVASION. These bills may be purchased, price twopence each – (*He breaks off, removing his hat.*) Ladies and gentlemen, it is upon us. Like a thief in the night in broad daylight it is upon us. (*All stand in a reverent silence. Distantly from the direction of the coast, a bugle sounds a military call. TIMOTHY at the top of his voice shouts.*) Humpage!

HUMPAGE: (*Awake.*) Sir!

TIMOTHY: Anything to report? Was that man asleep, can anyone tell me? Was he? Anything to report, Humpage?

HUMPAGE: Yes sir.

TIMOTHY: Something in sight?

HUMPAGE: Yes sir.

TIMOTHY: Something suspicious?

HUMPAGE: Oh, yes, sir!

TIMOTHY: Ships of war?

HUMPAGE: Oh, yes, yes, sir!

TIMOTHY: Troops?

HUMPAGE: Oh, sir – oh, sir – yes, yes, yes, sir! One, two, three, four, five – (*He continues to count aloud in a growing agony and panic as the scene proceeds.*)

TIMOTHY: Every man for himself!

LAMPRETT: What's that?

TIMOTHY: Every man for himself! (*He rushes into the house.*)

HUMPAGE: – thirty-seven, thirty-eight, thirty-nine, forty. Oh, God! Forty, forty-one, forty-two –

(*The action within the garden becomes confused. From the general activity the following can be heard.*)

LAMPRETT: Humpage!

HUMPAGE: – fifty-seven, fifty-eight – yes, sir? – fifty-nine, sixty –

LAMPRETT: You must on no account, allow this diversion to distract you from your primary duty.

HUMPAGE: No, sir – sixty-five, sixty-six, sixty-seven –

LAMPRETT: Fires, Humpage, fires!

HUMPAGE: Yes, sir. Seventy, seventy-one –

(*BREEZE speaks to HUMPAGE.*)

BREEZE: You want to be careful up there, you know.

LAMPRETT: Don't distract him, if you please.

BREEZE: Sorry, sir.

LAMPRETT: No point in alarming him. We must all take our chance. What are you going to do?

BREEZE: I shall have to look after Mr Matthews.

LAMPRETT: Well, if you'll take my advice –

(*HESTER is speaking to JONATHAN.*)

HESTER: Are you prepared to fight for your life, little boy? If we meet the enemy squarely, my dear, will he run away? Bless your innocent face, you're laughing! Is it at me? Or do you laugh at all of us? Let me confide something to you –

(*DORCAS is speaking to EDWARD.*)

EDWARD *and* DORCAS: Don't be frightened. (*They laugh.*)

DORCAS: Perhaps this will stop you from going away. I hope so.

EDWARD: You'd even have a battle to keep me with you?

DORCAS: Anything – anything! What is a battle!

EDWARD: The people here – what are they going to do?

DORCAS: Talk, I expect. We always do, every one of us. (*And indeed they are. HESTER to JONATHAN.*)

HESTER: – for that's what the old song tells us, and it is true, believe me. (*And, turning to LAMPRETT.*) Lamprett, what are your intentions?

LAMPRETT: What's that, my dear?

HESTER: Your intentions. What are they in this emergency?

LAMPRETT: To stand by, my dear, until required.

HESTER: And when will that be?

LAMPRETT: It will be when the first spark, flash, flame, scintillation, blaze or conflagration is reported. And then –

BREEZE: Excuse me, sir.

LAMPRETT: What is it?

BREEZE: Do you think it would be wise to wake Mr Matthews now?

LAMPRETT: Wake him?

BREEZE: He's sleeping at the moment and he does so dislike being woken. Could you again advise me, Mr Bellboys? Does the emergency warrant so grave a liberty?

LAMPRETT: As waking him? I should say so. Wouldn't you, my dear?

HESTER: Yes, Breeze. I think you may wake him.

BREEZE: Thank you, ma'am. (*He crosses to HALLAM and stands looking down at him.*)

HESTER: This will make it necessary for me to expedite my departure, Lamprett. At any moment you may be seeing the last of me.

LAMPRETT: I hope not, my dear.

HESTER: Temporarily, I mean.

LAMPRETT: I must have a word with Hallam. (*He goes to HALLAM, who, gently shaken by BREEZE, is coming to consciousness.*)

BREEZE: Excuse me, sir. The invasion.

HALLAM: Thank you, Sam. (*He discovers LAMPRETT standing over him.*)

LAMPRETT: Hallam!

HALLAM: My dear fellow?

LAMPRETT: (*He holds out his hand.*) Goodbye.

HALLAM: You're off?

LAMPRETT: Certainly not! I'm standing by.

HALLAM: Then why – ?

LAMPRETT: The situation is grave.

HALLAM: Yes, yes! Goodbye.

LAMPRETT: The lieutenant of my brigade was burnt to a cinder two months ago in what was merely a civil conflagration. Don't tell the women.

HALLAM: About your lieutenant?

LAMPRETT: No, no. About the danger to me at the moment.

HALLAM: Of course. Not a word, I assure you.

LAMPRETT: Thank you.

(*They shake hands. LAMPRETT then salutes and marches away with JONATHAN.*)

HUMPAGE: One hundred and fourteen – one hundred and fifteen!

HALLAM: What's that fellow doing?

BREEZE: Counting the enemy forces, I imagine.

HALLAM: Oh, dear!

BREEZE: Would you like to retire to a place of safety, sir?

HALLAM: I don't think so. I'm very comfortable here.

HESTER: What are you children going to do?

DORCAS: What do you suggest, Mama?

HESTER: I really don't know.

DORCAS: In that case we'll just sit here and wait for something to happen.

(*It does – in a tremendous cannonade from the beaches and, simultaneously, the appearance of TIMOTHY in the doorway of the house. He is dressed for his impersonation of Bonaparte: the resemblance is very startling. Firmly grasped in his right hand is the French phrase book.*)

TIMOTHY: Halte-là! Où est mon baton? Il n'est pas dans mon havresac! (*He roars with laughter.*) Good, eh? I'm really very pleased. But no nonsense! Humpage!

HUMPAGE: One hundred and sixteen.

TIMOTHY: One hundred and sixteen what?

HUMPAGE: Men, sir.

TIMOTHY: Nonsense! There are one hundred and seventy-five thousand men. You can't count, anyway – you know that. (*Again there is a bugle call from the beaches – followed this time by the rattle of musketry.*) Obviously no time to be lost. They are ashore. Humpage!

HUMPAGE: Sir!

TIMOTHY: You may ring the bell and put up the signals. I am ready.

HUMPAGE: Thank you, sir. (*He is galvanized into action.*)

(*The clangour of the great brass bell rings out. The signal flaps whirl and wave, finally coming to rest to show an ominous scarlet. LAMPRETT, in uniform, rushes in with JONATHAN.*)

LAMPRETT: No! Humpage! No! You'll call out the brigade! Ah! Damn the invasion.

HESTER: Lamprett!

LAMPRETT: Well, my dear, what shall I say to the men when they arrive?

TIMOTHY: If your men have any spirit they'll already be on the beaches fighting the French, and not waiting for you to show them some miserable little fire they can fight.

LAMPRETT: Oh, what a thing to say! My men are brave and good and true. Bless them! (*Then – very maliciously, he says:*) And if you, Timothy, think that by dressing yourself up as Lord Nelson –

TIMOTHY: (*Furious.*) Lord Nelson!

LAMPRETT: – and running away – if you think by that you are helping your country, then I'm a Dutchman.

TIMOTHY: You're a damned ignorant fool, I know that. Anyway, I've no time for a row with you. Hallam!

LAMPRETT: Well, don't say horrid things about my brigade, then. (*He moves to HESTER, who consoles him.*)

TIMOTHY: Hallam!

HALLAM: Timothy?

TIMOTHY: You recall your promise?

HALLAM: My –

TIMOTHY: (*He points to the well.*) The initial part of the plan.

HALLAM: Yes, indeed.

TIMOTHY: I am quite ready. If you will take the handle, I will grasp the rope and stand in the bucket. On the command from me – lower! (*HALLAM has moved to the well and now miserably takes hold of the handle.*) Got it? (*HALLAM nods.*) Right! (*TIMOTHY puts both feet into the bucket and takes hold of the rope. HALLAM takes the strain of his weight.*) Am I clear?

HALLAM: I think so.

TIMOTHY: A last word to everyone. Should I not return there must be no tears. I go on this mission of my own free will, giving my services –

HALLAM: Timothy!

TIMOTHY: – to my country with a good heart. Those that have gone before me and those that will come after me –

HALLAM: Timothy!

TIMOTHY: What is it, Hallam?

HALLAM: (*Breathlessly.*) Last words should be spoken before entering the bucket.

TIMOTHY: What? Oh, sorry! Well – (*He consults the phrase book.*) Au revoir, mes amis, au revoir. La! Descendons maintenant. (*HALLAM begins to lower. TIMOTHY and the bucket remain unmoving, the rope wreathing itself about TIMOTHY.*) Can you release me? I seem to be caught in something. (*In his little struggle, TIMOTHY glances at the sky. He is immediately transfixed.*) What's that?

(*Everyone looks up: they are lost in wonder.*)

HUMPAGE: It's a balloon!

HESTER: Bless me! What a pretty thing!

DORCAS: Edward – an air-balloon – above us.

HUMPAGE: You'd never get me into one of them.

TIMOTHY: That's an idea. I like that. (*He catches sight* of *LAMPRETT: He remembers.*) Lord Nelson! (*Suddenly he descends the well. There is a loud cry from everyone – followed by an explosion.*)

*CURTAIN*

# ACT TWO

*The scene is the same. The time: later the same day. The battle may have passed this way for there are sounds of military activity from a little way off. A drum rolls ominously and a voice shouts commands at intervals. Across the garden drifts a cloud of smoke and from an upper part of the house flies a tattered banner – a symbol of resistance it can only be supposed. HUMPAGE remains at his post. The garden is otherwise empty, but the fire-engine has been brought in. This stands at the ready, pulsating with the need for action. From the engine a length of hose runs out of the garden below the house. After a moment LAMPRETT appears rolling in the hose which he stores away on the engine. He adjusts a complication of valves: the engine becomes silent and still, and some kind of order is restored. LAMPRETT sits on the engine and looks hopefully at HUMPAGE, who shakes his head.*

LAMPRETT: Then we can but wait. For I'll not believe that this day – so-called Armageddon – can pass without our being needed.
(*JONATHAN comes into the garden. LAMPRETT speaks to him.*) Nothing yet, I'm afraid. (*JONATHAN sits beside LAMPRETT.*) Could you grasp that lever there? Thank you. It controls something. I have to look after it like a child, you know. For example, the cold atmosphere makes the thing fret in a quite distressing manner. But today is very warm. (*He pauses.*) Ironic, isn't it, that the only place we have a fire is inside the engine. But I've long ceased to believe in the art of reasoning. When I was a young man at the university I studied logic and it led to dreadful conclusions. Such fearful results came from attempting to arrange my thoughts. No, I cannot tell you! However, on some subjects my mind is clear. (*The MAIDSERVANT has come into the garden from the house carrying the necessities for a picnic meal, which she proceeds to lay out on the ground.*) I'm an example of the man of learning turned man of action by necessity. Yet, I will confess, there are times when I'm tempted to retire,

put up my feet, draw my cap over my eyes and let the world burn away around me.

(*HESTER comes from the house.*)

HESTER: Pippin!

MAID: Yes, ma'am?

HESTER: As much food as possible, I think. We cannot tell how many we shall be called upon to feed and succour on a day like this.

MAID: Very good, ma'am.

HESTER: I thought, Lamprett, we'd eat out here. A fine, if rather noisy day. I don't want people tramping all over the house, you know.

LAMPRETT: Quite right.

HESTER: We should have eaten before this but the household arrangements are a little awry. Forgive me.

LAMPRETT: More than understandable in the circumstances.

HESTER: Thank you, my dear. (*He is looking at the fire-engine.*)

LAMPRETT: Is the engine in your way?

HESTER: Well, perhaps –

LAMPRETT: Yes, I can see you wish me to move it.

HESTER: We are all aware of its usefulness. But at meal times, do you think –

LAMPRETT: Very well. (*LAMPRETT and JONATHAN move the engine from the garden.*)

HESTER: Pippin, run into the house. You'll find some wine in the cooler. Bring it to me. (*The MAID goes into the house. HESTER sits on the ground beside the picnic meal.*) There is great comfort, I find, in resorting to good food during a crisis. Man's behaviour to man would be less ungenerous if everyone ate regular meals. For when conversation fails how much better to resort to the knife and fork than to the sword and trumpet.

HUMPAGE: Are you speaking to me?

HESTER: Not necessarily. (*LAMPRETT returns with JONATHAN.*) Come along. Everything is ready.

LAMPRETT: How charming! It would appear it takes a siege to return us to the pleasures of our youth.

HESTER: Indeed, it must be thirty years, Lamprett, since you and I sat together in the sun.

LAMPRETT: There has been much to do in that time. Come, little boy, don't be shy.

HESTER: Join us, please.

(*JONATHAN joins them at the meal. The MAID comes from the house, carrying the wine.*)

LAMPRETT: Ah! You anticipate my wishes. A glass of wine to rinse from me the staleness of approaching age. Have some, little boy –

HESTER: With water!

LAMPRETT: – but always remember – 'Drink not the third glass – which thou canst not tame when once it is within thee.'

(*They laugh gently at the child. The MAID returns to the house.*)

HESTER: Tell me, Lamprett, is it reprehensible that we should enjoy a moment's peace?

LAMPRETT: I should say not, my dear. Let us enjoy it whilst we can. You may be assured we shall be brought to rude fact at any moment by some disgraceful incident.

HESTER: Which reminds me to ask you something. But first – I'll just take the merry thought from the chicken.

LAMPRETT: These bouches are delicious. What was it you wished to ask?

HESTER: Concerning rude fact, I fear.

LAMPRETT: Never mind. We must face it.

HUMPAGE: Excuse me.

HESTER: What was at the bottom of the well?

HUMPAGE: Excuse me.

LAMPRETT: What is it? (*To HESTER.*) Harsh reality, alas, is ever with us.

HUMPAGE: Might I have some form of protection?

LAMPRETT: Protection against what?

HUMPAGE: Missiles, I think they're called.

LAMPRETT: Are you being shot at? At this very moment – are you being shot at?

HUMPAGE: No, sir.

LAMPRETT: But you think it may happen soon?

HUMPAGE: Yes, sir. And I fear for my life.

(*LAMPRETT takes a dish from among the picnic, empties it, and carries it to HUMPAGE.*)

LAMPRETT: Try wearing this. It will afford you some kind of protection.

HUMPAGE: Yes, sir.

LAMPRETT: You cannot expect both to look handsome and be safe, can you?

HUMPAGE: No, sir.

LAMPRETT: Is it comfortable?

HUMPAGE: No, sir.

LAMPRETT: But you think it will do?

HUMPAGE: Yes, sir.

LAMPRETT: Good. (*An afterthought.*) It doesn't obscure your vision, does it?

HUMPAGE: No, sir.

LAMPRETT: (*A second afterthought.*) It is a saucepan, you know.

HUMPAGE: Yes, sir. (*He adjusts the headgear.*)

LAMPRETT: Must look after the servants in this business. Quite incapable of doing so themselves. You were saying, my dear – before that absurd interruption by Humpage complaining of the danger of his somewhat exposed position? (*He glances at HUMPAGE who is immediately suffused by shame.*) You were saying? –

HESTER: I asked – what was at the bottom of the well?

LAMPRETT: Darkness and dirt, and a most peculiar, rather interesting smell.

HESTER: No water?

LAMPRETT: Oh, dear no!

HESTER: And, as you said, no Timothy.

LAMPRETT: Not a sign of him.

HESTER: May I say, Lamprett, that I consider you showed the most admirable courage in volunteering to descend the well in search of Timothy.

LAMPRETT: Well, after all, he is my brother. And it provided an excuse for doing something I've always wanted to do.

HESTER: Descend the well?

LAMPRETT: Yes. Now I have, so to speak, broken the ice I may make it a regular habit.

HESTER: Have you any idea what Timothy is about?

LAMPRETT: No idea at all.

HESTER: What was the purpose of the uniform he was wearing?

LAMPRETT: Ah, that! Foolish of me to mistake it for an impersonation of Lord Nelson – it was obviously the uniform of the Consular Service. From that we can draw but one conclusion.

HESTER: Which is – ?

LAMPRETT: That he is attempting to escape the country.

(*There is a loud explosion a little way off.*)

HESTER: Do you think we shall ever see him again?

LAMPRETT: I very much doubt that. It would appear that he was successful in getting away. I shall, of course, take over the administration of the estate from today and – (*Through the open orchard gate there rolls, very slowly, a cannon-ball. It traverses the garden and comes to rest at LAMPRETT's* feet.) – I may say that under my direction –

HESTER: What is that?

LAMPRETT: A cannon-ball, my dear. Under my direction things here will be very different. I've never agreed to the subordination of certain public services, such as the fire brigade, to ephemeral activities such as agriculture. My views – (*There is a loud explosion.*) – will now be put into practice and I think we can look forward – (*Through the open gate a second cannon-ball comes fairly bounding into the garden. It comes to rest by the first.*) – to an era which will be without parallel –

HESTER: Lamprett!

LAMPRETT: My dear?

HESTER: Shut the gate.

(*He does so, saying:*)

LAMPRETT: – an era without parallel in the history of the county.

HESTER: Where is everyone?

LAMPRETT: Whom do you mean by everyone?

HESTER: Well, Dorcas and her blind soldier. And Hallam – Hallam Matthews, where is he?

LAMPRETT: The last I saw of him was when he was being led away by his servant after his regrettable behaviour with Timothy and the well. I've no idea where they were making for. (*HALLAM and BREEZE come into the garden from the orchard.*) But wherever it was, they are returned.

HALLAM: Hester. Lamprett.

HESTER: How are you, Hallam?

HALLAM: Shaken, but recovering.

HESTER: I'm pleased to hear that.

HALLAM: What is happening?

LAMPRETT: At the moment? Well, the battle – if it can be called such – appears to have moved somewhat to the west. With regards to the general situation it is fluid. Anything may happen.

HALLAM: Oh, dear!

LAMPRETT: Don't fret, my dear fellow. I am now in charge

HALLAM: Any sign of Timothy?

LAMPRETT: None. Apparently he was successful in his escape.

HALLAM: Escape! No, no, my dear Lamprett, you have misunderstood his intentions.

LAMPRETT: I think not –

HALLAM: But I can assure you –

LAMPRETT: No more, if you please! The subject is delicate. What I do not understand is this: an invasion in force but no fires. Not one. I cannot believe that Bonaparte and his generals can have underestimated the effect upon a civil population of a good wholesome blaze. But that is apparently the case. Not a fire within sight. (*Shouting.*) Is there, Humpage?

HUMPAGE: No sir.

LAMPRETT: Although how you should know with that pot crammed over your eyes in that preposterous fashion is beyond me! (*HUMPAGE prises the saucepan from his forehead.*) Better! Anything to report?

HUMPAGE: No sir.

LAMPRETT: (*To HALLAM.*) You see?

HALLAM: I admit that things seem unnaturally quiet.

LAMPRETT: The lull, perhaps, before the storm.

HALLAM: Please don't say that!

(*DORCAS and EDWARD come in from the orchard.*)

DORCAS: Ah, Mama! Have you recovered Uncle Timothy yet?

HESTER: Don't be frivolous, my dear.

DORCAS: Là! Descendons maintenant! Bump! (*She laughs.*)

HALLAM: Oh, horrid, horrid, heartless child.

DORCAS: Do the present remarkable and unforeseen circumstances upset your plans, dear Mama?

LAMPRETT: What's the child saying?

DORCAS: A simple question, Papa. Does the loss of Uncle Timothy prevent Mama from taking up her duties as Sergeant-Major to the Amazons of Norfolk? Or do we all, in that very English way, refuse to admit that 'Something has happened' and proceed to carry on as if nothing ever could – happen, I mean – that we didn't ourselves decree?

HESTER: Whatever is the matter with you, Dorcas?

DORCAS: I'm happy, Mama.

HESTER: That's no excuse for talking the most utter nonsense.

DORCAS: But there's no excuse for anything, Mama, is there, ever.

HALLAM: Hadn't you better lie down for a while?

DORCAS: A very immodest suggestion, Mr Matthews, in the circumstances. I'm in love.

HALLAM: God bless my soul!

LAMPRETT: This is no time to be falling in love, Dorcas. At any other time – yes, yes! – your mother and I would be only too pleased, but now there is much to be done. (*He speaks to JONATHAN.*) Come with me, little boy.

DORCAS: Where are you taking Jonathan?

LAMPRETT: I'm instructing him in the rudimentary principles of fire-fighting. He knows nothing about it. Quite ignorant. It is ridiculous this business of not letting children play with fire when they are babies. (*He goes out with JONATHAN.*)

HESTER: Hallam, I'm wondering if I might borrow your servant, Breeze, for a short while.

HALLAM: Most certainly, my dear Hester, but take care not to damage him.

HESTER: The reason is this: among the accoutrements Lady Jerningham has sent to me is a large brass breastplate. This is in a quite shockingly dilapidated condition. It occurred to me that Breeze might be the very person to refurbish it.

BREEZE: Certainly, ma'am.

HALLAM: That's right, Sam. Go with Mrs Bellboys and do your best. What is your experience with breastplates?

BREEZE: Very limited, sir.

HALLAM: Never mind. Do all you can.

HESTER: None of us can do more.

(*BREEZE follows HESTER into the house.*)

HALLAM: I am contemplating the effect on my digestion of eating during a battle. (*He fusses over the little meal before him.*)

DORCAS: Mr Matthews –

HALLAM: Yes?

DORCAS: Mr Matthews, you're not really so deeply concerned about yourself, are you?

HALLAM: (*He smiles.*) No.

DORCAS: I know you're not. Then why –

HALLAM: Yes?

DORCAS: I mean to say – why pretend?

HALLAM: What an inquisitive child you are! You must learn to accept things – attitudes – especially if you're going to be in love. More important then than at any other time: for love itself is only a delicious pose to gain for ourselves the comfort we all so deeply need.

DORCAS: Oh, I know all about love –

HALLAM: You do?

DORCAS: – yes – but what has been puzzling me is why you play the fool all the time.

HALLAM: Everyone does so.

DORCAS: Nonsense!

HALLAM: Everyone attempts to be other than they are.

DORCAS: I don't believe it. What about the saints?

HALLAM: Worse than any. It is clowning, you know. A most consequent factor of life.

EDWARD: (*He speaks* to *DORCAS.*) He means, I think, that we find the reality unbearable. That factor within us – ah! – the infrangible burden to carry: self-knowledge. And so we escape, childlike, into the illusion. We clown and posture but not to amuse others – no – to comfort ourselves. The laughter is incidental to the tragic spectacle of each man attempting to hide his intolerable self.

HALLAM: In arguments you treat me as a museum piece which occasionally needs dusting, eh?

EDWARD: (*He laughs.*) Bless you! I may be wrong. What we call the illusion – you and I – which is the laughter and the happiness and the sudden flowering of love, perhaps that is the reality. Who knows and – by God! today who cares? (*He swings DORCAS up in his arms, laughing.*) Do you love me?

DORCAS: Yes.

EDWARD: How much?

DORCAS: That much.

EDWARD: Not enough.

DORCAS: No?

EDWARD: To defend me against myself.

HALLAM: (*Observing them.*) We fight even our love from a catena of unprepared positions retiring ever deeper upon ourselves. The battle lost, we pretend the sacred citadel taken by the enemy is nothing more than a paper palace.

DORCAS: Oh, do be quiet, Mr Matthews! (*DORCAS and EDWARD, their heads together, begin to whisper and laugh. HALLAM continues.*)

HALLAM: Rather than reveal our human imperfections we will turn ourselves, even for the beloved, into a fair-booth from which we offer for sale at extravagant cost the gayest and most useless toys. We cry our wares hoping the naked baby cowering at the back of the booth will not be noticed. We never give up our rattles: our thumbs will go to our mouths on our deathbeds. (*There is a pause*: *DORCAS and EDWARD still whisper together.*) Dorcas?

DORCAS: Yes?

HALLAM: Go a little way off.

DORCAS: Why?

HALLAM: Don't ask questions. Just go a little way off for a little while.

DORCAS: Something I shouldn't hear?

HALLAM: Yes. (*Then he smiles.*) Remember, I told you that the clowns must sometimes sit in the sun and gossip. Go, for a moment.

DORCAS: All right. (*She wanders away.*)

HALLAM: You will not think badly of me?

EDWARD: If you destroy my illusion? No, I am accustomed to destruction. Go on.

HALLAM: The King –

EDWARD: You know His Majesty?

HALLAM: Yes. He is not in London at the moment. He is, I understand, at Weymouth, sea-bathing.

EDWARD: I shall await his return.

HALLAM: If you do you will find him – how shall I put it? – oh, he will see you, my dear Sterne, he will see you. He will be, alas, his very kind and charming self. He will ask you innumerable questions every one of which he will answer for you. He will grant any request you may care to put to him, fully and without qualification. But it will be no good, Sterne, it will be no good.

EDWARD: Why not?

HALLAM: Because – dear, sweet, kindly soul – he is not quite right in the head. At the moment we refer to his eccentricity. In a few years we shall call it something else.

EDWARD: But he's the King of England!

HALLAM: Yes.

EDWARD: But, I say, he is the King of England.

HALLAM: Is the illusion so great?

EDWARD: I didn't know.

HALLAM: Very few do. (*There is a pause.*) She is waiting for you.

EDWARD: Dorcas?

HALLAM: Yes.

EDWARD: Why did you send her away?

HALLAM: Because, Mr Sterne, you will go to London, you will see His Majesty and you may – you may very well be the instrument that will stop this war.

EDWARD: In spite of what you have told me?

HALLAM: In spite of anything I might have told you. (*He calls.*) Dorcas!

(*She returns to EDWARD. JONATHAN has come into the garden.*)

DORCAS: Have you finished with my beloved?

HALLAM: Yes. Yes.

EDWARD: Thank you, Mr Matthews.

HALLAM: Off you go. You don't need me. (*EDWARD and DORCAS move across the garden. JONATHAN, standing beside them as they pass, for a moment, stretches out a hand towards them. But, of course, he is unseen by EDWARD and even, in her own blindness, by DORCAS. They go out by the gateway and the boy stares after them. HALLAM, now by the alcove, speaks to him.*) What is it? Didn't they see you? (*The boy shakes his head.*) Well, you're really very small, you know. Hasn't that got anything to do with it? You're right, it hasn't. But you mustn't be hurt: upset. Come here. (*The boy, unmoving, again shakes his head.*) Now, why not? Do you think I'm going to talk to you? To try to tell you why – why – why things happen. Do I look like a great talker? I suppose I do: I am. But come here. We'll sit together in absolute silence. Or do you like music to pass the time? (*HALLAM takes from an inner pocket a tiny pipe – a recorder – ludicrously small in comparison with his bulk. He plays a snatch of a hornpipe. The child turns to him.*) An unexpected accomplishment, eh? (*He continues to play and then holds out the pipe to JONATHAN.*) Try. (*JONATHAN, taking the pipe, blows a single note.*) Were someone to overlook us now they would take it that Innocence conversed with Experience. In that latter part what can I say to you? I feel I should say something, don't you? The situation requires it. Very well, then: retain the defensive weapons of your childhood always, my dear. They are invaluable, these delights and amusements. They are many, too. And all so simple. Indeed, what is this? Only a wooden pipe with some holes in it. But thrust a current of air through it – there is a sound – and you smile and smile as you are smiling now. What is more – (*GEORGE SELINCOURT, accompanied by three of his fencibles – the Reverend JOSEPH BROTHERHOOD, JAMES GIDDY and RUFUS PIGGOTT – marches into the garden. They are, each one of them, in a state of considerable alarm and confusion. Each is armed to a certain degree: there is not an element of uniformity about their clothes. GEORGE SELINCOURT shepherds them forward, crying out.*)

SELINCOURT: Now, please, gentlemen, please! Sort yourselves out! The first principle of modern warfare is to accept an unexpected occurrence with equity, dignity and discipline. Discipline, Piggott! (*PIGGOTT is greeting HUMPAGE with enthusiasm.*) And we do not consort with members of other units. Now, then. (*The tiny Corps is lined up and now stands to attention.*) Oh, good! Very, very good! (*SELINCOURT, for only a moment, is lost in admiration.*) Your hat, Reverend Sir – (*He speaks to BROTHERHOOD.*) – perhaps just a trifle forward. (*BROTHERHOOD adjusts his hat.*) Excellent! Excellent! Now, gentlemen, the situation which has arisen has quite confounded my original plans for today. I have therefore rearranged my notions with speed and skill. The mark of the modern soldier, gentlemen. Giddy!

GIDDY: Sir!

SELINCOURT: You will mount guard over this gate. (*GIDDY falls out to take up his place.*) Piggott!

PIGGOTT: What?

SELINCOURT: You will mount guard on some object over there. (*PIGGOTT falls out to take up his place.*) And you, Reverend Sir, will you be so kind as to keep an eye on the front door of this house. (*BROTHERHOOD takes up this position.*) This, gentlemen, is to prevent any possible attack on my rear. Ever vulnerable according to the textbooks. (*He regards his men.*) Excellent – excellent! (*From the alcove, whilst speaking to JONATHAN, HALLAM's voice is raised.*)

HALLAM: – and there, my dear, you find the music of civilised conversation. The counterpoint of voices, the fugue of argument, the bravura passage – in cadenza – myself, for example – the coda of peroration. Magnificent! We must guard – (*SELINCOURT has approached the alcove, but in his excessive wariness he now trips and tumbles headlong at HALLAM's feet. HALLAM acknowledges his presence but continues to speak to JONATHAN.*) – we must guard our right to practise this. Will you remain such a silent boy, I wonder?

SELINCOURT: Excuse me –

HALLAM: Yes?

SELINCOURT: You are the gentleman I saw earlier today.

HALLAM: Am I?

SELINCOURT: You are.

HALLAM: You must forgive me but I cannot recall ever having seen you in my life before.

SELINCOURT: Come, come! Only a little time ago I saw you.

HALLAM: You did, sir?

SELINCOURT: And now I want to see you again.

HALLAM: And so you shall. Can I help you up?

SELINCOURT: No, no! I can manage. (*He gets up.*) First, I must ask you not to be afraid of, or intimidated by, my fencibles.

HALLAM: Certainly not. You may rest assured on that point. (*A pause.*) Where are they? (*SELINCOURT indicates BROTHERHOOD, GIDDY and PIGGOTT. HALLAM peers from the alcove.*) Ah, yes. Fencibles, eh? Is that all you have?

SELINCOURT: No, indeed not! There are ninety-six at the ready on the beaches and cliffs, every one alert, crafty and massively courageous. The gentlemen you see here are my personal bodyguard. Mr Matthews –

HALLAM: That is my name.

SELINCOURT: Mr Matthews, at our previous meeting today I grievously misled you.

HALLAM: I'm very sorry to hear that.

SELINCOURT: Through no fault of my own, may I add?

HALLAM: No, no!

SELINCOURT: The fact is –

HALLAM: Yes?

SELINCOURT: Shall I come straight to the point?

HALLAM: Please do.

SELINCOURT: Time is short.

HALLAM: Yes, indeed.

SELINCOURT: Very well, then. This that you hear – (*Obligingly, in the distance, there is a roll of drums and a bugle call.*) this is no elementary exercise in tactics, no mere manoeuvre, but the Real Thing!

HALLAM: You mean –

SELINCOURT: I mean, sir, that Napoleon Bonaparte has landed in England!

(*There is a suitable pause.*)

HALLAM: You've seen him?

SELINCOURT: No, not myself. But Mr Brotherhood, here, has seen him in circumstances which – but he might care to explain himself. He is the local Rector, you know. Mr Brotherhood! (*BROTHERHOOD comes forward.*) Tell your story again, Mr Brotherhood.

(*BROTHERHOOD proceeds to do so in a commendably military manner.*)

BROTHERHOOD: Sir: whilst sitting at a point of vantage on the cliff top and partaking of a small alfresco meal –

SELINCOURT: I provide my men with rations for the field.

HALLAM: Bravo!

SELINCOURT: At my own expense, of course. Proceed, Mr Brotherhood.

BROTHERHOOD: – an alfresco meal which I was interested to note was wrapped in some pages of George Herbert's poems, I was suddenly confronted by what, at first, I took to be an apparition. This fiend seemed to rise from the ground before my eyes. I was about to pronounce an exorcism when the creature shouted: 'Me voici, Monsieur!' The combination of the French tongue and sudden recognition of the uniform worn gave me to understand that I was confronted by none other than the French Emperor, Bonaparte.

HALLAM: (*Fascinated.*) What did you do?

BROTHERHOOD: I ran at once to my superior officer.

SELINCOURT: That's me. We returned to the place together and there was no sign of anyone. But – and I think this important – someone had stolen Mr Brotherhood's bag of biscuits.

HALLAM: Was Bonaparte alone when you saw him, Mr Brotherhood?

SELINCOURT: Ah! That is the confusing point. Bonaparte has landed here, but where are his men?

HALLAM: I can honestly disclaim that I'm concealing them.

SELINCOURT: A confusing point, but I have the solution.

HALLAM: Yes?

SELINCOURT: His men are under the sea.

HALLAM: *Under* the sea!

SELINCOURT: Yes. Bonaparte, intrepid fellow that he is – we must admit that – come, in fairness we must admit it – Bonaparte has come ashore to spy out the lie of the land. His armies wait for his signal and then when it is given they will pour from the tunnel in their thousands.

HALLAM: Tunnel, sir!

SELINCOURT: The tunnel beneath the sea, Mr Matthews. You must have read your newspapers. The method of Bonaparte's arrival has long been a matter for conjecture. Some – and I must admit myself to have once been of their number – some favoured the monster bridge to have been constructed by his engineers. A vast project thrown across the breadth of the Channel, and over which Bonaparte's armies would have marched in their thousands. You may return to your post, Reverend Sir.

BROTHERHOOD: Sir! (*He goes back to the door of the house and takes up a defensive attitude.*)

SELINCOURT: Another school of thought – profoundly unimaginative – took it that he would transport his armies on a series of giant rafts. (*He whispers.*) Mr Brotherhood once confided to me that he was of the opinion that by some diabolical power the French would walk to England.

HALLAM: On the water?

SELINCOURT: Yes.

HALLAM: God bless my soul!

SELINCOURT: He's a very good man: he believes in the Devil. The last conjecture – which we can now substantiate as fact – was that Bonaparte would arrive through a vast tunnel bored beneath the sea. This he has done. His armies doubtless wait below for his signal. (*He looks at the ground with some satisfaction.*) Rather like standing on a volcano, isn't it?

HALLAM: Then all, I take it, is lost.

SELINCOURT: Certainly not!

HALLAM: What are you going to do?

(*BREEZE has come into the garden from the house.*)

BREEZE: Mr Matthews, sir.

HALLAM: Just a moment, Sam. (*To SELINCOURT.*) What are you going to do?

SELINCOURT: All that is necessary. I told you that the French armies await a signal from their Emperor.

HALLAM: Yes.

SELINCOURT: That signal will never be given. We shall prevent it. We shall catch him – oh, yes, by heaven! – the hunt is up and we shall catch him. Meantime, I've given instructions for the signal fires to be lighted. There they are, burning well. One, two, three, four – and there goes another – and yet another. (*LAMPRETT runs into the garden. He is properly accoutred, wearing his helmet and carrying another in his hand. He sees JONATHAN and, going to him, crams the second helmet on the wretched child's head before snatching him up. He then goes out at a run with the boy literally tucked beneath his arm. SELINCOURT has observed this: he shakes his head.*) First sign of panic. (*He turns to HALLAM.*) As for your accepted duties, Mr Matthews, I have your materials here.

HALLAM: I beg your pardon?

(*SELINCOURT has taken a large roll of invasion posters from GIDDY.*)

SELINCOURT: You will remember – (*He unrolls a poster before HALLAM.*) – and my plea is: run, Mr Matthews, run! Through every town, village and hamlet spread the news with feverish haste. Run, Mr Matthews, run till you drop! Twelve shillings.

HALLAM: What's that?

SELINCOURT: There are one hundred posters. At the authorized reduction, that is twelve shillings. (*HALLAM produces a sovereign.*) I've no change.

HALLAM: Neither have I.

SELINCOURT: I'll owe it to you. (*He takes the sovereign leaving HALLAM clasping the bundle of posters.*) We must be off! Squad! (*The FENCIBLES assemble in some kind of order.*) Off we go!

(*And off they go except the Reverend MR BROTHERHOOD, who lags behind to ask:*)

BROTHERHOOD: Are you Hallam Matthews, author of 'A Critical Enquiry into the Nature of Ecclesiastical Cant'?

HALLAM: 'With a Supplementary Dissertation on Lewd Lingo.' Yes, I am.

BROTHERHOOD: You should be ashamed! (*Then he, too, is gone.*)

BREEZE: Can I relieve you of those, sir.

HALLAM: What's that, Sam? Oh, yes, thank you very much. (*He gives* the *roll of posters* to *BREEZE.*)

BREEZE: Forgive me if I anticipate, sir, but do you wish me to run through the countryside with a feverish haste?

HALLAM: No, Sam, I don't want you to do anything of the kind.

BREEZE: I overheard your conversation with that gentleman, sir. I was just inside that door. I wasn't going to show myself, but I saw you were getting into difficulties.

HALLAM: God bless you, Sam.

BREEZE: I suppose it's Sir Timothy they've seen, sir, and mistaken him, as is only natural in that get-up, for Boney.

HALLAM: I suppose so. And yet –

(*They stare at each other.*)

BREEZE: I know what you're thinking, sir. Suppose it isn't Sir Timothy they've seen. Suppose –

HALLAM: Bonaparte has really landed.

BREEZE: That's what you were thinking, wasn't it, sir?

HALLAM: Of course not! Don't be a fool, Sam! From a tunnel! Do you read the newspapers?

BREEZE: Yes, sir. And they said it was a likelihood.

HALLAM: No, Sam, no! I shall go mad if you put such ideas into my head. We must work on the assumption that it is Sir Timothy these fellows have seen.

BREEZE: Very good, sir.

(*There is a distant call*: Hulloa!)

HALLAM: Now, what are we going to do. Have you any suggestions?

BREEZE: Well, sir, it seems to me that the best thing we can do is to get hold of Sir Timothy and keep him quiet until this thing blows over.

HALLAM: I defer to you, Sam. But surely – correct me if I am wrong – surely the point is this: where is Timothy?

BREEZE: That is the point, sir.

(*Again comes the cry*: Hulloa!)

HALLAM: I suppose the only thing to do –

BREEZE: Just a minute, sir. Did you hear anything?

HALLAM: No.

BREEZE: I thought I heard –

(*Again*: Hulloa there!)

HALLAM: Yes! Yes, indeed.

BREEZE: Oh, what a fool I am! (*He goes to the well, and looking down, calls*:) Hullo, down there! (*He is joined by HALLAM, they peer into the well.*)

TIMOTHY: No, no! Hullo, up here, if you please! (*He is above them in the gondola of a gaily painted balloon. He is very happy.*)

HALLAM: Oh, my God!

TIMOTHY: Fortunes of war! Captured from the enemy with amazing astuteness. Do I flatter myself? No, I do not. (*HESTER comes from the house.*)

HESTER: Oh, so you're back.

HALLAM: Do you never tread the surface of this earth nowadays, Tim?

TIMOTHY: What an invention! The French have ideas about war. We cannot deny it. Humpage!

HUMPAGE: Sir!

TIMOTHY: May I inform you that in your present position you are completely out of date.

HUMPAGE: Thank you, sir.

TIMOTHY: Hallam, my dear fellow, would you care to come up with me for a while.

HALLAM: Never!

TIMOTHY: You must move with the times. Do you know, I can now literally have my head in the clouds.

HESTER: Where did you get it?

TIMOTHY: From the enemy. Found it in a field being guarded by one French soldier. Typical specimen, unshaven and dirty, armed with a form of bill-hook. Didn't appear to understand his own language. I spoke to him – with kindness, you know – and asked him where he came from. 'C'est à Bordeaux que vous avez été élevé, je crois, n'est-ce-pas?' I said. The fellow just stared at me his mouth wide open like an idiot, and then ran away. I suppose he'd never seen an Emperor before. Then I jumped in here, released the anchor, and took to the air. But to national affairs. Hallam, come a little closer. I wish to be secret.

(*BREEZE comes forward.*)

BREEZE: Now then, sir, don't you think it would be rather nice if you were to get out of that balloon and come and have a lie down for a while? I'm sure things are going very well at the moment, and so you can take a little time off.

TIMOTHY: You're quite right. Things are going exceedingly well. But I must not spare myself. I'm needed in the thick of it.

HESTER: Do be careful, Timothy.

BREEZE: I feel you should conserve your energy, sir, for the last great effort.

TIMOTHY: Which is almost upon us, my dear fellow. No, no! I must go on, weary as I am. I could do with a little refreshment. I've had nothing but a few biscuits since breakfast.

BREEZE: Well, you get down from there, sir, and I'll go into the house and see what I can find.

TIMOTHY: You do that, but I must remain here ready for instant departure.

HALLAM: It's no good, Sam, no good at all.

TIMOTHY: When I have reported I shall be away again.

HALLAM: (*Suddenly shouting.*) Timothy, get out of that balloon at once!

BREEZE: Now, now, sir, that's not going to help.

HALLAM: I'm sorry, Sam.

TIMOTHY: Tell the family that I am well – desperately tired but well and, as yet, unharmed. I have made contact with the enemy troops twice, and a more slovenly, cowardly, uncouth crew I never did see. I don't know why there's been all this fuss about encountering Bonaparte's much-vaunted army.

BREEZE: Probably, sir, because –

TIMOTHY: Oh, we shan't have any difficulty finishing them off by nightfall. Now then, is there anything else? I don't think so. I brought this report back because I didn't want any of you to worry about me. Tell the others, will you, Hallam. Yes, I think that's all. Stand clear! I am about to ascend! (*He begins involved and useless activity about the gondola of the balloon. HESTER returns to the house.*)

HALLAM: Well, Sam?

BREEZE: Well, sir?

HALLAM: This is an unexpected development.

BREEZE: Yes sir.

HALLAM: There can be no harm in it, I suppose.

BREEZE: Not a bit, sir. The old gentleman will be as safe as houses up there. In a couple of days we can send to fetch him from round about Chichester.

HALLAM: Better than the tunnel, do you think.

BREEZE: Oh, much better, sir. I shouldn't let him go down there again, if I were you.

TIMOTHY: Hallam –

HALLAM: My dear fellow?

TIMOTHY: Can you see anything which might control levitation or propulsion?

HALLAM: Throw something out. Yourself, for example. (*TIMOTHY jumps up and down in the gondola. This has no effect. There is a bugle call from the beaches.*)

TIMOTHY: They're on the move! The French armies! No time to be lost! (*He stares about the balloon in impotent fury.*) Damned useless object! (*Then.*) Humpage!

HUMPAGE: Sir!

TIMOTHY: Pull that thing there and see what happens. (*He points to a ratline from the balloon swinging dangerously near to HUMPAGE's head. HUMPAGE hesitates.*) Well, go on, man – pull it!

(*HUMPAGE does so. The balloon begins to descend. TIMOTHY in sudden realization of this, turns on HUMPAGE.*)

TIMOTHY: You've broken it!

HALLAM: (*To BREEZE.*) He has, you know.

TIMOTHY: You've let all the – whatever it was filled with – out! (*HUMPAGE gives another tug at the rope.*) Oh, leave it alone. (*He suddenly understands the exact situation. He is descending the well.*) But I don't want to go down here again!

HUMPAGE: We don't want you to go, sir.

TIMOTHY: Then do something!

(*Nothing is done. TIMOTHY, in the gondola of the balloon, descends the well. SELINCOURT enters.*)

SELINCOURT: Some fool is going round putting out all my signal fires!

HALLAM: That must be so awkward.

SELINCOURT: Awkward! It's disastrous! I'm very, very angry.

HALLAM: Oh, dear!

SELINCOURT: Do you know anything about it?

HALLAM: Nothing – nothing.

SELINCOURT: One man and a little boy ruining everything! (*During this the balloon has gently risen from the well, the gondola empty of TIMOTHY, and begins to float away. SELINCOURT notices this.*) What's that?

HALLAM: A balloon.

SELINCOURT: Yours?

HALLAM: No, yours.

SELINCOURT: Ah, yes. Keep an eye on it. (*He runs from the garden to return immediately.*) I'd better tell you. In a moment we are sealing the entrance to the tunnel.

HALLAM: How?

SELINCOURT: With a ton of explosive. (*He goes out.*)

HALLAM: A ton of explosive! Quickly, Sam! (*They move to the well.*) Come back to us, Timothy!

BREEZE: Don't alarm him, sir.

HALLAM: I thought, perhaps, a word of encouragement –

BREEZE: Not at the moment. (*He calls down the well.*) Sir Timothy!

HALLAM: I'd give half my debts to hear that voice again. Come, Sam, one last great effort.

(*Together they shout down the well.*)

BREEZE: I fear it's useless, sir.

HALLAM: You have done me a disservice, Sam.

BREEZE: I'm sorry, sir.

HALLAM: In allowing me to carry the joke too far.

(*In the distance there is a blast on a trumpet. SELINCOURT shouts.*)

SELINCOURT: Stand back! One-two-three-four-five-six.

(*There is a tremendous reverberating explosion a short way off: also great pandemonium from the FENCIBLES which fades in the distance.*)

HALLAM: Is there anything we can do, Sam?

BREEZE: It doesn't look like it, sir.

(*But they go off in the direction of the explosion as the MAIDSERVANT comes from the house.*)

MAID: Oh, you're still there, Mr Humpage.

HUMPAGE: Yes, my dear.

MAID: There was a noise, but if you're still there everything must be all right.

HUMPAGE: From the way things are going I shall be up here until the end of time.

MAID: You're the bravest man I know, Mr Humpage.

HUMPAGE: Thank you, my dear.

(*HESTER appears in the doorway of the house, and EDWARD and DORCAS come in from the orchard.*)

EDWARD: Everything still here?

DORCAS: Yes, still here.

HESTER: I thought it was your father.

DORCAS: It may well have been.

(*HESTER is regarding a wisp of smoke rising from the well.*)

HESTER: What is he doing down there now?

DORCAS: You mustn't go down, Mama!

HESTER: Don't be absurd, child. I've no intention of doing so. Your father is quite capable of managing his own affairs. No one seems to understand that. (*He is about to return to the house when*:) Dorcas –

DORCAS: Mama?

HESTER: You told me earlier – and I was a little sharp with you – that you are in love.

DORCAS: Yes, Mama.

HESTER: I can only presume it to be with you, young man.

EDWARD: Yes.

HESTER: People sometimes smile at the memory of your father and myself, but let me say this to you: remember the first day, my dears. It will mean much to you in the future.

EDWARD: I understand you very well. I'm leaving this evening.

(*With a cry DORCAS tears herself from EDWARD leaving him standing alone. She runs out to the orchard. Immediately, HESTER calls.*)

HESTER: Dorcas! Dorcas, come back! At once! Do you hear me – at once! (*After a moment DORCAS, silent, reappears at the orchard entrance. HESTER takes DORCAS's hand and passes her to EDWARD.*) You need not part for a while, my dears – not for a little while. (*DORCAS and EDWARD go out to the orchard. HESTER turns to the MAIDSERVANT.*) Don't stand agape, Pippin. Continue with your preparations.

MAID: Yes, ma'am.

(*As HESTER and the MAID go into the house HALLAM and BREEZE escorted by SELINCOURT and surrounded by the FENCIBLES return to the garden.*)

HALLAM: Listen, sir – I've no wish to be caught further in your machinations.

SELINCOURT: Not mine, Mr Matthews, but the Devil's. Ask Mr Brotherhood.

BROTHERHOOD: True.

SELINCOURT: For we have unearthed him. He is on the run, among us at this very moment. Everyone alert!

(*HALLAM and BREEZE merely look mystified.*)

HALLAM: Mr –

SELINCOURT: Selincourt.

HALLAM: (*With grave patience.*) Mr Selincourt. Kindly explain yourself. Once again.

SELINCOURT: Certainly. Our explosion – which you heard –

HALLAM: Yes.

SELINCOURT: – was only partially successful.

HALLAM: Continue.

SELINCOURT: Our proposition was, as I told you –

HALLAM: To seal –

SELINCOURT: Correct. To seal the entrance to the tunnel.

HALLAM: Well?

SELINCOURT: And to stifle the beast in the depths. Well, we set the charge –

HALLAM: A ton of explosive.

SELINCOURT: – and formed about the tunnel entrance in a circle.

HALLAM: Admirable!

SELINCOURT: To prevent, you understand, any possible escape.

HALLAM: In the confusion. Yes, go on.

SELINCOURT: All was prepared –

HALLAM: But –

SELINCOURT: – we had overlooked one thing.

HALLAM: That being?

SELINCOURT: The size of the charge.

HALLAM: It was –

SELINCOURT: Too great; Piggott, here –

HALLAM: Brave fellow.

SELINCOURT: Lit the fuse.

(*A pause.*)

HALLAM: Yes?

SELINCOURT: The charge exploded and – here is the error –

HALLAM: Yes?

SELINCOURT: Bonaparte was ejected from the mouth of the tunnel like a bullet from a gun. He flew over our heads –

HALLAM: Amazing sight!

SELINCOURT: – to fall twenty yards beyond the bounds of my cordon.

HALLAM: Unhurt?

SELINCOURT: Apparently. The confusion among my men – understandably – was enormous. And in that confusion Bonaparte made off in this direction. But we shall catch him – never fear! – we shall catch him.

(*LAMPRETT and JONATHAN, very dirty, come in from the orchard. They are pleased with themselves.*)

LAMPRETT: An excellent day's work! Nine conflagrations totally extinguished.

SELINCOURT: You – you!

LAMPRETT: I cannot recall ever having see you before, sir.

HALLAM: (*Swiftly.*) Mr Selincourt – Mr Lamprett Bellboys.

SELINCOURT: You are the man who has been putting out all my fires.

LAMPRETT: Your fires, sir?

SELINCOURT: Yes.

LAMPRETT: The law holds that a fire, once under way, is public property, sir. Your fires, indeed! But tell me, do you mean you started them?

SELINCOURT: I was responsible.

LAMPRETT: Then you should be ashamed of yourself! A grown man going about the countryside wantonly starting fires.

SELINCOURT: Surely you understand that –

LAMPRETT: If you please, we will discuss the matter no further. They are out.

SELINCOURT: But –

LAMPRETT: Hush! (*He pats JONATHAN on the head.*) Good boy!

(*BREEZE has now made his way to the orchard gate. Suddenly he cries out:*)

BREEZE: Sir!

HALLAM: Yes?

BREEZE: (*Pointing through the orchard.*) There – there!

HALLAM: What?

BREEZE: There he goes!

HALLAM: Sam!

BREEZE: A small man –

SELINCOURT: Yes?

BREEZE: – in a cocked hat –

SELINCOURT: What?

BREEZE: Breeches.

SELINCOURT: My God!

BREEZE: There – there!

SELINCOURT: Bonaparte! (*He joins BREEZE at the orchard gate.*) I can see no one.

BREEZE: Just went down, sir, behind that hedgerow.

SELINCOURT: Fencibles! Follow-follow-follow-follow – (*And so shouting he runs out of the orchard, BROTHERHOOD, GIDDY and PIGGOTT taking after him. There is a pause.*)

HALLAM: My dear Sam, what are you doing? Did you *see* someone?

BREEZE: No, sir.

HALLAM: I thought not. Then why this extraordinary exhibition?

BREEZE: You'll know in a moment, sir.

(*It is a fraction of time and then BREEZE points the way from the cliff-top. TIMOTHY has appeared. He is very dirty and his clothes are in a most dilapidated state: he retains his hat and the impersonation is yet very recognizable. HALLAM goes to him.*)

HALLAM: My dear old friend!

TIMOTHY: Hallam! (*They embrace.*) Tried to blow me up, the devils. Inefficient fools! Ran into some kind of mine which went off and up I went like a rocket. Amazing sensation! Then, while they stood around gaping, I came to earth. Was rather stunned. Don't quite know what I did. Have they been here?

HALLAM: Yes. But, Tim, they are not – my word, I am pleased to see you! – listen, they are not –

BREEZE: Sir!

HALLAM: What is it, Sam?

BREEZE: Ask him if he's seen anyone like himself.

HALLAM: Why?

BREEZE: Well, sir, we just don't know, do we? Whether Sir Timothy is the one, or whether Boney really is here.

HALLAM: Of course. Listen, Timothy –

TIMOTHY: Um?

HALLAM: This is very important. Have you, in your travels, seen anyone looking like you?

(*There is a pause.*)

TIMOTHY: You mean someone has been impersonating me? (*He is suddenly very angry.*) Damned impertinence! Where is he? Before long I shan't be able to call my life my own.

(*LAMPRETT, who has been standing by regarding all this, comments –*)

LAMPRETT: Well, I'm sure no one else would wish to be credited with it.

(*– and leaves the garden taking JONATHAN with him. BREEZE who is still standing by the orchard gate, calls.*)

BREEZE: Look out, sir!

HALLAM: For what?

BREEZE: They are returning, sir.

HALLAM: Heavens! They mustn't see him like this. They'll probably shoot at sight.

BREEZE: They probably will, sir.

HALLAM: In here! (*He begins to bustle TIMOTHY towards the alcove.*)

TIMOTHY: My dear Hallam, I'd be very much obliged if you would refrain from jostling me. I'm extremely tired and –

HALLAM: They're here!

TIMOTHY: What's that?

(*HALLAM has piloted him into the alcove.*)

HALLAM: They're here!

TIMOTHY: Where?

HALLAM: Here!

(*SELINCOURT, BROTHERHOOD, GIDDY and PIGGOTT march through the garden. TIMOTHY speaks to HALLAM.*)

TIMOTHY: Pour la famille, mon cher, pour la famille!

(*He then steps from the alcove to confront SELINCOURT and*

*the FENCIBLES.*) Messieurs! Je suis votre Empereur. Je suis Napoléon Bonaparte. Retirez! Les armées de France sont vaincrent! Retournez à vos domestiques! Allons! Je suis un prisonnier et – (*Then the FENCIBLES, recovered from their amazement, fall upon him. The confusion is indescribable. At last, TIMOTHY stands pinioned by the FENCIBLES whilst SELINCOURT triumphant parades before him.*)

SELINCOURT: Aha! Mon petit tyrant! Aha! Mon bête sauvage! (*He tweaks TIMOTHY's nose.*)

TIMOTHY: God damn you!

SELINCOURT: Oh, you speak English.

TIMOTHY: Non.

SELINCOURT: Well, anyway, we've got you, disgusting little pest.

TIMOTHY: Are you English?

SELINCOURT: Of course I'm English.

TIMOTHY: Then what the hell are you doing? Hallam!

SELINCOURT: Are you Napoleon Bonaparte?

TIMOTHY: Oui! Non! No!

SELINCOURT: Of course you deny it. Mr Brotherhood, do you identify this man as the one who stole your biscuits?

BROTHERHOOD: I do.

SELINCOURT: Then, Napoleon Bonaparte, in the King's name I declare you to be my prisoner.

TIMOTHY: Well, if I'm Napoleon Bonaparte who in hell are you?

SELINCOURT: My name is George Selincourt and I am commander of the local forces.

TIMOTHY: Dear God! I'm Bellboys.

SELINCOURT: Who?

TIMOTHY: Timothy Bellboys.

SELINCOURT: So you're Timothy Bellboys, are you? Well, well, well! (*Suddenly very intimidating.*) Impersonation, eh? A knowledge of the local gentry is not going to help you. What have you done with the poor old gentleman –

TIMOTHY: Poor old gentleman!

SELINCOURT: Yes! What have you done with him? Murdered him probably, and stuffed his frail old body into some hole in the ground. What harm had he ever done to you? (*TIMOTHY, in an excess of fury, attempts to break loose from the FENCIBLES.*) Hold him! Hold him!

TIMOTHY: I tell you I am Timothy Bellboys! Ask my friend, Hallam Matthews, there.

(*SELINCOURT turns doubtfully to HALLAM.*)

SELINCOURT: Can you identify this man, sir?

HALLAM: Certainly, Lord Nelson. (*Then, with BREEZE, he retires a little way off.*)

SELINCOURT: (*To BROTHERHOOD.*) What do you think?

BROTHERHOOD: It is very difficult to know what to think.

TIMOTHY: Or what to think with, apparently.

SELINCOURT: It will not help to be abusive. We are only trying to determine the truth.

TIMOTHY: And whilst you are, as you put it, determining the truth, the French may be preparing to assault the beaches.

SELINCOURT: That is all taken care of. Mr Brotherhood –

TIMOTHY: Taken care of! You do not impress me, sir.

SELINCOURT: Mr Brotherhood – (*SELINCOURT and BROTHERHOOD confer in whispers. TIMOTHY speaks to PIGGOTT.*)

TIMOTHY: Will you have a care! You are pinching my arm quite unmercifully. I think you take a delight in it, you horrid fellow.

(*SELINCOURT and BROTHERHOOD have reached a decision.*)

SELINCOURT: Now, sir –

TIMOTHY: Well?

SELINCOURT: Are you willing to answer a few questions to prove your identity?

TIMOTHY: No.

SELINCOURT: Then I'm afraid I must insist. Mr Brotherhood here, is going to help me.

TIMOTHY: Help you with the questions?

SELINCOURT: Yes.

TIMOTHY: Is anyone going to help me with the answers?

SELINCOURT: Certainly not.

TIMOTHY: Well, unless I'm released you'll get nothing from me.

SELINCOURT: (*To GIDDY and PIGGOTT.*) Release him. (*They do so, and TIMOTHY comes forward.*) Now, sir, at Mr Brotherhood's suggestion I am going to put to you several questions which only an Englishman could answer. Are you ready?

TIMOTHY: Yes.

SELINCOURT: One. What is a Wykehamist?

TIMOTHY: I am a Wykehamist.

(*SELINCOURT looks at BROTHERHOOD who shakes his head.*)

BROTHERHOOD: Inconclusive.

TIMOTHY: I can make a guess as to what you are.

SELINCOURT: Two. What was the second question, Mr Brotherhood?

BROTHERHOOD: What is a New Leicester?

TIMOTHY: A cow.

BROTHERHOOD: Oh, very good!

SELINCOURT: Is he right?

BROTHERHOOD: Yes.

TIMOTHY: Aha! Go on.

SELINCOURT: Three. Now this requires action. Watch carefully. If I was to do this – (*With an underarm action he bowls an imaginary ball to TIMOTHY.*) – what would you do?

TIMOTHY: (*Very intent.*) Do it again.

(*SELINCOURT repeats the action.*)

SELINCOURT: Well, what would you do?

TIMOTHY: This! (*With an imaginary bat TIMOTHY strikes the imaginary ball and then proceeds to run madly between two points some ten yards apart touching down at each imaginary wicket.*)

SELINCOURT: Stop! Stop! (*TIMOTHY stops.*) Do you play?

TIMOTHY: Cricket? Of course. Do you?

SELINCOURT: Yes, indeed.

TIMOTHY: God bless my soul! What's your name again?

SELINCOURT: Selincourt.

TIMOTHY: Not Stumper Selincourt?

(*At this SELINCOURT positively simpers.*)

SELINCOURT: I must confess that I am sometimes known by that appellation – on the field.

TIMOTHY: But you're famous.

SELINCOURT: Oh come.

TIMOTHY: Yes, you are. And these brave fellows – (*He indicates BROTHERHOOD, GIDDY and PIGGOTT.*) – are they some of your team?

SELINCOURT: Yes. We have a side, in its infancy yet, but give us a few weeks. I've been working hard with them since my arrival here from Somerset.

TIMOTHY: Then we must play, Stumper Selincourt. Well, well! Hallam, this is Stumper Selincourt.

(*HESTER comes from the house. She is dressed in what appears to be a suit of golden armour and is accompanied by the tiny MAIDSERVANT who, dressed for travelling, bears the baggage.*)

HESTER: Ah! gentlemen – (*Everyone seeing HESTER is momentarily lost in admiration.*) – what is this? A congress of war?

TIMOTHY: We were talking about cricket.

HESTER: At a time like this? I feel you must be joking, Timothy.

HALLAM: The immediate danger would appear to have passed, Hester.

HESTER: Nonsense, Hallam! East Anglia is in turmoil. I set off at once. (*She calls.*) Lamprett!

(*LAMPRETT comes in and recognizes his wife.*)

LAMPRETT: Oh!

HESTER: Don't be afraid. I'm away now.

(*They embrace.*)

LAMPRETT: Goodbye. Come back soon.

TIMOTHY: Breeches or not, Hester, you appear to be amply protected.

HESTER: We can but take care. And if one goes down one should go down magnificently. An Englishman's prerogative.

(*SELINCOURT comes to attention as HESTER and the MAID march out.*)

TIMOTHY: I say, are you hungry?

SELINCOURT: A little.

TIMOTHY: I am, damnably. Come inside and we'll find some food. Give us a chance to talk. Now that we've met we must arrange something at once. Come along, all of you. (*The FENCIBLES go into the house.*) I've quite a fair side, although now my sister-in-law has gone it will be weaker, but I think we can give you a game. In fact, I'm sure we can. (*He takes SELINCOURT to the door of the house.*) By the way, this business of my being Bonaparte –

SELINCOURT: Never mind that nonsense!

TIMOTHY: What! (*He roars with laughter.*) Show you my bat. Not bad. Made it myself. (*With SELINCOURT he goes into the house.*)

HALLAM: And so, Sam, there is always a basis for understanding however remote it may appear, however dissimilar the two parties, however hopeless the situation.

BREEZE: Yes, sir.

HALLAM: Comforting, isn't it?

BREEZE: Yes, sir.

HALLAM: And what, pray, are you smiling at?

BREEZE: Nothing, sir.

HALLAM: You mustn't have these secret thoughts, you know. Very disturbing.

BREEZE: Sorry, sir.

HALLAM: And you, Lamprett – a good day?

LAMPRETT: Excellent! I'm just cleaning up the engine – oh, it has done magnificently! – and then I shall go to my bed. It has been a somewhat busy day for you, too, I suppose.

HALLAM: Unwittingly, I have sometimes been caught up in the general action.

(*BREEZE laughs.*)

LAMPRETT: Well, you must enjoy the remainder of your stay with us.

HALLAM: Thank you, Lamprett.

(*LAMPRETT goes out.*)

BREEZE: Will you come in now, sir?

HALLAM: Not for a while, I think. I propose to revel for a time in this most unaccustomed peace.

BREEZE: Very good, sir. (*He goes into the house.*)

HALLAM: Humpage!

HUMPAGE: Sir!

HALLAM: Anything to report?

HUMPAGE: No, sir.

HALLAM: Thank God. (*He wanders a little way off. From within the house comes a subdued burst of men's laughter. Suddenly, the day is gone, it is evening and from the long shadows come EDWARD and DORCAS.*)

DORCAS: But yesterday was just another day – nothing to tell about it.

EDWARD: Nothing?

DORCAS: Nothing at all. The sun shone as it has today, but not so brightly and to no purpose whatever. Yesterday was just – oh, any old day. There are times you remember and times you forget – but your life is made up of the times you remember. Come, let us sit here. (*She draws EDWARD towards the alcove.*) We shall be safe and sound – oh, quite secure and secret. (*They enter the alcove.*)

EDWARD: What is this place?

DORCAS: I used to play here when I was a baby. Yes, it is a good place for us to be together for I have been happy here. It was my world within a world – peopled by folk who were all like me – and that is simple to understand for I was everyone.

EDWARD: I am a stranger.

DORCAS: No, no! We all greet you. (*Lightly, she kisses him.*)

EDWARD: Have you ever been unhappy?

DORCAS: Oh, yes, deeply. Indeed, so very unhappy that I have wept and had to seek comfort.

EDWARD: Which you have always found?

DORCAS: Of course. Oh, look!

EDWARD: I'm looking with all my heart. What is this new wonder you have to show me?

DORCAS: Only my name – Dorcas – scored upon this seat. Oh, that was done many years ago. (*She takes up a stone and begins to mark the seat.*)

EDWARD: What are you doing?

DORCAS: I'm putting your name – Edward – here with mine. Isn't that a clever thing to do?

EDWARD: Indeed it is.

(*As DORCAS works, she asks*:)

DORCAS: You're going away?

EDWARD: Yes.

DORCAS: Soon?

EDWARD: Yes.

(*A pause.*)

DORCAS: Not before I've finished your name?

EDWARD: Not before then, perhaps, but soon – soon.

DORCAS: I shall be a long time. (*EDWARD smiles.*) Perhaps – if I cut very slowly – (*A pause.*) – I cannot come with you?

EDWARD: No.

DORCAS: There! (*She throws down the stone.*)

EDWARD: Finished?

(*DORCAS turns to him, her face distraught.*)

DORCAS: Yes. Oh, yes. (*She cries out.*) But we all love you – why can't you remain?

EDWARD: Poor Dorcas.

DORCAS: Forgive me. I don't understand.

EDWARD: Then –

DORCAS: Speak in simple words, if you please.

EDWARD: If you tear the words from me, as you are doing now, they are bound to be tattered.

DORCAS: Go on.

EDWARD: For me there is no escape – not even by returning, my darling. There is only a little purpose – the ending of a war to be achieved and then this broken thing I call myself can be discarded, happily relinquished. I am only a scarecrow to frighten away the spirit of hatred. That done I can be left to weather and fall apart in some deserted place.

DORCAS: But do you love me now?

EDWARD: Yes.

DORCAS: For a little while do you love me?

EDWARD: Yes.

DORCAS: Tell me – tell me!

EDWARD: I love you. I love you.

(*She stares at him.*)

DORCAS: Then – goodbye.

(*Out of the falling darkness HALLAM speaks.*)

HALLAM: Circumstances deal with us in a way we cannot approve. As you grow older you will understand that.

EDWARD: Where's the child? (*He calls.*) Jonathan!

(*LAMPRETT comes in with JONATHAN. The child is dressed as he was on arrival.*)

LAMPRETT: I thought you'd be off soon. He's all ready.

EDWARD: Thank you, sir.

LAMPRETT: (*To JONATHAN.*) Got everything? (*The BOY nods.*) Well, thank you very much for your help today. I think we can say we did well. There's only one word of advice I should like to give you and it is this. Out there in the world people will always be telling you not to get caught between two fires. Pay no attention to them. (*Then, very sadly, he adds.*) I'm only joking, you know. Off with you.

HALLAM: Mr Sterne.

EDWARD: Ah! You're there, Mr Matthews.

HALLAM: You're going.

EDWARD: Yes.

HALLAM: I believe you to be wise. Yes, I really believe that. Goodbye. (*EDWARD and JONATHAN go, leaving DORCAS.*) You know about them, do you, Lamprett – their journey?

LAMPRETT: Yes, the child told me today.

HALLAM: I reasoned with the man. I gave him the cold fact as to why he must fail – and yet he goes on. And damn it, Lamprett, I'm glad he goes on. This would be hell if we acted always to reason and cold fact. Did you tell the child?

LAMPRETT: That the child of Bethlehem no longer lives? No. It occurred to me to do so – but no, I decided against it.

HALLAM: Why, I wonder?

LAMPRETT: Because our destination is unimportant, Hallam. We journey forward only to discover the reason for our travelling.

HALLAM: Thank you, Lamprett. I feel I should have said that.

(*TIMOTHY comes from the house. He has changed from his uniform of impersonation and now wears a dressing robe. He carries a cricket bat.*)

TIMOTHY: What are you all doing out here?

HALLAM: Nothing, and it's absolutely delightful.

TIMOTHY: I say, Hallam, this Selincourt is an amazing fellow. Tells me he once stumped Richard Nyren. You know, the captain of Hambledon.

HALLAM: Really!

TIMOTHY: Yes, he did. And he's as modest as milk about it. By the way, we're arranging a match for next Sunday. Think you'll be here then?

HALLAM: I doubt that, Tim.

TIMOTHY: Pity. Now that Hester's gone I've got to find another player and – (*He holds up his bat.*) – I thought you might care to –

HALLAM: No.

TIMOTHY: I could teach you in an afternoon.

HALLAM: No, Timothy.

TIMOTHY: Then Humpage will have to come down.

HUMPAGE: Can I believe my ears?

LAMPRETT: No, you cannot, Humpage. Whatever can you be thinking of, Timothy. Humpage has his duties.

TIMOTHY: Yes, I suppose so. (*HUMPAGE groans.*) Well, Lamprett, I'll have to show you, I suppose. (*He gives the bat to LAMPRETT.*) Try not to make too big a fool of yourself. Oh, God! You're holding it by the wrong end, man.

LAMPRETT: Well, I can't see.

TIMOTHY: Come inside and I'll show you. I hope you're enjoying your stay with us, Hallam.

HALLAM: I am, very much – at the moment.

TIMOTHY: Don't seem to have had a chance to say it before, but I'll say it now. We're very pleased to see you, Hallam. Aren't we, Lamprett?

LAMPRETT: Of course.

TIMOTHY: There's some food and drink inside when you're ready for it.

HALLAM: Bless you, Tim.

TIMOTHY: You're happy, then?

HALLAM: Very happy, thank you.

TIMOTHY: Good. Now, Lamprett, as a beginner you'll have to go in the outfield.

LAMPRETT: Where's that?

TIMOTHY: You'll find out.

LAMPRETT: Is it a dangerous game?

TIMOTHY: Well, you want to look out for your knuckles, you know – (*Together TIMOTHY and LAMPRETT go into the house. The garden becomes darker. A great branched candlestick, ablaze, is placed in the window of a ground floor room of the house. From within the house comes a second burst of laughter and, for a moment, a single voice is raised in a snatch of song. Distantly, from the beaches, a bugle sounds the Stand Down. DORCAS can be seen against the night sky looking out over the countryside. After a moment she enters the garden to move to HALLAM and sit beside him. They remain together in silence for a considerable time. At last HALLAM speaks to her.*)

HALLAM: Not tears to end the day.

(*When DORCAS speaks her voice is high and clear.*)

DORCAS: I'm not crying. Didn't you know, Mr Matthews, that you do not cry over spilt milk or lost lovers.

HALLAM: I'm sorry.

DORCAS: It's quite all right. (*There is a pause.*) You don't mind if I sit here with you for a while?

HALLAM: Not at all, darling.

DORCAS: Please don't be kind to me.

HALLAM: I'm sorry.

DORCAS: And please don't continue to be sorry. You have given no offence. I shall sit here for a while because I don't know where to go. I've not yet made up my mind, you understand? (*In the slight pause the sudden rush of an evening breeze seems to disturb the stillness of the garden.*) Can you see me?

HALLAM: Yes.

DORCAS: It is getting dark. Day's end. Nightfall. I suppose there will be a tomorrow. (*A pause.*) I cannot believe that I shall wake to find the sun high. (*A pause.*) Do you know a song beginning 'All my past life is mine no more – '?

HALLAM: 'All my past life is mine no more;
The flying hours are gone,
Like transitory dreams given o'er,
Whose images are kept in store
By memory alone.'

Yes, I know that.

DORCAS: I wondered if you did. There is no need to talk if you do not wish.

(*BREEZE comes from the house.*)

BREEZE: Mr Matthews –

HALLAM: I'm here, Sam.

BREEZE: That's everything, then, sir.

HALLAM: Thank you, Sam.

BREEZE: Thank you, sir. Goodnight, Miss Bellboys.

DORCAS: Goodnight.

BREEZE: Goodnight, sir.

HALLAM: Goodnight, Sam. God rest you.

(*BREEZE goes out by the orchard. It is now almost dark but for the light of the night sky and the blaze of candles in the window. From within the house a spinet strikes up a tune and men's voices, gay and gentle, begin to sing. HUMPAGE, stirs in his sleep and the brass bell sounds once, softly. Then, with an infinite tenderness, HALLAM takes up the melody being sung in the house on his pipe. The tune ends. A single star stands in the sky.*)

*CURTAIN*